BREAD MACHINE

BREAD MACHINE

how to prepare and bake the perfect loaf

JENNIE SHAPTER

HERMES HOUSE

This edition published by Hermes House
an imprint of Anness Publishing Limited
Hermes House, 88-89 Blackfriars Road, London SE1 8HA

A CIP catalogue record for this book is available from the British Library

PUBLISHER: Joanna Lorenz
EXECUTIVE EDITOR: Linda Fraser
EDITOR: Rebecca Clunes
DESIGNER: Nigel Partridge
PHOTOGRAPHER AND STYLIST: Nicki Dowey
HOME ECONOMIST: Jennie Shapter
TYPESETTER: Diane Pullen
PRODUCTION CONTROLLER: Wendy Lawson

Previously published as *The Ultimate Bread Machine Cookbook*

Printed and bound in China

© Anness Publishing Limited 2000, 2001
Updated © 2003
1 3 5 7 9 10 8 6 4 2

Front cover shows Sweet Potato Bread, for recipe see page 160
and Coconut Milk Sugar Buns, for recipe see page 199

NOTES
Standard spoon and cup measures are level.

Large eggs are used unless otherwise stated.

CONTENTS

INTRODUCTION

In recent years there has been a huge upsurge in the popularity of home-baked bread. Men and women are coming home from work to the comforting aroma of freshly baked bread once only associated with an idyllic childhood. But making and eating home-baked bread is not only the stuff of dreams. No. The bread that stands cooling in many of our kitchens is real. It has a beautiful golden crust, an even crumb and a delicious flavor. It looks

BELOW: To many people, a Farmhouse Loaf is the traditional bread they associate with their childhood.

and tastes as if aching effort went into its making, but nothing could be further from the truth. Much of today's tastiest bread is made at home with the aid of an easy-to-operate machine, which takes the hard work out of bread making while retaining all the pleasure.

The first automatic domestic bread-maker appeared on the market in Japan in the late 1980s, and since then bread machines have gained popularity all over the world. These excellent appliances have helped to rekindle the pleasure of making homemade bread, by streamlining the process and making it incredibly

simple. All the "home baker" needs to do is to measure a few ingredients accurately, put them into the bread machine pan and push a button or two.

At first it is easy to feel overwhelmed by all the settings on a bread machine. These are there to help you bake a wide range of breads, both sweet and savory, using different grains and flavorings. In time you'll understand them all, but there's no need to rush. Start by making a simple white loaf and watch while your machine transforms a few ingredients first into a silky, smooth dough and finally into a golden loaf of bread.

No matter what make of machine you have, it is important to focus on the bread, not the machine. Even the best type of machine is only a kitchen aid. The machine will mix, knead and bake beautifully, but only after you have added the necessary ingredients and programmed it. The machine cannot think for itself; it can only carry out your instructions, so it is essential that you add the correct ingredients in the right proportions, in the order specified in the instructions for your particular breadmaking machine, and that you choose the requisite settings. Do not become frustrated if your first attempts do not look one hundred per cent perfect; they will probably still taste wonderful. Get to know your bread machine and be willing to experiment to find the correct ratio of dry ingredients to liquids. There are a number of variables, including the type of ingredients used, the climate and the weather, which can affect the moisture level, regardless of the type of machine you are using.

When you make bread by hand you can feel whether it is too wet or dry, simply by kneading it. However, when you use a bread machine, you need to adopt a different strategy to determine if your bread has the right moistness and, if not, how you may adjust it to produce a perfect loaf.

After the machine has been mixing for a few minutes, take a quick look at the dough—it should be pliable and soft. When the machine stops kneading, the

dough should start to relax back into the shape of the bread machine pan. Once you have made a few loaves of bread you will soon recognize what is an acceptable dough, and you will rapidly progress to making breads with different grains, such as rye, buckwheat or barley, or breads flavored with vegetables such as potatoes or zucchini. The range of both savory and sweet breads you ultimately will be able to produce will only be limited by your imagination. Creative thinking can produce some magical results.

The breads in this book are either made entirely by machine or the dough is made in the machine, then shaped by hand and baked in a conventional oven. Teabreads are mixed by hand and baked in the bread machine. Where the loaves are made automatically you will usually find three separate lists of ingredients, each relating to a different size of machine. The small size is recommended for bread machines that are designed for loaves using 3–3¼ cups of flour, the medium size for machines that make loaves using 4–4½ cups of flour and the large size for bread machines that are capable of making loaves using up to 6 cups of flour. Refer to your manu-

BELOW: Mix the dough for Pistolets in the machine and shape by hand.

ABOVE: Babka is a traditional Polish Easter cake.

facturer's handbook if you are not sure of the capacity of your machine. If only one set of ingredients is given for a loaf that is to be made automatically, relate these to the size of your machine to make sure it is suitable for the job.

Where a bread machine is used solely for preparing the dough, which is then shaped by hand and baked conventionally, quantities are not so crucial, and only one set of ingredients is given.

It is very pleasurable to shape your own loaves of bread, and setting the machine to the "dough-only" cycle takes all the hard work out of the initial mixing and kneading. The machine provides an

ideal climate for the initial rising period, leaving you to bring all your artistry to bear on transforming the dough into rolls, shaped breads or yeasted cakes. Once you master the technique, you can make breads from all around the world, including Middle Eastern flatbreads, American Doughnuts, Chinese-style Chicken Buns, French Brioches, and Jewish Challah—to name but a few. Sourdoughs and breads made from starters are becoming increasingly popular, and there is a whole chapter illustrating how the bread machine can be used to help you make them. It is also possible to make gluten-free breads, but as this is a specialized area, it is best to follow the instructions given by your manufacturer, or contact their helpline, if you wish to do this.

A BAKERY IN YOUR KITCHEN

Bread making is a tremendously satisfying activity. With the help of your machine, delectable breads you will not find at the bakery or supermarket can be made with very little effort. From basic breads containing little more than flour, yeast and water to more elaborate loaves based on stoneground flours milled from a variety of grains—the possibilities are endless. What's more, you know precisely what goes into the bread, and can tailor loaves to your family's own tastes, adding sweet or savory ingredients.

For everyday use, basic white loaves, possibly enriched with milk or egg, or flavorful multi-grain and Light Whole-wheat Breads are perfect for breakfast, whether freshly baked or toasted, and these can also be used for sandwiches and quick snacks. These types of bread are the easiest to make in your machine and are the ones you are likely to make over and over again. In time, however, you will probably progress to baking loaves with added ingredients such as potato, to provide, for example, an enhanced lightness to the dough. Leftover rice makes a tasty bread; and another delicious treat is the New England Anadama Bread, made from a blend of white, whole-wheat and corn-meal flours flavored with molasses.

BELOW: Strawberry Teabread

ABOVE: Hazelnut Twist Cake

With the addition of other grains, you can make more complex, hearty loaves. Breads containing oats, rye, wheatgerm and wild rice, perhaps with added whole seeds and grains, can all be baked in the bread machine. These provide extra fiber and are a good source of complex carbohydrates, and are thus a wonderfully healthy option as well as being tasty. Try Multigrain Bread, a flavor-packed healthy loaf made from multi-grain, rye and whole-wheat flours with whole oats. Alternatively, experiment with a mixed-seed bread such as Four Seed Bread. The added seeds not only contribute crunchiness and flavor, but are also very nutritious.

The bread machine will happily incorporate such ingredients as caramelized onions, sun-dried tomatoes, char-grilled peppers, crisp bacon, slivers of ham and other cured meats, fresh chopped herbs and grated or crumbled cheese, to produce mouthwatering vegetable and other savory breads. Spices and nuts, and dried, semi-dried and fresh fruits can also be added to make classic fruit loaves. Try succulent Cranberry and Orange Bread or Mango and Banana Bread. Other sweet breads include crunchy Buckwheat and Walnut Bread and—every chocolate lover's dream—Three Chocolate Bread.

You can also cook succulent teabreads, Honey Cake, Gingerbread, Madeira Cake and Passion Cake, to name but a few, which provides an alternative to using your traditional oven for one small cake. Fresh fruits such as strawberries and raspberries plus more exotic offerings can also be used as flavorings for these afternoon treats, as can traditional dried fruits, such as apricots, dates, prunes, and raisins.

These breads, mixed, proved and baked automatically, illustrate just a part of the bread machine's capabilities. You can also use the dough only setting to make an endless variety of doughs for hand-shaping. Classic French breads, such as Fougasse, Couronne and baguettes, or rustic breads, such as Pain de Campagne and Pain de Seigle are all possible, as are Italian breads, such as Ciabatta, Pan all'Olio and Breadsticks (grissini). You will be able to experiment in making flatbreads such as Indian Naan, Middle Eastern Lavash and Pita Breads, or Italian Focaccia, Stromboli, Sfincione or pizzas.

Sweet yeast doughs also work well in a bread machine. Try making Strawberry Chocolate Savarin, Apricot and Vanilla Slices, Peach Brandy Babas or Austrian Coffee Cake, as well as strudels and classic festive breads such as Polish Babka (Easter bread) or a Finnish Festive Wreath. You can even impress your friends by baking the traditional Italian Christmas bread, Mocha Panettone.

There are endless shaped rolls, buns and pastries to try out, from Pain au Chocolat to English Chelsea Buns, and the Chinese-style Chicken Buns, topped with sesame seeds. These breads can be easily shaped by hand after the machine has mixed and proved the dough, and then baked to golden perfection in a conventional oven.

BELOW: A flavored bread, such as Grainy Mustard and Beer Loaf, is delicious served with cheese and pickles as a simple lunch.

GETTING DOWN TO BASICS

A bread machine is designed to take the hard work out of making bread. Like most kitchen appliances, it is a labor-saving device. It will mix the ingredients and knead the dough for you, and allows the bread to rise and bake at the correct time and temperature.

For most breads, all you will need to do is to measure the ingredients for your chosen bread, put them into the pan in the correct order, close the lid, select a suitable baking program and opt for light, medium or dark crust. You may also choose to delay the starting time, so that you have freshly baked bread for breakfast or when you return from work. Press the Start button and in a few hours you will have a beautifully baked loaf, the machine having performed the kneading, rising and baking cycles for you.

Bread machines offer a selection of programs to suit different types of flour and varying levels of sugar and fat. You can explore making a whole variety of raw

BELOW: The three different sizes of bread machine pans that are available. From left to right: large, small and medium.

ABOVE: The shape of the kneading blade varies among different models of bread machine.

doughs for shaping sweet and savory breads, sourdough breads, mixed-grains, Continental-style breads and many more.

All bread machines work on the same basic principle. Each contains a removable nonstick bread pan, with a handle, into which a kneading blade is fitted. When inserted in the machine, the pan fits onto a central shaft, which rotates the blade. A lid closes over the bread pan so that the ingredients are contained within a controlled environment. The lid includes an air vent and may have a window, which can be useful for checking the progress of your bread. The machine is programmed by using the control panel.

The size and shape of the bread is determined by the shape of the bread pan. There are two shapes currently available; one rectangular and the other square. The rectangular pan produces the more traditional shape, the actual size varying from one manufacturer to another. The square shape is mostly to be found in smaller machines and produces a tall loaf, which is similar to a traditional rectangular loaf that has been stood on its end. The vertical square loaf can be turned on its side for slicing, if preferred, in order to give smaller slices of bread.

The size of the loaf ranges from about 1 pound 2 ounces to 3 pounds, depending on the machine, with most large machines offering the option of baking smaller loaves as well. One machine will make small, medium and large loaves.

BUYING A BREAD MACHINE

There is plenty of choice when it comes to selecting a bread machine to buy. Give some thought to which features would prove most useful to you, then shop around for the best buy available in your price range. First of all, consider the size of loaf you would like to bake, which will largely be governed by the number in your family. Remember that a large bread machine will often make smaller loaves but not vice versa.

You will need to consider whether the shape of the bread is important to you, and choose a machine with a square or rectangular bread pan accordingly.

Are you likely to want to make breads with added ingredients? If so, a raisin beep is useful. Does the machine have special flour cycles for whole-wheat loaves? Would this matter to you? Another feature, the dough cycle, adds a great deal of flexibility, as it allows you to make hand-shaped breads. Extra features, such as jam-making and rice-cooking facilities, are very specialized and only you know whether you would find them worth having.

One important consideration is whether the manufacturer offers a well-written manual and an after-sales support system or help line. If these are available, any problems or queries you might have can be answered quickly, which is particularly useful if this is your first machine.

A bread machine takes up a fair amount of room, so think about where you will store it, and buy one that fits the available space. If the bread machine is to be left on the work surface and aesthetics are important to you, you'll need to buy a machine that will be in keeping with your existing appliances. Most bread machines are available in white or black, or in stainless steel.

Jot down the features important to you, listing them in order of preference. Use a simple process of elimination to narrow your choice down to two or three machines, which will make the decision easier.

BELOW: A typical bread machine. Although each machine will have a control panel with a different layout, most of the basic features are similar. More specialized cycles vary from machine to machine.

BUILT-IN SAFETY DEVICES

Most machines include a power failure override mode which can prove to be extremely useful. If the machine is inadvertently unplugged or there is a brief power cut the program will continue as soon as the power is restored. The maximum time allowed for loss of power varies from 10 to 30 minutes. Check the bread when the power comes back on; depending on what stage the program had reached at the time of the power cut, the rising or baking time of the loaf may be affected.

An overload protection is available in some models. This will take over if the kneading blade is restricted by hard dough and will stop the motor to protect it. It will automatically re-start after about 30 minutes, but it is important to rectify the problem dough first. Either start again or cut the dough into small pieces and return it to the bread pan with a little more liquid to soften the dough.

HOW TO USE YOUR BREAD MACHINE

The instructions that follow will help you to achieve a perfect loaf the first time you use your bread machine. The guidelines are general, that is they are applicable to any bread machine, and should be read in conjunction with the manual provided for your specific machine. Make sure you use fresh, top quality ingredients; you can't expect good results with old flour or out-of-date yeast.

1 Stand the bread machine on a firm, level, heat-resistant surface. Place away from any heat source, such as a stove or direct sunlight, and also in a draft-free area, as these factors can affect the temperature inside the machine. Do not plug the bread machine into the power socket at this stage. Open the lid. Remove the bread pan by holding both sides of the handle and pulling upwards or twisting slightly, depending on the design of your particular model.

2 Make sure the kneading blade and shaft are free of any bread crumbs left behind when the machine was last used. Fit the kneading blade on the shaft in the base of the bread pan. The blade will only fit in one position, as the hole in the blade and the outside of the shaft are D-shaped.

3 Pour the water, milk and/or other liquids into the bread pan, unless the instructions for your particular machine require you to add the dry ingredients first. If so, reverse the order in which you add the liquid and dry ingredients, putting the yeast in the bread pan first.

4 Sprinkle the flour over, ensuring that it covers the liquid completely. Add any other dry ingredients specified in the recipe, such as evaporated milk. Add the salt, sugar or honey and butter or oil, placing them in separate corners so they do not come into contact with each other.

5 Make a shallow indentation in the center of the flour (but not down as far as the liquid) with the tip of your finger and add the yeast. If your indentation reached the liquid below the dry ingredients, then the yeast would become wet and would be activated too quickly. Wipe away any spills from the outside of the bread pan.

6 Place the pan inside the machine, fitting it firmly in place. Depending on the model of your machine, the pan may have a designated front and back, or clips on the outer edge that need to engage in the machine to hold the bread pan in position. Fold the handle down and close the lid. Plug into the socket and switch on the power.

7 Select the program you require, including crust color and loaf size, if available. Press Start. The kneading process will begin, unless your machine has a "rest" period to settle the temperature first.

8 Towards the end of the kneading process the machine will beep to alert you to add any additional ingredients, such as dried fruit. Open the lid, add the extra ingredients, and close the lid again.

9 At the end of the cycle, the machine will beep once more to let you know that the dough is ready or the bread is cooked. Press Stop. Open the lid of the machine. If you are removing baked bread, remember to use oven mitts to lift out the bread pan, as it will be extremely hot. Avoid leaning over and looking into the machine when you open the lid as the hot air escaping from the machine could cause you discomfort.

BELOW: A basic white bread is an excellent choice for the novice bread maker. If you follow these instructions and measure the ingredients carefully, you are sure to achieve a delicious loaf of bread. Once you have gained confidence, experiment with the recipe, by adding other ingredients or changing the crust color.

10 Still using oven mitts, turn the pan upside down and shake it several times to release the bread. If necessary, tap the bottom of the pan on a heatproof board.

11 If the kneading blade for your bread machine is not of the fixed type, and comes out inside the bread, use a heat-resistant utensil to remove it, such as a wooden spatula. It will come out easily.

12 Place the bread on a wire rack to cool. Unplug the bread machine and let it cool before using it again. Refer to the manufacturer's manual for guidance. If you use the bread machine again too soon, your second loaf will not be a success. Wash the pan and kneading blade, and wipe down the machine if necessary. All parts of the bread machine must be cool and dry before you store it.

PROGRAMS

BASIC CONTROLS

It will take you a little while and some practice to become familiar with and confident about using your new bread machine. Most manufacturers now produce excellent manuals, which are supplied with their machines. The manual is a good place to start, and should also be able to help you if you come up against a problem. Programs obviously differ slightly from machine to machine, but an overview will give you a general idea of what is involved.

It is important to understand the function of each control on your bread machine before starting to make a loaf of bread. Each feature may vary slightly between different machines, but they all work in a similar manner.

START AND STOP BUTTONS

The Start button initiates the whole process. Press it after you have placed all the ingredients required for the bread-making procedure in the bread pan and after you have selected all the required settings, such as loaf type, size, crust color and delay timer.

The Stop button may be the same control or a separate one. Press it to stop the program, either during the program, if you need to override it, or at the end to turn off the machine. This cancels the "keep warm" cycle at the end of baking.

TIME DISPLAY AND STATUS INDICATOR

A window displays the time remaining until the end of the program selected. In some bread machines the selected program is also shown. Some models use this same window or a separate set of lights to indicate what is happening inside the machine. It gives information on whether the bread machine is on time delay, kneading, resting, rising, baking or warming.

PROGRAM INDICATORS OR MENU

Each bread machine has a number of programs for different types of bread. Some models have more than others. This function allows you to choose the appropriate program for your recipe and indicates which one you have selected. These programs are discussed in more detail later.

PRE-HEAT CYCLE

Some machines start all programs with a warming phase, either prior to mixing or during the kneading phase. This feature can prove useful on colder days or when you are using larger quantities of ingredients such as milk, straight from the refrigerator, as you do not have to wait for them to come to room temperature before making the bread.

DELAY TIMER

This button allows you to pre-set the bread machine to switch on automatically at a specified time. So, for example, you can have freshly baked bread for breakfast or when you return from work. The timer should not be used for dough that contains perishable ingredients such as fresh dairy products or meats, which deteriorate in a warm environment.

CRUST COLOR CONTROL

The majority of bread machines have a default medium crust setting. If, however, you prefer a paler crust or the appearance of a high-bake loaf, most machines will give you the option of a lighter or darker crust. Breads high in sugar, or that contain eggs or cheese, may color too much on a medium setting, so a lighter option may be preferable for these.

WARMING INDICATOR

When the bread has finished baking, it is best to remove it from the machine immediately. If for any reason this is not possible, the warming facility will switch on as soon as the bread is baked, to help prevent condensation of the steam, which otherwise would result in a soggy loaf. Most machines continue in this mode for an hour, some giving an audible reminder every few minutes to remove the bread.

LEFT: French Bread can be baked in the machine on a French bread setting, or the dough can be removed to make the traditional shape by hand.

Reminder Lights

A few models are fitted with a set of lights which change color after being activated, to serve as your reminder that certain essential steps have been followed. This helps to ensure that the kneading blade is fitted, and that basic ingredients such as liquid, flour and yeast have been placed in the bread pan.

Loaf Size

On larger bread machines you may have the option of making up to three different sizes of loaf. The actual sizes vary between individual machines, but approximate to small, medium and large loaves of around 1 pound, 1½ pounds and 2 pounds respectively. However, this control in some machines is for visual indication only and does not alter the baking time or cycle. Check the manufacturer's instructions.

Baking Programs

All machines have a selection of programs to help ensure you produce the perfect loaf of bread. The lengths of kneading, rising and baking times are varied to suit the different flours and to determine the texture of the finished loaf.

Basic or Normal

This mode is the most commonly used program, ideal for white loaves and mixed grain loaves where white bread flour is the main ingredient.

Rapid

This cycle reduces the time to make a standard loaf of bread by about 1 hour and is handy when speed is the main criterion. The finished loaf may not rise as much as one made on the basic program and may therefore be a little more dense.

Whole Wheat

This is a longer cycle than the basic one, to allow time for the slower rising action of doughs containing a high percentage of strong whole-wheat flour. Some machines also have a multigrain mode for breads made with cereals and grains such as

ABOVE: Sun-dried tomatoes can be added to the dough at the raisin beep to make deliciously flavored bread.

multi-grain and rye, although it is possible to make satisfactory breads using either this or the basic mode, depending on the percentages of the flours.

French

This program is best suited for low-fat and low-sugar breads, and it produces loaves with an open texture and crispier crust. More time within the cycle is devoted to rising, and in some bread machines the loaf is baked at a slightly higher temperature.

Sweet Bread

A few bread machines offer this feature in addition to crust color control. It is useful if you intend to bake breads with a high fat or sugar content, which tend to color too much.

Cake

Again, this is a feature offered on a few machines. Some will mix a quick non-yeast teabread-type cake and then bake it; others will mix yeast-raised cakes. If you do not have this facility, teabreads and non-yeast cakes can easily be mixed in a bowl and cooked in the bread pan on a "bake-only" cycle, if your machine has one.

Bake

This setting allows you to use the bread machine as an oven, either to bake cakes and prepared dough from the supermarket or to extend the standard baking time if you prefer your bread to be particularly well done.

Sandwich

This facility, which enables you to bake a loaf with a soft crust that is particularly suitable for sandwich slices, is available on one or two models only.

Raisin Beep

Additional ingredients can be added mid-cycle on most programmes. The machine gives an audible signal—usually a beep—and some machines pause late in the kneading phase so that ingredients such as fruit and nuts can be added. This late addition reduces the risk of them being crushed during the kneading phase.

If your machine does not have this facility, you can set a kitchen timer to ring 5 minutes before the end of the kneading cycle and add the extra ingredients then.

Dough Programs

Most machines include a dough program: some models have dough programs with extra features.

Dough

This program allows you to make dough without machine-baking it, which is essential for all hand-shaped breads. The machine mixes, kneads and proves the dough, ready for shaping, final rising and baking in a conventional oven. If you wish to make different shaped loaves or rolls, buns and pastries, you will find this facility invaluable.

Other Dough Programs

Some machines include cycles for making different types of dough, such as a rapid dough mode for pizzas and Focaccia or a longer mode for whole-wheat dough and bagel dough. Some dough only cycles also include the raisin beep facility.

BAKING, COOLING AND STORING

A bread machine should always bake a perfect loaf of bread, but it is important to remember that it is just a machine and cannot think for itself. It is essential that you measure the ingredients carefully and add them to the bread pan in the order specified by the manufacturer of your machine. Ingredients should be at room temperature, so take them out of the refrigerator in good time, unless your machine has a pre-heat cycle.

Check the dough during the kneading cycles; if your machine does not have a window, open the lid and look into the bread pan. The dough should be slightly tacky to the touch. If it is very soft add a little more flour; if the dough feels very firm and dry add a little more liquid. It is also worth checking the dough toward the end of the rising period. On particularly warm days your bread may rise too high. If this happens it may rise over the bread pan and begin to travel down the outside during the first few minutes of baking. If your bread looks ready for baking before the baking cycle is due to begin, you have two options. You can either override and cancel the program, then re-program using a bake only cycle, or you can try pricking the top of the loaf with a toothpick to deflate it slightly and let the program continue.

Different machines will give different browning levels using the same recipe. Check when you try a new recipe and make a note to select a lighter or darker setting next time if necessary.

BELOW: Use a toothpick to prick dough that has risen too high.

REMOVING THE BREAD FROM THE PAN
Once the bread is baked it is best removed from the bread pan immediately. Turn the bread pan upside down, holding it with oven mitts or a thick protective cloth—it will be very hot—and shake it several times to release the bread. If removing the bread is difficult, rap the corner of the bread pan on a wooden board several times or try turning the bottom of the shaft underneath the bottom of the bread pan. Don't try to free the bread by using a knife or similar metal object, or you will scratch the nonstick coating.

If the kneading blade remains inside the loaf, you should use a heat-resistant plastic or wooden implement to remove it. The metal blade and the bread will be too hot to use your fingers.

ABOVE: Multi-grain Bread is made with honey, which acts as a preservative. The loaf should stay moist for longer.

BELOW: Use a serrated bread knife when slicing bread so that you do not damage the texture of the crumb.

TO SERVE BREAD WARM
Wrap the bread in foil and place in an oven preheated to 350°F for 10–15 minutes, to heat through. This is also a method that can be used to freshen bread.

COOLING
Place the bread on a wire rack to allow the steam to escape and leave it for at least 30 minutes before slicing. Always slice bread using a serrated knife to avoid damaging the crumb structure.

STORING
Cool the bread, then wrap it in foil or place it in a plastic bag and seal it, to preserve the freshness. If your bread has a crisp crust, this will soften on storage, so until it is sliced it is best left uncovered. After cutting, put the loaf in a large paper bag, but try to use it fairly quickly, as bread starts to dry out as soon as it is cut. Breads containing eggs tend to dry out even more quickly, while those made with honey or added fats stay moist for longer.

BELOW: Parker House Rolls can be frozen after baking, as soon as they are cool. They taste delicious warm, so refresh them in the oven just before serving.

ABOVE: If you are freezing bread to be used for toasting, slice the loaf first.

Ideally, freshly baked bread should be consumed within 2–3 days. Avoid storing bread in the refrigerator as this causes it to go stale more quickly.

Freeze cooked breads if you need to keep them longer. Place the loaf or rolls in a freezer bag, seal and freeze for up to 3 months. If you intend to use the bread for toast or sandwiches, it is easier to slice

ABOVE: Store bread with a crisp crust in a large paper bag.

it before freezing, so you can remove only the number of slices you need. Thaw the bread at room temperature, still in its freezer bag.

With some loaves, however, freezing may not be a sensible option. For example, very crusty bread, such as French Couronne, tends to come apart after it has been frozen and thawed.

STORING BREAD DOUGHS
If it is not convenient to bake bread dough immediately you can store it in an oiled bowl that has been covered with plastic wrap, or seal it in a plastic bag. Dough can be stored in the refrigerator for up to 2 days if it contains butter, milk or eggs and up to 4 days if no perishable ingredients are included.

Keep an eye on the dough and punch it down occasionally. When you are ready to use the dough, bring it back to room temperature, then shape, prove and bake it in the normal way.

You can make dough in your machine, shape it, then keep it in the refrigerator overnight, ready for baking conventionally next morning for breakfast. Cover with oiled plastic wrap as usual.

Bread dough can be frozen in a plastic bag for up to 1 month. When you are ready to use it, thaw the dough overnight in the refrigerator or at room temperature for 2–3 hours. Once the dough has thawed, place it in a warm place to rise, but bear in mind that it will take longer to rise than freshly made dough.

ABOVE: Store dough in the refrigerator in an oiled bowl covered in plastic wrap or in a plastic bag.

ABOVE: Prepare rolls the night before and store in the fridge, ready to bake the following morning.

HAND-SHAPED LOAVES

One of the most useful features a bread machine can have is the dough setting. Use this, and the machine will automatically mix the ingredients, and will then knead and rest the dough before providing the ideal conditions for it to rise for the first time. The whole cycle, from mixing through to rising, takes around 1¾ hours, but remember it will vary slightly between machines.

PUNCHING DOWN

1 At the end of the cycle, the dough will have almost doubled in bulk and will be ready for shaping. Remove the bread pan from the machine.

2 Lightly flour a work surface. Gently remove the dough from the bread pan and place it on the floured surface. Punch down or deflate the dough to relieve the tension in the gluten and expel some of the carbon dioxide.

3 Knead the dough lightly for about 1–2 minutes; shape into a tight ball. At this stage, a recipe may suggest you cover the dough with oiled plastic wrap or an upturned bowl and leave it to rest for a few minutes. This allows the gluten to relax so dough will be easier to handle.

SHAPING

Techniques to shape dough vary, depending on the finished form of the bread you wish to make. The following steps illustrate how to form basic bread, roll and yeast pastry shapes.

BAGUETTE

1 To shape a baguette or French bread, flatten the dough into a rectangle about 1 inch thick, either using the palms of your hands or a rolling pin.

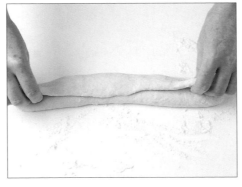

2 From one long side fold one-third of the dough down and then fold over the remaining third of dough and press gently to secure. Repeat twice more, resting the dough in between folds to avoid tearing.

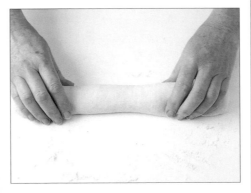

3 Gently stretch the dough and roll it backward and forward with your hands to make a long roll of even thickness and the required length.

4 Place the baguette dough between a folded floured dish towel, or in a banneton, and leave in a warm place to rise. The dish towel or banneton will help the baguette to keep the correct shape as it rises.

BLOOMER

1 Roll the dough out to a rectangle 1 inch thick. Roll up from one long side and place it, seam side up, on a floured baking sheet. Cover and let rest for 15 minutes.

2 Turn the loaf over and place on a floured baking sheet. Using your fingertips, tuck the sides and ends of the dough under. Cover; set aside to finish rising.

LOAF

Roll the dough out to a rectangle the length of the bread tin and three times as wide. Fold the dough widthways, bringing the top third down and the bottom third up. Press the dough down well, turn it over and place it in the pan.

COTTAGE LOAF

1 To shape a cottage loaf, divide the dough into two pieces, approximately one-third and two-thirds in size. Shape each piece of dough into a plump round ball and place on lightly floured baking sheets. Cover with inverted bowls and let rise for 30 minutes, or until 50 percent larger.

2 Flatten the top of the large loaf. Using a sharp knife, cut a cross about 1½ inches across in the center. Brush the area lightly with water and place the small round on top.

3 Using one or two fingers or the floured handle of a wooden spoon, press the center of the top round, penetrating into the middle of the dough beneath.

TWIST

1 To shape bread for a twist, divide the dough into two equal pieces. Using the palms of your hands, roll each piece of dough on a lightly floured surface into a long rope, about 1½–2 inches thick. Make both ropes the same length.

2 Place the two ropes side by side. Starting from the center, twist one rope over the other. Continue in the same way until you reach the end, then pinch the ends together and tuck the join underneath. Turn the dough around and repeat the process with the other end, twisting the dough in the same direction as the first.

ITALIAN BREADSTICK

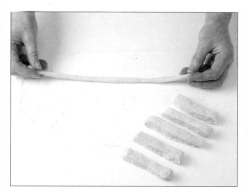

To shape a breadstick, roll the dough to a rectangle about ½ inch thick, and cut out strips that are about 3 inches long and ¾ inch wide. Using the palm of your hand, gently roll each strip into a long thin rope.

It may help to lift each rope and pull it very gently to stretch it. If you are still finding it difficult to stretch the dough, let it rest for a few minutes and then try again.

COURONNE

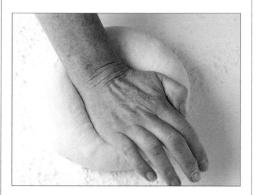

1 Shape the dough into a ball. Using the heal of your hand make a hole in the center. Gradually enlarge the center, turning the dough to make a circle, with a 5–6 inch cavity.

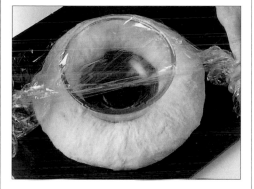

2 Place on a lightly oiled baking sheet. Put a small, lightly oiled bowl in the center of the ring to prevent the dough from filling in the center during rising.

SCROLL

Roll out the dough using the palms of your hands, until it forms a rope about 10 inches long with tapered ends. Form into a loose "S" shape, then curl the ends in to make a scroll. Leave a small space to allow for the final rising.

CROISSANT

1 To shape a croissant, roll out the dough on a lightly floured surface and then cut it into strips that are about 6 inches wide.

2 Cut each strip along its length into triangles with 6 inch bases and 7 inch sides.

3 Place with the pointed end toward you and the 6 inch base at the top; gently pull each corner of the base to stretch it slightly.

4 Roll up the dough with one hand from the base while pulling, finishing with the dough point underneath. Finally, curve the corners around in the direction of the pointed end to make the curved croissant shape.

BRAIDED ROLL

1 To shape a braided roll, place the dough on a lightly floured surface and roll out. Divide the dough into balls, the number depending on the amount of dough and how many rolls you would like to make.

2 Divide each ball of dough into three equal pieces. Using your hands, roll into long, thin ropes of equal length and place them side by side.

3 Pinch one of the ends together and braid the pieces of dough. Finally, pinch the remaining ends together and then tuck the join under.

BRAIDED LOAF

1 Place the dough on a lightly floured surface. Roll out and shape into a rectangle. Using a sharp knife, make diagonal cuts down each of the long sides of the dough, about ⅔ inch wide. Place the filling in the center of the uncut strip.

2 Fold in the end strip of dough, then fold over alternate strips of dough to form a braid over the filling. Tuck in the final end to seal the braid.

RISING

After the dough has been shaped, it will need to be left to rise again. This is sometimes referred to as proving the dough. Most doughs are left in a warm place until they just about double in bulk. How long this takes will vary —depending on the ambient temperature and richness of the dough—but somewhere between 30 and 60 minutes is usual.

Avoid leaving dough to rise for too long (over-proving) or it may collapse in the oven or when it is slashed before baking. Equally, you need to let it rise sufficiently, or the finished loaf will be heavy.

To test if the dough is ready to bake, press it lightly with your fingertip; it should feel springy, not firm. The indentation made by your finger should slowly fill and spring back.

ABOVE: A dough that has been shaped and placed in a bread pan to rise. The unproved dough should reach just over halfway up the pan.

ABOVE: Leave the dough in a warm, draft-free place to rise. This should take between 30 and 60 minutes. Once risen, the dough will have almost doubled in bulk.

SLASHING

Slashing bread dough before baking serves a useful purpose as well as adding a decorative finish, as found on the tops of traditional loaf shapes such as bloomers and baguettes. When the dough goes into the oven it has one final rise, known as "oven spring", so the cuts or slashes allow the bread to expand without tearing or cracking the sides.

The earlier you slash the dough the wider the splits will be. Depth is important, too: the deeper the slashes the more the bread will open during baking. Most recipes suggest slashing just before glazing and baking. If you think a bread has slightly over-risen keep the slashes fairly shallow and gentle to avoid the possibility of the dough collapsing.

Use a sharp knife or razor blade to make a clean cut. Move smoothly and swiftly to avoid tearing the dough. Scissors can also be used to make an easy decorative finish to rolls or breads.

SLASHING A SPLIT LOAF OR FARMHOUSE LOAF

A long slash, about ½ inch deep, can be made along the top of the dough just before baking. You can use this slashing procedure for both machine and hand-shaped loaves. Using a very sharp knife, plunge into one end of the dough and pull the blade smoothly along the entire length, but make sure you do not drag the dough.

If flouring the top of the loaf, sprinkle with flour before slashing.

SLASHING A BAGUETTE

To slash a baguette, cut long slashes of equal length and depth four or five times along its length. A razor-sharp blade is the best tool for slashing breads. Used with care, a scalpel is perfectly safe and has the advantage that the blades can be changed to ensure you always have a sharp edge.

USING SCISSORS TO SLASH ROLLS

Rolls can be given quick and interesting finishes using a pair of sharp pointed scissors. You could experiment with all sorts of ideas. Try the following to start you off.
• Just before baking cut across the top of the dough first in one direction then the other to make a cross.
• Make six horizontal or vertical cuts equally spaced around the sides of the rolls. Leave for 5 minutes before baking.
• Cut through the rolls in four or five places from the edge almost to the center, just before baking.

ABOVE: Top rolls: making a cross; middle rolls: horizontal cuts around the side; bottom rolls: cuts from the edge almost to the center.

BAKING BREAD WITH A CRISP CRUST

For a crisper crust, it is necessary to introduce steam into the oven. The moisture initially softens the dough, so that it can rise, resulting in a crispier crust. Moisture also improves the crust color by encouraging caramelization of the natural sugars in the dough. Standing the loaf on a baking stone or unglazed terracotta tiles also helps to produce a crisp crust, the effect being similar to when breads are cooked in a clay or brick oven. The porous tiles or stone hold heat and draw moisture from the bottom of the bread while it is baking.

1 About 30 minutes before you intend to bake, place the baking stone on the bottom shelf of the oven, then preheat the oven. Alternatively line the oven shelf with unglazed terracotta tiles, leaving air space all around to allow for the free circulation of the hot air.

2 When ready to bake, using a peel (baker's shovel), place the bread directly on the tiles or baking stone.

3 Using a water spray bottle, mist the oven walls two or three times during the first 5–10 minutes of baking. Open the oven door as little as possible, spray the oven walls and quickly close the door to avoid unnecessary heat loss. Don't spray the oven light, fan or heating elements.

GLAZES

Both machine-baked breads and hand-shaped loaves benefit from a glaze to give that finishing touch. Glazes may be used before baking, or during the early stages of baking to give a more golden crust or to change the texture of the crust. This is particularly noticeable with hand-shaped breads. However, good results may also be obtained with loaves baked in the bread machine. Glazes may also be applied after baking to give flavor and a glossy finish. Another important role for glazes is to act as an adhesive, to help any topping applied to the loaf stick to the surface of the dough.

For machine-baked breads, the glaze should either be brushed onto the loaf just before the baking cycle commences, or within 10 minutes of the start of the baking cycle. Apply the glaze quickly, so there is minimal heat loss while the bread machine lid is open. Avoid brushing the edges of the loaf with a sticky glaze as this might make the bread stick to the pan.

Glazes using egg, milk and salted water can also be brushed over freshly cooked loaves. Brush the glaze over as soon as the baking cycle finishes, then leave the bread inside the machine for 3–4 minutes, to allow the glaze to dry to a shine. Then remove the loaf from the machine and pan in the usual way. This method is useful if you want to sprinkle a topping over.

For hand-shaped loaves, you can brush with glaze before or after baking, and some recipes, such as Parker House Rolls, will suggest that you do both.

GLAZES USED BEFORE OR DURING BAKING

For a crust with a glossy shine to the loaf, apply a glaze before or during baking.

MILK

Brush milk on loaves, such as potato breads, where a softer golden crust is desired. Milk is also used for bridge rolls, buns and flatbreads where a soft crust is desirable. It can also be used on baps and soft morning rolls before dusting with flour.

OLIVE OIL

This is mainly used with Mediterranean-style breads, such as Focaccia, Stromboli and Fougasse. It adds flavor and a shiny finish; and the darker the oil the fuller the flavor, so use extra virgin olive oil for a really deep taste. Olive oil can be used before and/or after baking.

BELOW: French Fougasse is brushed with olive oil just before baking.

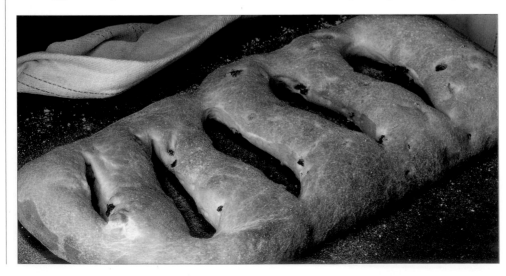

BUTTER

Rolls and buns are brushed with melted butter before baking to add color, while also keeping the dough soft. Parker House Rolls are brushed before and after baking, while Bubble Corn Bread is drizzled with melted butter before being baked. Butter adds a rich flavor to the breads glazed with it.

SALTED WATER

Mix 2 teaspoons salt with 2 tablespoons water and brush over the dough immediately before baking. This gives a crisp baked crust with a slight sheen.

EGG WHITE

Use 1 egg white mixed with 1 tablespoon water for a lighter golden, slightly shiny crust. This is often a better alternative to egg yolk for savory breads.

EGG YOLK

Mix 1 egg yolk with 1 tablespoon milk or water. This classic glaze, also known as egg wash, is used to give a very golden, shiny crust. For sweet buns, breads and yeast cakes add 1 tablespoon sugar, for extra color and flavor.

GLAZES ADDED AFTER BAKING

Some glazes are used after baking, often on sweet breads, cakes and pastries. These glazes generally give a glossy and/or sticky finish, and also help to keep the bread or cake moist. They are suited to both machine and hand-shaped breads.

BUTTER

Breads such as Italian Panettone and stollen are brushed with melted butter after baking to soften the crust. Clarified butter is also sometimes used as a glaze to soften flatbreads such as Naan.

HONEY, MALT SYRUP, MOLASSES AND GOLDEN SYRUP

Liquid sweeteners can be warmed and brushed over breads, rolls, teabreads and cakes to give a soft, sweet, sticky crust. Honey is a traditional glaze and provides a lovely flavor, for example. Both malt syrup and molasses have quite a strong flavor, so use these sparingly, matching them to compatible breads such as fruit loaves and cakes. Or you could mix them with a milder-flavored liquid sweetener such as golden syrup, to reduce their impact slightly.

SUGAR GLAZE

Dissolve 2–3 tablespoons granulated sugar in the same amount of milk or water. Bring to a boil then simmer for 1–2 minutes, until syrupy. Brush over fruit loaves or buns for a glossy sheen. For extra flavor, use rose water.

SYRUPS

Yeast cakes, such as Savarin, are often drizzled with sugar syrup, flavored with liqueurs, spirits or lemon juice. The syrup moistens the bread, while adding a decorative topping at the same time.

PRESERVES

Jam or marmalade can be melted with a little liquid. Choose water, liqueur, spirits (such as rum or brandy) or fruit juice, depending on the bread to be glazed. The liquid thins the preserves and adds flavor. It can be brushed over freshly baked warm teabreads, Danish Pastries and sweet breads to a give a glossy, sticky finish. Dried fruit and nuts can then be sprinkled on top.

Select a flavored jam to complement your bread or teacake. If in doubt, use apricot jam.

CONFECTIONERS' SUGAR GLAZE

Mix 2–3 tablespoons confectioners' sugar with 1 tablespoon fruit juice, milk, light cream (flavored with natural vanilla extract) or water and drizzle over sweet breads, cakes and pastries. You can also add a pinch of spice to the confectioners' sugar to bring out the flavor of the loaf. Maple syrup can be mixed with sugar for glazing nut-flavored breads.

LEFT: The glossy top to Hot Cross Buns is achieved by glazing after baking with a mixture of milk and sugar.

TOPPINGS

In addition to glazes, extra ingredients can be sprinkled over breads to give the finished loaf further interest. Toppings can alter the appearance, flavor and texture of the bread, so are an important part of any recipe. They also allow you to add your own individual stamp to a bread by using a topping of your own invention.

Machine-baked breads can be sprinkled with a topping at various stages: at the beginning of the baking cycle, about 10 minutes after baking begins, or immediately after baking while the bread is still hot. If you choose to add the topping at the beginning of baking, only open the lid for the shortest possible time, so heat loss is limited to the minimum. Before you add a topping, brush the bread with a glaze. This will ensure that the topping sticks to the loaf. Most machine breads are brushed with an egg, milk or water glaze.

If applying a topping to a bread after baking, remove the bread pan carefully from the machine and close the lid to retain the heat. Using oven gloves, quickly loosen the bread from the pan, then put it back in the pan again (this will make the

ABOVE: Flaked almonds have been sprinkled over the top of this Raspberry and Almond Teabread, giving a broad hint of its delicious flavor and adding extra crunch.

final removal easier) then brush the loaf with the glaze and sprinkle over the chosen topping. Return the bread in the pan to the bread machine for 3–4 minutes, which allows the glaze to bake on and secure the topping. With this method, the chosen topping will not cook and brown in the same way it would were it added at the beginning of baking.

When using grain as a topping, the general rule is to match it to the grain or flour used in the bread itself; for example, a bread containing millet flakes or millet seeds is often sprinkled with millet flour.

If a flavoring has been incorporated into the dough, you may be able to top the loaf with the same ingredient, to provide a hint of what is inside. Try sprinkling a little grated Parmesan onto a cheese loaf about 10 minutes after baking begins, or, for a loaf containing herbs, add an appropriate dried herb as a topping immediately after baking.

LEFT: Rolled oats and wheat grain are sprinkled on to Sweet Potato Bread just before it begins to bake to give the loaf a delightful rustic look.

FLOUR

To create a farmhouse-style finish, brush the loaf with water or milk glaze just before baking—or within 10 minutes of the start of baking—and dust lightly with flour. Use white flour, or wholewheat or multi-grain for a more rustic finish.

CORNMEAL OR POLENTA

Use cornmeal, polenta, semolina or other speciality flours as a finish for breads containing these flours, such as Zucchini Country Grain Bread.

ROLLED OATS

These make a decorative finish for white breads and breads flavored with oatmeal. Rolled oats are best added just before or at the very beginning of baking.

SMALL SEEDS

Seeds can be used to add flavor and texture in addition to a decorative finish. Try sesame, poppy, aniseed, caraway or cumin seeds. If adding sesame seeds immediately after baking, lightly toast until golden before adding.

LARGE SEEDS

Gently press pumpkin or sunflower seeds onto the top of a freshly glazed loaf to give an attractive finish and a bonus crunch.

PEPPER AND PAPRIKA

Freshly ground black pepper and paprika both add spiciness to savory breads. This tasty topping can be added before, during or after baking.

SALT

Brush the top of a white loaf with water or egg glaze and sprinkle with coarse sea salt, to give an attractive and crunchy topping. Sea salt is best applied at the beginning of baking or 10 minutes into the baking cycle.

WHEAT AND OAT BRAN FLAKES

These add both texture and fiber to bread as well as visual appeal. Sprinkle them over the top of the loaf after glazing at the beginning of baking.

CONFECTIONERS' SUGAR

Dust cooked sweet breads, teabreads or cakes with confectioners' sugar for a finished look. If you wish, add ½ teaspoon spice before sprinkling for added flavor.

HAND-SHAPED BREAD

All of the toppings used on machine-baked breads can also be added to breads that are hand-shaped and baked in an oven. There are several methods that can be used for adding a topping to hand-shaped rolls and breads.

SPRINKLING WITH FLOUR

If you are using flour, this should be sprinkled over the dough immediately after shaping and again before slashing and baking, to give a rustic finish. Match the flour to the type of bread being made. Unbleached white bread flour is ideal for giving soft rolls and breads a fine finish. Use cornmeal, ground rice or rice flour for crumpets and muffins and brown, whole-wheat and multi-grain flours on whole grain breads.

GROUND RICE OR RICE FLOUR

Muffins are enhanced with a ground rice or rice flour topping.

WHOLE-WHEAT FLOUR

Whole-wheat flour toppings complement whole grain dough whether made into loaves or rolls.

ABOVE: An Easter Tea Ring is glazed with confectioners' sugar and orange juice, then sprinkled with pecans and candied orange.

ROLLING DOUGH IN SEEDS

Sprinkle seeds, salt or any other fine topping on a work surface, then roll the shaped but unproved dough in the chosen topping until it is evenly coated. This is ideal for coating whole wheat breads with wheat flakes or pumpkin seeds. After rolling, place the dough on the sheet for its final rising.

SESAME SEEDS

Dough sticks can be rolled in small seeds for a delicious crunchy topping.

ADDING A TOPPING AFTER A GLAZE

Some toppings are sprinkled over the bread after glazing and immediately before baking. In addition to the toppings suggested for machine-baked breads, these toppings can be used:

CANDIED FRUITS

Whole or chopped candied fruits make an attractive topping for festive buns and breads. Add the fruits after an egg glaze. Candied fruits can also be used after baking, with a confectioners' sugar or jam glaze to stick the fruits to the bread.

NUTS

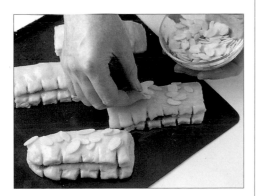

Just before baking, brush sweet or savory breads and rolls with glaze and sprinkle with chopped or flaked almonds, chopped cashews, chopped or whole walnuts or pecans.

SMALL SEEDS AND GRAINS

Seeds and grains such as black onion seeds, mustard seeds and millet grain all add texture and taste to breads. Try them as a topping for loaves and flatbreads such as Lavash and Naan.

VEGETABLES

Brush savory breads and rolls with an egg glaze or olive oil and then sprinkle with finely chopped raw onion, raw peppers, sun-dried tomatoes or olives for an extremely tasty crust.

CHEESE

Grated cheeses, such as Parmesan, Cheddar or Pecorino, are best for sprinkling onto dough just before baking, resulting in a chewy, flavorful crust.

FRESH HERBS

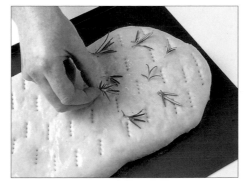

Use fresh herbs, such as rosemary, thyme, sage or basil for Italian-style flatbreads. Chopped herbs also make a good topping for rolls.

USING SUGAR AS A TOPPING

Sugar is available in many forms, so chose one appropriate for your topping.

DEMERARA SUGAR

Before baking, brush buns and cakes with butter or milk, then sprinkle with demerara sugar for a crunchy finish.

SUGAR COATING

Yeast doughs that are deep-fried, such as Doughnuts and Saffron Braids can be sprinkled or tossed in a sugar coating. Toss doughnuts in sugar that has been mixed with a little ground cinnamon or freshly grated nutmeg, or flavored using a vanilla bean.

DUSTING WITH CONFECTIONERS' SUGAR

Use a fine sieve to sprinkle cooked buns and yeast cakes, such as Devonshire Splits and Calas, with confectioners' sugar. Large cakes and breads such as Kugelhopf and Strudel also benefit from a light dusting of confectioners' sugar, as do fruit-filled Savarins. If serving a bread or cake warm, dust with confectioners' sugar when ready to serve to avoid the topping soaking into the bread.

USING SOURDOUGHS AND STARTERS

For bread to rise, some sort of raising agent – or leaven – must be used. In most cases, this will be yeast, or perhaps baking soda, but it is also possible to initiate the fermentation process naturally, by the action of wild yeasts, present in the air, on a medium such as flour or potatoes. When this is done, the mixture that results is called a starter.

There are two basic starters: a natural leaven and a yeasted starter. The former uses only airborne yeast spores, which create a lactic fermentation, as when milk turns sour. A yeasted starter includes a small amount of baker's yeast to kick-start the fermentation and develop a desired strain of yeast.

Sourdoughs are made using starters which develop over several days to produce a distinctive tanginess or "soured" flavor. Depending on how starters are made, how long they are left to ferment and how they are used, different flavors as well as textures can be achieved. Many of the Continental breads owe their flavors and textures to starters, which also influence their keeping qualities.

BREADMAKING METHODS

There are three basic methods of making breads: the direct method, the sourdough method, and the sponge method.

In the direct method, the flour, water and yeast are mixed, and once the dough has risen, the bread is baked in the shortest possible time. This is the conventional way of bread making.

The sourdough method is a much lengthier process. First, a starter must be made – this takes several days – and then this must be mixed with additional flour and other ingredients, often in several stages, called "refreshments," a process that takes at least 24 hours.

The sponge method is a compromise between the previous two. The dough is made using baker's yeast. A portion of the dough is mixed and allowed to ferment before the remaining ingredients are added. The process enhances the flavor and texture of the finished bread.

THE SOURDOUGH METHOD

Sourdough breads can be made from either a natural leaven or a yeasted starter. Most natural sourdough cultures can be turned into a starter within about 5 days. Flour and water are the basic ingredients, but other ingredients may be added to encourage the fermentation, such as malt extract (syrup), honey, sour milk, ground cumin or even a little baker's yeast.

The French term for this flour and water mixture is a "chef." The chef is left to ferment for 2–3 days, which brings about a lactic acid action, giving rise to the basic sour flavor. Once this dough is aerated and slightly sour, it is mixed or "refreshed" with more flour and water, to feed the fermentation process. After another 24 hours or so it is refreshed again, and becomes a natural leavener, or levain. This is left to ferment for about 8 hours more, when it is ready for use in the final bread dough.

Bread made by this method will taste slightly sour and will have a dense moist crumb, chewy crust and extremely good keeping qualities. Sourdough starters have varying textures, so do not worry if you come across different consistencies. Often American starters tend to be less stiff.

THE FRENCH SPONGE METHOD

The French sponge or poolish is made with yeast and some of the flour and water from the bread recipe, but no salt to retard the fermentation. The poolish is usually fermented for a minimum of 2 hours, and for up to 8 hours. Usually less yeast is used than with the direct method so the dough rises more slowly, giving it time to ripen and develop a springy texture. It combines the chewiness of a sourdough with the lightness of a basic bread.

The wetter the mix, the quicker it will rise, as the flour and water will provide less resistance for the yeast.

THE ITALIAN SPONGE METHOD

The Italian sponge or biga takes at least 12 hours, often longer, to ripen, allowing time for the dough to develop and rise to three times its original bulk before collapsing. The longer it is left the more developed the flavor will be. These breads have an open, holey, slightly moist and chewy texture. Their flavor and aroma tend to be yeasty and champagne-like. Ciabatta is a perfect example.

MAKING AN ITALIAN SPONGE

1 The flour, water and yeast for the biga are added to the bread machine and mixed as usual.

2 It is allowed to rise for several hours until it has tripled in size. After 12 hours it should be starting to collapse.

3 When the dough collapses, it is ready to be combined with the remaining ingredients for the bread.

THE OLD DOUGH METHOD

A variation of the direct method, this approach is exactly what its name suggests. A small piece of dough is removed from a batch of risen dough and set aside for adding to the dough for the next loaf of bread. This is a quick and easy alternative to making a starter and will add texture and improve the taste of the bread to which it is added.

The old dough method is perfect for the bread machine. Make a batch of dough using the regular dough cycle. When the bread is ready for shaping, pull off about 4 ounces of the dough, place it in a bowl and cover with plastic wrap. If using within 4 hours leave at room temperature; if not, put the bowl in the refrigerator, but let the dough return to room temperature before using it. It can either be kneaded into a batch of dough which will be shaped by hand or added with the ingredients for a machine-baked bread.

If you are adding old dough to a loaf which is to be baked in a machine, reduce the flour and liquid slightly when you make up the new batch of dough. The following recipe is suitable for a medium or large machine. If you have a smaller machine reduce the quantities by a quarter. You can increase the quantities by a quarter for a large machine if you like.

ABOVE: San Francisco-style Sourdough is made from airborne spores of yeast, and has no baker's yeast added to it. The variety of yeast strains in the atmosphere will mean that the bread tastes slightly different from place to place.

USING THE OLD DOUGH METHOD

1 Tear about 4 ounces dough off bread that is ready for shaping. Place in a bowl and cover with plastic wrap. Set aside at room temperature or, if not using within 4 hours, in the refrigerator. Return to room temperature before using.

2 Pour 1¼ cups water into the bread machine pan. Add the old dough which has been reserved. However, if the instructions for your machine specify that the dry ingredients are to be placed in the bread pan first, reverse the order in which you add the dry ingredients and the water and reserved dough.

3 Sprinkle 4 cups unbleached white bread flour over. Add 1½ teaspoons salt, 1 tablespoon granulated sugar and 2 tablespoons butter, placing these ingredients in separate corners of the bread pan.

4 Make a small indentation in the center of the flour and add 1 teaspoon rapid-rise active dry yeast.

5 Set the bread machine to the basic/normal setting, medium crust. Press Start. At the end of the baking cycle, remove the bread from the pan and turn out onto a wire rack to cool.

MAKING A YOGURT STARTER

Variations on the basic flour and water starter can be made to add complexity and uniqueness to the flavor and texture of bread. This yogurt starter will give a flavor similar to that of San Francisco-style Sourdough because the lactose in the milk products sours in a similar way.

1 Place 5 tablespoon plain yogurt in a bowl. Pour ¾ cup skim milk into a saucepan and heat gently.

2 Stir the milk into the yogurt. Cover with plastic wrap and leave in a warm place for 8–24 hours, or until thickened. Stir in any clear liquid that may have separated and risen to the surface.

REPLENISHING A STARTER

After making the starter for the first time, use or replenish within 3–4 days. When half has been used, replenish with ½ cup white bread flour and 3 tablespoons skim milk and 1 table-spoon natural yogurt or ¼ cup skim milk. If used daily, the starter can be kept at room temperature. If not, store in the refrigerator; bring back to room temperature before use.

3 Gradually mix in 1 cup organic white bread flour, stirring well to incorporate it evenly.

BELOW: French Couronne is made using a chef starter which becomes a levain, a natural leavener.

4 Cover and leave in a warm place for 2–3 days, until the mixture is full of bubbles and smells pleasantly sour. (Uncover to check the aroma of the starter.) Use instead of the usual starter for San Francisco-style Sourdough or incorporate into a basic bread recipe.

2 Stir the starter and use the amount required in the recipe. If your purpose in bringing the starter to room temperature is just so that you can feed it, pour half of the starter into a measuring cup, note the volume, then throw it away. This is so you will know how much to replenish.

USING A STARTER IN YOUR BREAD MACHINE

You can try adding a sourdough starter to one of your favorite recipes for a more complex flavor. Add it to a basic white, whole-wheat, mixed grain or rye bread. Here are a few pointers:

• Always bring the starter back to room temperature before using if it has been stored in the refrigerator.

• If your starter was made from a mixture of roughly half flour and half liquid, when you add it to the recipe, reduce the liquid in the recipe by the quantity of liquid in the starter, that is by half the total volume of the starter.

• The starter can be used in two ways. Try it in doughs that are made in the bread machine but shaped by hand and baked in the oven, or use it in a dough that is made and baked in the machine. If the latter, check the dough during the rising stage to make sure it is not rising too high; you can always override the program and set the machine to the bake only program, if available.

• If the dough hasn't risen as much as you would like, you will need to bake it in the oven. Remove the dough from the bread machine and shape it by hand. Let it rise until it has almost doubled in size, then bake in the normal way.

ABOVE : Ciabatta is made using the Italian sponge method.

REFRESHING A SOURDOUGH STARTER

Each time you use a sourdough starter, it needs to be replenished. Also, if you are not likely to be using it for some time, it is important to "feed" the starter regularly, with flour and liquid, to keep it active. The amount of flour and water you add to the starter to replenish it should equate to what was removed, either to be used in dough or discarded.

Once established, a sourdough starter can be kept in the refrigerator almost indefinitely. In fact, the flavor of the sourdough starter gets better with age. If your starter begins to turn pink or develops a mold, however, discard it and start again.

1 Take the starter from the refrigerator. It should be at room temperature before it's added to a recipe or fed.

3 Replenish the starter by adding a quantity of flour and water (in equal parts by volume). Use organic white or whole-wheat bread flour, or a combination of both. Whole-wheat flour develops a more intense sour flavor. Add a quantity that equates to the amount of starter that has been removed. Mix until smooth.

4 Cover and leave in a warm place for a few hours until it starts to ferment. Place in the refrigerator until needed.

GETTING THE BEST FROM YOUR MACHINE

Even the most comprehensive bread-machine manual cannot possibly cover all the hints and tips you will need. As you gain experience and confidence you will be able to solve more and more of any little problems that crop up. Here are a few pointers to help you along the road to successful baking.

TEMPERATURE AND HUMIDITY
The bread machine is not a sealed environment, and temperature and humidity can affect the finished results. On dry days, dry ingredients contain less water and on humid days they hold more.

The temperature of the ingredients is a very important factor in determining the success of machine-baked bread. Some machines specify that all ingredients should be at room temperature; others state that ingredients can be added from the refrigerator. Some machines have pre-heating cycles to bring the ingredients to an optimum temperature of around 68–77°F, before mixing starts. It is recommended that you use ingredients at room temperature. Water can be used straight from the cold tap. Lukewarm water may be beneficial for the rapid bake cycle on cold days.

Hot weather can mean that doughs will rise faster, so on very hot days start with chilled ingredients, using milk or eggs straight from the refrigerator.

Icy winter weather and cold draughts will inhibit the action of the yeast, so either move your machine to a warmer spot, or warm liquids before adding them to the bread pan. On very cold days, let the water stand at room temperature for about half an hour before adding the other ingredients to the pan, or add a little warm water to bring it up to a temperature of around 68°F, but no hotter.

QUALITY PRODUCE
Use only really fresh, good quality ingredients. The bread machine cannot improve poor quality produce. Make sure the yeast is within its use-by date. Yeast beyond its expiration date will produce poor results.

MEASURING INGREDIENTS

Measure both the liquids and the dry ingredients carefully. Most problems occur when ingredients are inaccurately measured, when one ingredient is forgotten or when the same ingredient is added twice. Before you start cooking, make sure you have all the necessary ingredients on hand.

Do not exceed the quantities of flour and liquid recommended for your machine. Mixing the extra ingredients may overload the motor and if you have too much dough it is likely to rise over the top of the pan.

FOLLOW THE INSTRUCTIONS
Always add the ingredients in the order suggested by the manufacturer. Whatever the order, keep the yeast dry and separate from any liquids added to the bread pan.

ADDING INGREDIENTS

Cut butter into pieces, especially if it is fairly firm, and/or when larger amounts than usual are required in the recipe. If a recipe requires ingredients such as cooked vegetables or fruit or toasted nuts to be added, let them cool to room temperature before adding them.

USING THE DELAY TIMER

Perishable ingredients such as eggs, fresh milk, cheese, meat, fruit and vegetables may deteriorate, especially in warm conditions, and could present a health risk. They should only be used in breads that are made immediately. Only use the delay timer for bread doughs that contain non-perishable ingredients.

CLEANING YOUR MACHINE
Unplug the machine before starting to clean it. Wipe down the outside regularly using a mild dishwashing detergent and a damp, soft cloth. Avoid all abrasive cleansers and materials, even those that are designated for use on nonstick items, and do not use alcohol-based cleansers.

BREAD PAN AND KNEADING BLADE
Clean the bread pan and blade after each use. These parts should not be washed in the dishwasher as this might affect the nonstick surface and damage the packing around the shaft. Avoid immersing the bread pan in water. If you have difficulty extracting the blade from the pan, fill the bottom of the pan with lukewarm water and let it soak for a few minutes. Remove the blade and wipe it with a damp cloth. Wash the bread pan with mild dishwashing detergent then rinse thoroughly. Store the bread machine with the kneading blade removed from the shaft. The bread machine and components must be completely dry before putting away.

ABOVE. A Multi-grain loaf should be baked on the whole-wheat setting, which has a longer rising cycle.

SPECIAL CONSIDERATIONS

Breads made with whole grains and heavier flours such as whole-wheat, rye or oatmeal, or with added ingredients such as dried fruits and nuts, are likely to rise more slowly than basic white loaves and will be less tall. The same applies to breads with a lot of fat or egg. Breads that include cheese, eggs or a high proportion of fats and/or sugar are more susceptible to burning. To avoid overcooked crusts, select a light bake crust setting.

WATCHING THE DOUGH

Keep a flexible rubber spatula next to the machine and, if necessary, scrape down the sides of the pan after 5–10 minutes of the initial mixing cycle. The kneading blade sometimes fails to pick up a thick or sticky dough from the corners of the pan.

COOLING THE BREAD

It is best to remove the loaf from the pan as soon as the baking cycle finishes, or it may become slightly damp, even with a "stay warm" program.

CHECKING THE DOUGH

Check the dough within the first 5 minutes of mixing, especially when you are trying a recipe for the first time. If the dough seems too wet and, instead of forming a ball, sticks to the sides of the pan, add a little flour, a spoonful at a time. However, the bread machine requires a dough that is slightly wetter than if you were mixing it by hand. If the dough is crumbly and won't form a ball, add liquid, one spoonful at a time. You will soon get used to the sound of the motor and notice if it is laboring due to a stiff mix. It is also worth checking the dough just before baking, to make sure it isn't about to rise over the top of the bread machine pan.

ABOVE: Dough is too wet and requires more flour.

SAFETY

1 Read the manufacturer's advice and instructions before operating your machine. Keep any instruction manuals provided with your machine handy for future reference.
2 If you touch the machine while it is in operation, be careful. The outside walls become hot when it is in baking mode.
3 Position the machine on a firm, level, heat-resistant surface, away from any other heat source.
4 Do not stand the bread machine in direct sunlight and allow at least 2–3 inches clearance on all sides when not in use.
5 Do not place anything on top of the machine lid.
6 Do not use the machine outdoors.
7 Do not immerse the machine, cord or plug in water and avoid using it near a source of water.
8 Be careful to keep your fingers away from the blade while the machine is kneading the dough, and never reach inside the machine during the baking cycle.
9 Keep the machine out of the reach of small children and make sure there is no trailing cord.
10 Unplug the machine before cleaning or moving it, and when it is not in use. Allow the bread machine to cool completely before cleaning and storing it.

ABOVE: Dough is too dry and requires more water.

ADAPTING RECIPES FOR USE IN A BREAD MACHINE

After you have cooked a number of the recipes from this book you may wish to branch out and adapt some of your own favorites. This sample recipe is used to explain some of the factors you will need to take into consideration.

INGREDIENTS

Read the list of ingredients carefully before you start, and adjust if necessary.

MALT EXTRACT (SYRUP) AND GOLDEN SYRUP

High sugar levels and/or dried fruit may cause the bread to over-brown. Reduce the malt extract (syrup) and golden syrup quantities by one-third and increase other liquids to compensate. Machine breads usually require the inclusion of sugar. Allow 1–2 teaspoons per 2 cups flour.

BUTTER

High fat levels mean that the bread will take longer to rise. Reduce to ¼ cup per 4 cups flour. You may need to add an extra 2 tablespoons liquid.

FLOUR

This recipe uses white flour, but remember that a whole-wheat loaf works better if you replace half the whole-wheat flour with white flour.

YEAST

Replace fresh yeast with rapid-rise active dry yeast. In a whole-wheat bread, for example, start by using 1 teaspoon for up to 3¼ cups flour or 1½ teaspoons for up to 6 cups flour.

MILK

Use skim milk at room temperature where possible. If you wish to use the time delay cycle you should replace with nonfat dry milk.

DRIED FRUIT

Additions that enrich the dough, such as dried fruits, nuts, seeds and whole grains, make the dough heavier, and the bread will not rise as well. Limit them to about a quarter of the total flour quantity.

MALTED FRUIT LOAF

scant ¼ cup barley malt syrup
2 tablespoons golden syrup
6 tablespoons butter
4 cups unbleached white bread flour
1 teaspoon apple pie spice
¾ ounce fresh yeast
⅔ cup lukewarm milk
¼ cup currants
⅛ cup golden raisins
¼ cup dried apricots
2 tablespoon mixed chopped peel

FOR THE GLAZE
2 tablespoons milk
2 tablespoons caster sugar

MAKES 2 LOAVES

1 Grease two 1-pound loaf pans.
2 Melt the barley malt syrup, golden syrup and butter in a saucepan. Let the mixture cool.
3 Sift the flour and spice into a large bowl; make a central well. Cream the yeast with a little of the milk; blend in the rest. Add the yeast mixture with the malt syrup to the flour and make a dough.
4 Knead the dough on a floured surface until smooth and elastic, about 10 minutes. Place in an oiled bowl and cover with oiled plastic wrap. Let it rise in a warm place for 1½–2 hours, until doubled in bulk.
5 Turn the dough out onto a lightly floured surface and punch down.
6 Gently knead in the dried fruits.
7 Divide the dough in half; shape into two loaves. Place in the pans and cover with oiled plastic wrap. Let it rise for 1–1½ hours or until the dough reaches the top of the pans.
8 Meanwhile, preheat the oven to 400°F. Bake the loaves for 35–40 minutes, or until golden. When cooked, transfer to a wire rack.
9 Gently heat the milk and sugar for the glaze in a saucepan. Brush the warm loaves with the glaze.

METHOD

Use a similar bread machine recipe as a guide for adapting a conventional recipe.

STEP 1

Obviously, you can only make one machine-baked loaf at a time. Make 1 large loaf or reduce the quantity of ingredients if your machine is small.

STEP 2

There is no need to melt the ingredients before you add them, but remember to chop the butter into fairly small pieces.

STEP 3

When adding ingredients to the bread pan, pour in the liquid first then sprinkle the flour over, followed by the apple pie spice. (Add the liquid first unless your machine requires dry ingredients to be placed in the bread pan first.)

Add rapid-rise active dry yeast to a small indentation in the center of the flour, but make sure it does not touch the liquid underneath. Place salt and butter in separate corners of the pan.

If your recipe calls for egg, add it with the liquid. Use water straight from the tap and other liquids at room temperature.

STEPS 4, 5, 7 AND 8

Ignore these steps: the bread machine will automatically mix, rise and cook the dough. Use a light setting for the crust due to the sugar, fat and fruit content of the Malted Fruit Loaf. Ordinary breads, such as a white loaf, need a medium setting; loaves that contain whole-wheat flour should be baked on the whole-wheat setting.

STEP 6

If you are adding extra ingredients, such as dried fruit, set the machine on raisin setting and add when it beeps. If you do not have this facility, add the ingredients 5 minutes before the end of the kneading cycle.

STEP 9

Make the glaze as usual and brush over the loaf at the end of the baking cycle.

USEFUL GUIDELINES

Here are a few guidelines that are worth following when adapting your own favorite recipes.

• Make sure the quantities will work in your machine. If you have a small bread machine it may be necessary to reduce them. Use the flour and water quantities in recipes in the book as a guide, or refer back to your manufacturer's handbook.

• It is important that you keep the flour and the liquid in the correct proportions, even if reducing the quantities means that you end up with some odd amounts. You can be more flexible with spices and flavorings such as fruit and nuts, as exact quantities are not so crucial.

• Monitor the recipe closely the first time you make it and jot down any ideas you have for improvements next time.

• Check the consistency of the dough when the machine starts mixing. You may need to add one or two extra spoonfuls of water, as breads baked in a machine

ABOVE: Some conventional recipes call for you to knead ingredients, such as fried onions, into a dough. When adapting for a bread machine, add to the dough at the raisin beep.

BELOW: Use a similar bread machine recipe to help you adapt a bread you usually make conventionally. For example, if you have a favorite rutabagas bread recipe, try adapting a machine recipe for parsnip bread.

require a slightly softer dough, which is wet enough to relax back into the shape of the bread pan.

• If a dough mixes perfectly in your machine but then fails to bake properly, or if you want bread of a special shape, use the dough cycle on your machine, then shape by hand before baking in a conventional oven.

• Look through bread machine recipes and locate something that is similar. This will give you some idea as to quantities, and which program you should use. Be prepared to make more adjustments after testing your recipe for the first time.

USING BREAD MIXES

Packaged bread mixes can be used in your machine. Check your manual, as some manufacturers may recommend specific brands.

• Check that your machine can handle the amount of dough the bread mix makes. If the package quantity is only marginally more than you usually make, use the dough cycle and then bake the bread conventionally.

• Select an appropriate setting; for instance, use the normal or rapid setting for white bread.

1 Place the recommended amount of water in the bread pan.

2 Spoon over the bread mix and place the pan in the machine.

3 Select the program required and press Start. Check the consistency of the dough after 5 minutes, adding a little more water if the mixture seems too dry.

4 At the end of the baking cycle, remove the cooked bread from the bread pan and turn out onto a wire rack to cool.

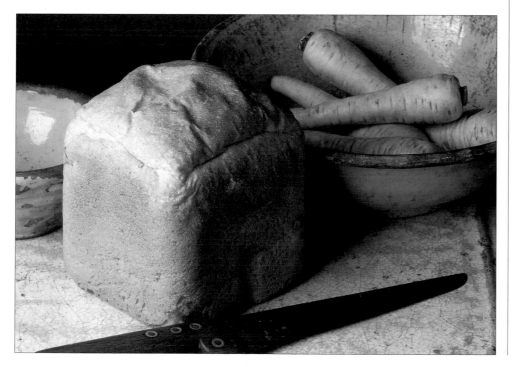

TROUBLESHOOTING

Bread machines are incredibly easy to use and, once you have become familiar with yours, you will wonder how you ever did without it. However, they are machines and they cannot think for themselves. Things can go wrong and you need to understand why. Here are a few handy troubleshooting tips.

BREAD RISES TOO MUCH

• Usually caused by too much yeast; reduce by 25 percent.
• An excess of sugar will promote yeast action; try reducing the quantity of sugar.
• Did you leave out the salt or use less than was recommended? If so, the yeast would have been uncontrolled and a tall loaf would have been the likely result.
• Too much liquid can sometimes cause a loaf to over-rise. Try reducing the liquid by 1–2 tablespoons next time.
• Other possibilities are too much dough or too hot a day.

BREAD DOES NOT RISE ENOUGH

• Insufficient yeast or yeast that is past its expiration date.
• A rapid cycle was chosen, giving the bread less time to rise.

• The yeast and salt came into contact with each other before mixing. Make sure they are placed in separate areas when added to the bread pan.
• Too much salt inhibits the action of the yeast. You may have added salt twice, or added other salty ingredients, such as salted nuts or feta cheese.
• Whole-grain and whole-wheat breads tend not to rise as high as white flour breads. These flours contain bran and wheat germ, which makes the flour heavier.
• You may have used all-purpose flour instead of a bread flour, which has a higher gluten content.
• The ingredients were not at the correct temperature. If they were too hot, they may have killed the yeast; if they were too cold, they may have retarded the action of the yeast.
• Insufficient liquid. In order for dough to rise adequately, it needs to be soft and pliable. If the dough was dry and stiff, add more liquid next time.
• The lid was open during the rising stage for long enough to let warm air escape.
• No sugar was added. Yeast works better where there is at least 1 teaspoon sugar to feed it. Note, however, that high sugar levels may retard yeast action.

BREAD DOES NOT RISE AT ALL

• No yeast was added or it was past its expiration date.
• The yeast was not handled correctly and was probably killed by adding ingredients that were too hot.

THE DOUGH IS CRUMBLY AND DOESN'T FORM A BALL

• The dough is too dry. Add extra liquid a small amount at a time until the ingredients combine to form a pliable dough.

THE DOUGH IS VERY STICKY AND DOESN'T FORM A BALL

• The dough is too wet. Try adding a little extra flour, a spoonful at a time, waiting for it to be absorbed before adding more. You must do this while the machine is still mixing and kneading the dough.

BREAD MIXED BUT NOT BAKED

• A dough cycle was selected. Remove the dough, shape it and bake it in a conventional oven or bake it in the machine on the "bake only" cycle.

BREAD COLLAPSED AFTER RISING OR DURING BAKING

• Too much liquid was added. Reduce the amount by 1–2 tablespoons next time, or add a little extra flour.
• The bread rose too much. Reduce the amount of yeast slightly in the future, or use a quicker cycle.
• Insufficient salt. Salt helps to prevent the dough from over-rising.
• The machine may have been placed in a draft or may have been knocked or jolted during rising.
• High humidity and warm weather may have caused the dough to rise too fast.
• Too much yeast may have been added.
• The dough may have contained a high proportion of cheese.

THERE ARE DEPOSITS OF FLOUR ON THE SIDES OF THE LOAF

• The dry ingredients, especially the flour, stuck to the sides of the pan during kneading, and then adhered to the rising dough. Next time, use a flexible rubber spatula to scrape down the sides of the pan after 5–10 minutes of the initial mixing cycle, if necessary, but take care to avoid the kneading blade.

CRUST IS SHRIVELLED OR WRINKLED

• Moisture condensed on top of the loaf while it was cooling. Remove from the bread machine as soon as it is cooled.

CRUMBLY, COARSE TEXTURE

• The bread rose too much; try reducing the quantity of yeast slightly next time.
• The dough didn't have enough liquid.
• Too many whole grains were added. These soaked up the liquid. Next time, either soak the whole grains in water first or increase the general liquid content.

BURNT CRUST

• There was too much sugar in the dough. Use less or try a light crust setting for sweet breads.
• Choose the sweet bread setting if the machine has this option.

PALE LOAF

• Add milk, either dried or fresh, to the dough. This encourages browning.
• Set the crust color to dark.
• Increase the sugar slightly.

CRUST TOO CHEWY AND TOUGH

• Increase the butter or oil and milk.

BREAD NOT BAKED IN THE CENTER OR ON TOP

• Too much liquid was added; next time, reduce the liquid by 1 tablespoon or add a little extra flour.
• The quantities were too large and your machine could not cope with the dough.
• The dough was too rich; it contained too much fat, sugar, eggs, nuts or grains.
• The bread machine lid was not closed properly, or the machine was used in too cold a location.
• The flour may have been too heavy. This can occur when you use rye, bran and whole-wheat flours. Replace some of it with white bread flour next time.

CRUST TOO SOFT OR CRISP

• For a softer crust, increase the fat and use milk instead of water. For a crisper crust, do the opposite.
• Use the French bread setting for a crisper crust.
• Keep a crisper crust by lifting the bread out of the pan and turn it out onto a wire rack as soon as the baking cycle finishes.

AIR BUBBLE UNDER THE CRUST

• The dough was not mixed well or didn't deflate properly during the punch down cycle between risings. This is not likely to be a consistent problem, but if it persists, try adding an extra spoonful of water.

ADDED INGREDIENTS WERE CHOPPED UP INSTEAD OF REMAINING WHOLE

• They were added too soon and were chopped by the kneading blade. Add on the machine's audible signal, or 5 minutes before the end of the kneading cycle.
• Leave chopped nuts and dried fruits in larger pieces.

ADDED INGREDIENTS NOT MIXED IN

• They were probably added too late in the kneading cycle. Next time, add them a couple of minutes sooner.

THE BREAD IS DRY

• The bread was left uncovered to cool too long and dried out.
• Breads low in fat dry out rapidly. Increase the fat or oil in the recipe.
• The bread was stored in the refrigerator. Next time place in a plastic bag when cool and store in a bread bin.

BREAD HAS A HOLEY TEXTURE

• The dough was too wet; use less liquid.
• Salt was omitted.
• Warm weather and/or high humidity caused the dough to rise too quickly.

A STICKY LAYERED UNRISEN MESS

• You forgot to put the kneading blade in the pan before adding the ingredients.
• The kneading blade was not correctly inserted on the shaft.
• The bread pan was incorrectly fitted.

SMOKE EMITTED FROM THE MACHINE

• Ingredients were spilled on the heating element. Remove the bread pan before adding ingredients, and add any extra ingredients carefully.

OTHER FACTORS

Creating the ideal conditions for your bread machine is largely a matter of trial and error. Take into account the time of year, the humidity and your altitude. Bread machines vary between models and manufacturers, and flour and yeast may produce slightly different results from brand to brand or country to country. Breads made in Australia, for example, often need slightly more water than those made in Britain.

You will soon get to know your machine. Watch the dough as it is mixing and check again before it begins to bake. Make a note of any tendencies (do you generally need to add more flour? does the bread often over-rise?) and adapt recipes accordingly.

FLOUR

The largest single ingredient used in bread, the right flour is the key to good bread making. Wheat is the primary grain for grinding into flour. Apart from rye, wheat is the only flour with sufficient gluten to make a well-leavened bread.

WHEAT FLOURS

Wheat consists of an outer husk or bran that encloses the wheat kernel. The kernel contains the wheat germ and the endosperm, which is full of starch and protein. It is these proteins that form gluten when flour is mixed with water. When dough is kneaded, gluten stretches like elastic to trap the bubbles of carbon dioxide, the gas released by the action of the yeast, and the dough rises.

Wheat is defined as either soft or hard, depending on its protein content, and is milled in various ways to give the wide range of flours we know today.

Wheat is processed to create many sorts of flour. White flours, for example, contain about 75 percent of the wheat kernel. The outer bran and the wheat germ are removed to leave the endosperm, which is milled into a white flour. Unbleached flour is the best type to use, as it has not been chemically treated to make it unnaturally white. This type is gradually replacing much of the bleached flour.

RIGHT: Clockwise from top: stone-ground, French, self-rising and all-purpose flour

ABOVE: Clockwise from top left: multigrain, stoneground whole-wheat bread flour, brown, stoneground white flour

ALL-PURPOSE FLOUR

A multi-purpose flour, all-purpose flour contains less protein and gluten than bread flour, typically around 9.5–10 percent. Sometimes a small amount of this type of flour is mixed with bread flour to achieve a closer-grained texture, but the main use for all-purpose flour is in quick teabreads, when chemical raising agents such as baking powder are added to give a light, airy crumb.

WHITE BREAD FLOUR

This flour is milled from hard wheat flour, which has a higher protein level than soft wheat flour. Levels vary between millers but the typical figure is around 12 percent. Some types of bread flour have lower levels—around 10.5–11 percent—but these have ascorbic acid added to act as a dough enhancer.

SELF-RISING FLOUR

This is not used in traditional breads, but is ideal for quick teabreads and cakes cooked in the bread machine. Sodium bicarbonate and calcium phosphate are mixed into the flour and act as rising agents.

FINE FRENCH BREAD FLOUR

Used principally for baking in France, this unbleached light flour is very fine and thus free-flowing. A small amount is often added to French bread recipes to reduce the gluten content slightly and achieve the texture associated with baguettes and other French specialities.

ORGANIC FLOURS

Organic white flour is produced using only natural fertilizers, and the wheat has not been sprayed with pesticides. Organic bread flours can be used in any recipe, and are recommended when developing natural yeasts for starters and sourdoughs.

WHOLE-WHEAT FLOURS

Because it is made from the complete wheat kernel, including the bran and wheat germ, whole-wheat is coarse textured and full-flavored with a nutty taste. For making machine breads, you should use whole-wheat bread flour, with a protein content of around 12.5 percent. Plain whole-wheat flour can be used with baking powder or baking soda for teabreads. Loaves made with 100 percent whole-wheat bread flour tend to be very dense. The bran inhibits the release of gluten, so whole-wheat doughs rise more slowly. For these reasons, many machine recipes recommend blending whole-wheat bread flour with some white bread flour.

Stoneground flour results when complete wheat grain is ground between two stones. Whole-wheat flours that are not stoneground have the bran and wheat germ removed during milling. They are replaced at the end of processing.

BROWN BREAD FLOUR

This flour contains about 80–90 percent of the wheat kernel, with some of the bran removed. It is a good alternative to whole-wheat flour, as it produces a loaf with a lighter finish, but with a denser texture and fuller flavor than white bread.

GRANARY FLOUR

A combination of whole-wheat, white and rye flours mixed with malted wheat grains, this adds texture and contributes a flavor that is slightly sweet and nutty. Malthouse is similar to Granary flour.

ABOVE: Left to right: semolina, spelt

SPELT FLOUR

Rich in nutrients, this is made from spelt grain, an ancient precursor of modern wheat. It is best used in combination with white bread flour. Even though it contains gluten, some gluten-intolerant people can digest it, so it is included in some diets for people who are allergic to wheat.

SEMOLINA

A high gluten flour, semolina is made from the endosperm of durum or hard winter wheat before it is fully milled into a fine flour. It can be ground to a coarse granular texture or a finer flour. The finer flour is traditionally used for making pasta, but also makes a delicious bread when combined with other flours. If 100 percent semolina is used, a heavy loaf will result.

OTHER WHEAT GRAINS

WHEAT BRAN

This is the outer husk of the wheat, which is separated from white flour during processing. It adds fiber, texture and flavor. You can add a spoonful or two to your favorite recipe or use it in place of part of the white bread flour.

WHEAT GERM

The germ is the embryo or heart of the wheat grain kernel. Use in its natural state, or lightly toasted, giving a nutty flavor. Wheat germ is a rich source of vitamin E and increases the nutritional value of bread. However, it inhibits the action of gluten, so do not use more than 2 tablespoons for every 2 cups flour.

CRACKED WHEAT

This is whole wheat kernel, broken into rather large pieces. It is quite hard, so you may like to soften it. Simmer in hot water for 15 minutes, then drain and cool. Add 1–2 tablespoons to a dough 5 minutes before the end of the kneading cycle.

BELOW: Clockwise from top left: bran, bulghur wheat, wheat germ, cracked wheat

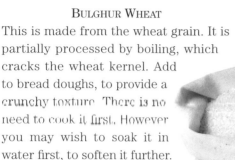

BULGHUR WHEAT

This is made from the wheat grain. It is partially processed by boiling, which cracks the wheat kernel. Add to bread doughs, to provide a crunchy texture. There is no need to cook it first. However you may wish to soak it in water first, to soften it further.

NON-WHEAT FLOURS

RYE FLOUR

Rye flour is used extensively in breads, partly because it grows well in climates that are cold and wet and not suitable for wheat cultivation. This is why so many of the Russian and Scandinavian breads include rye. Light and medium rye flours are produced from the endosperm while dark rye includes all the grain, resulting in a coarser flour that adds more texture to the bread. Rye contains gluten, but when used on its own produces a very heavy bread. Rye dough is very sticky and difficult to handle. For machine-made breads, rye flour must be combined with other flours. Even a small amount adds a distinctive tang.

MILLET FLOUR

Another high-protein, low-gluten grain, millet produces a light yellow flour with a distinctly sweet flavor and a slightly gritty texture. It tends to give breads a dry, crumbly texture, so you may need to add extra fat when using it. If using millet flour, boost the gluten content of the dough by using at least 75 percent white bread flour.

BARLEY

Barley seeds are processed to remove the bran, leaving a product called pearl barley. This is ground to make barley flour, which is mild, slightly sweet and earthy. It gives breads a soft, almost cake-like texture, as it has a very low gluten content. White flour must be combined with barley flour in a ratio of at least 3:1 for machine bread.

BUCKWHEAT FLOUR

This grayish-brown flour has a distinctive, bitter, earthy flavor. Buckwheat is the seed of a plant related to the rhubarb family. It is rich in calcium and vitamins A and B, high in protein but low in gluten. Traditionally used to make pancakes, Russian blinis and French galettes, it is best used in combination with other flours, to produce full-bodied and tasty multi-grain breads.

BELOW: Top to bottom: millet, buckwheat, barley

ABOVE: Left to right: polenta, cornmeal, millet

OTHER GRAINS

OATMEAL

When oats are cleaned and the outer husk has been removed, what remains is the oat kernel or groat. This is then cut into pieces to make either fine, medium or coarse oatmeal, or fully ground to make flour. All of these ingredients can be used in multi-grain breads, adding a rich flavor and texture. The coarser the oats, the more texture they will contribute to the

ABOVE: Top to bottom: oatmeal, rye

bread. Oatmeal is gluten-free, so it needs to be combined with wheat flour for bread making. The coarser textured oatmeal makes an attractive topping on breads and rolls.

POLENTA AND CORNMEAL
Dried corn kernels are ground to make coarse, medium and fine meal. The medium grain is known as polenta and the fine grain as cornmeal. For bread making, this flour has to be combined with white bread flour as it contains no gluten. Polenta and cornmeal add a sweet flavor and an attractive yellow color to the dough. For shaping the bread by hand, use polenta, which is slightly coarser and adds a pleasant finish to the bread.

MILLET GRAIN
This tiny, golden yellow, round grain is used in breads in Europe and Russia to give added texture. Include 1–2 table-spoons in a multi-grain bread, or even in a simple basic white loaf, for added inter-est. Millet grains make an attractive topping for breads such as Lavash. Millet flakes are also used in some breads.

RICE
Rice grains can be used in a variety of ways. Cooked long-grain rice can be added to doughs for bread with a moist crumb. Wild rice, although strictly an aquatic grass, will add a beautiful texture and fla-vor. Add it near the end of the kneading cycle to keep the grain intact and give attractive dark flecks of color to the bread. Ground rice and rice flour are milled from rice grains. Both brown and white rice flour are used, brown flour being more nutritious. Ground rice is more granular, similar to semolina. Either can replace some white bread flour in a recipe; they will add a

ABOVE: Clockwise from top left: ground rice, rice flour, wild rice, long grain rice

sweet flavor and chewy texture to the bread. Ground rice and rice flour can also be used as toppings. They are often dusted over English muffins or crumpets.

As rice is gluten-free, use only a small percentage of it with the bread flour.

ROLLED OATS
The inedible husk is removed from the oat kernel and the grain is then sliced, steamed and rolled to produce rolled oats. You can get jumbo-size oat flakes as well as traditional old-fashioned rolled oats. For bread making, use the old-fash-ioned oats rather than the "quick cook" oats. Add rolled oats to bread doughs to give a chewy texture and nutty taste, or use as a topping for an attractive finish on rolls and breads.

OAT BRAN
High in soluble fiber, this is the outer casing of the oat kernel. It acts in a similar way to wheat bran, reduc-ing the elasticity of the gluten, so use a maximum of 1 tablespoon per 1 cup flour. When using oat bran, you may need to add a little extra liquid to the dough.

LEFT: Clockwise from top right: jumbo oats, rolled oats, oat bran

LEAVENS AND SALT

Yeast is a living organism that, when activated by contact with liquid, converts the added sugar or sucrose, and then the natural sugars in the flour, into gases. These gases cause the bread to rise. As yeast is live, you must treat it with respect. It works best within the temperature range 70–97°F. Too hot and it will die; too cold and it will not activate. Yeast must be used before its expiration date, as old yeast loses its potency and eventually dies.

In most bread machine recipes dried yeast is used. In this book, all the recipes have been tested using rapid-rise active dry yeast, which does not need to be dissolved in liquid first. If you can find dried yeast especially made for use in bread machines, this will produce good results. You may need to adjust the quantities in individual recipes as variations occur between different brands of yeast.

ABOVE: Yeast is available in two forms, fresh and dry. From top to bottom: fresh yeast, dry yeast.

ABOVE: Add liquid to dissolve and activate fresh yeast.

Fresh yeast is considered by some bakers to have a superior flavor. It can be used with caution when baking in a bread machine, but is best used in the "dough only" cycle. It is hard to give exact quantities for breads, which will be made using a range of machines operating in different temperatures. The difficulty lies in preventing the bread from rising over the top of the bread pan during baking; doughs made from rapid-rise active dry yeast are easier to control where uniform results are required.

NATURAL LEAVENS

Long before yeast was sold commercially, sourdough starters were used to make breads. These were natural leavens made by fermenting yeast spores that occurred naturally in flour, dairy products, plant matter and spices. Breads are still produced by the same method today. Breads made using natural leavens have different flavors and textures from the breads made with commercial yeast.

BELOW: Buckwheat and Walnut Bread is made using rapid-rise active dry yeast, which gives good results.

ABOVE: Place active dry yeast in a shallow indentation in the flour.

ABOVE: Fresh yeast is dissolved before placing in the bread pan.

RIGHT: Left to right: cream of tartar, baking powder, baking soda

CHEMICAL LEAVENS

Raising agents other than yeasts can be used for bread. When using a bread machine, other raising agents are best used for teabreads and cakes that are mixed in a bowl, then baked in the bread pan.

Baking soda is an alkaline raising agent that is often used for quick breads. When moistened with liquid it gives off carbon dioxide, which makes the cake or quick bread rise. The heat from the oven cooks and sets the risen batter before it has a chance to collapse.

Cream of tartar is an acid, which is often combined with baking soda to boost the latter's leavening qualities. It also helps to neutralize the slightly soapy taste from the baking soda.

BELOW: Baking soda is the raising agent used for this Apricot, Prune and Peach Teabread

Baking powder is a ready-made mixture of acid and alkaline chemicals, usually baking soda and cream of tartar, but sometimes baking soda and sodium pyrophosphate. All these raising agents are fast acting. The bubbles are released the moment the powder comes into contact with a liquid, so such breads must be mixed and baked quickly.

SALT

Bread without salt tastes very "flat." While it is possible to make a saltless bread (there is, in fact, a famous saltless Tuscan bread which is eaten with salty cheese or preserved meats such as salami), salt is normally an indispensable ingredient. Salt has two roles: one is to improve the flavor and the other is to act as a yeast retardant, controlling the rate of fermentation, which in turn strengthens the gluten and stops the bread from rising too much and collapsing.

When adding salt to the bread pan, it is vital to keep it away from the yeast, as concentrated salt will severely impede the activity of the yeast.

Fine table salt and sea salt can both be used in bread that is to be baked in a machine. Coarse sea salt is best used as a topping. It can be sprinkled on top of unbaked breads and rolls to give a crunchy texture and agreeable flavor.

Salt substitutes are best avoided as few of these contain sodium.

DOUGH CONDITIONERS

These are added to breads to help stabilize the gluten strands and hold the gases formed by the yeast. Chemical conditioners are often added to commercially-produced bread, and you will also find bread improvers listed among the ingredients on fast action yeast packages.

Two natural dough conditioners which help to ensure a higher rise, lighter texture, and stronger dough are lemon juice and malt extract (syrup). Gluten strength can vary between bags of flour, so you can add some lemon juice to the dough to help to strengthen it, particularly when making wholegrain breads. You can add 1 teaspoon lemon juice with every 2 cups bread flour without affecting the flavour of the bread.

Malt extract (syrup) helps to break down the starch in wheat into sugars for the yeast to feed on and so encourages active fermentation. If you use up to 1 teaspoon malt extract with every 2 cups bread flour you will not effect a noticeable flavour change. If you like the flavour of malt extract, you can increase the amount used.

LIQUIDS

Some form of liquid is essential when making bread. It rehydrates and activates the yeast, and brings together the flour and any other dry ingredients to make the dough. Whatever the liquid, the temperature is important for successful machine breads. If your machine has a preheating cycle, cold liquids, straight from the refrigerator, can be used. If not, use liquids at room temperature, unless it is a very hot day. Water from the tap, providing it is merely cool, is fine. On a very cold day, measure the water and let it stand in the kitchen for a while to come to room temperature before you use it.

WATER

Water is the most frequently used liquid in bread making. Bread made with water has a crisper crust than when milk is included. Tap water is chemically treated, and if it has been heavily chlorinated and fluorinated this may well slow down the rising. Hard water can also affect the rise,

BELOW: Cranberry juice and orange juice may be used in breads.

because it is alkaline, which retards the yeast. If your breads are not rising very well and you have tried other remedies, then either boil some water and let it cool to room temperature or use bottled spring water.

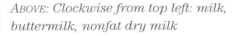

ABOVE: Clockwise from top left: milk, buttermilk, nonfat dry milk

MILK

Milk helps to enrich the dough and produces a loaf with a creamy-colored, tender crumb and a golden crust. Use whole, low-fat or skim milk, according to your preference.

You can also replace fresh milk with nonfat dry milk. This can be useful if you intend using the timer to delay the starting time for making bread, as, unlike fresh milk, the milk powder will not deteriorate. Sprinkle it on top of the flour in the bread pan to keep it separated from the water until mixing starts.

BUTTERMILK

Used instead of regular milk, this makes bread more moist and gives it an almost cake-like texture. Buttermilk is made from skim milk which is pasteurized, then cooled. After this a cultured bacteria is added which ferments it under controlled conditions to produce its slightly tangy, acidic, but pleasant flavor. This flavor is noticeable in the finished loaf.

YOGURT AND OTHER DAIRY PRODUCTS

Another alternative to milk, yogurt also has good tenderizing properties. Use plain yogurt or try flavored ones, such as lemon or hazelnut in similarly flavored breads.

Soured cream, cottage cheese and soft cheeses such as ricotta, fromage frais and mascarpone can all be used as part of the liquid content of the bread. They are valued more for their tenderizing properties than for their flavor.

COCONUT MILK

Use 50:50 with water to add flavor to sweet breads and buns.

FRUIT JUICES

Fruit juices such as orange, mango, pineapple or cranberry can be added to the dough for fruit flavored breads to enhance their fruitiness.

VEGETABLE JUICES AND COOKING LIQUIDS

The liquid left over from cooking vegetables will add flavor and extra nutritional value to breads and is particularly useful when making savory breads. Potato water has several benefits. The extra starch acts as an additional food for the yeast, and produces a greater rise and also a softer, longer-lasting loaf.

Vegetables themselves contain liquid juices and when added to a bread machine will alter the liquid balance.

SOAKING JUICES

When dried vegetables such as mushrooms, especially wild ones, and sun-dried tomatoes are rehydrated in water, a

ABOVE: Ciders, beers and liqueurs all add a rich, interesting flavor to breads.

flavorful liquid is produced. This is much too good to waste. Rehydrate the vegetables, drain off the liquid and add it as part of the liquid in a savory bread. In sweet breads, the liquid drained from dried fruits that have been plumped up in fruit juices, spirits and liqueurs is equally useful.

BEERS, ALES, CIDERS AND LIQUEURS

All of these can be added to bread recipes. Beers and ales, in particular, have a great affinity with dark, heavy flours. The added sugars stimulate the yeast by providing more food. Dark beers and ales impart a stronger flavor.

EGGS

If a bread recipe includes eggs, these should be considered part of the liquid content. Eggs add color, improve the structure and give the bread a rich flavor, although they are inclined to dry out more quickly than plain bread. It is worth adding extra fat to compensate for this. All the recipes in this book use medium eggs unless stated otherwise.

ABOVE: Use soaking and cooking liquids in savoury breads.

FATS AND SWEETENERS

FATS

Whether solid (butter, margarine) or liquid (oil), small amounts of fats are often added to breads. They enrich doughs and add flavor, and, with eggs, they give a soft, tender texture to the crumb. Fats help to extend the freshness of the loaf, and in rich doughs, help to cancel out the drying effect that eggs can cause.

In small amounts, fat contributes to the elasticity of the gluten, but use too much and the opposite effect will result. The fat coats the gluten strands and this forms a barrier between the yeast and flour. This slows down the action of the yeast, and hence increases the rising time. For this reason it is best to limit the amount of fat in a machine-baked bread, or risk a heavy, compact loaf.

When making rich, brioche-style bread, it is best to use the bread machine only for making the dough. It may be necessary to use the cycle twice. Afterwards, shape the dough by hand and let it rise for as long as required, before baking the bread conventionally.

SOLID FATS

Butter, margarine or lard can all be used in small quantities (of up to 1 tablespoon) without adding any noticeable flavor to the dough. Where a recipe calls for a larger quantity of fat, use butter, preferably unsalted. If you only have salted butter, and you are using quite a lot of it, you may need to reduce the amount of salt added to the dough. Cut the butter into small pieces so that it will mix in better. Avoid letting the fat come into contact with the yeast as it may inhibit the dissolving of the yeast.

BELOW: Left to right: olive oil, sunflower oil, hazelnut oil and walnut oil can all be used to impart a slightly different flavor to bread.

Where butter is layered in yeast pastry for croissants and Danish pastries, it is important to soften it so it has the same consistency as the dough.

Although it is possible to use low-fat spreads in breadmaking, there is not much point in doing so, as they may contain up to 40 percent water and do not have the same properties as butter.

LIQUID FATS

Sunflower oil is a good alternative to butter if you are concerned about the cholesterol level, while olive oil can be used where flavor is important. Use a fruity, full-flavored extra virgin olive oil.

Nut oils, such as walnut and hazelnut, are quite expensive and have very distinctive flavors, but are wonderful when teamed with similarly flavored breads.

Solid fats and oils are interchangeable in many bread recipes. If you wish to change a solid fat for a liquid fat or oil the amount of liquid in the dough may need to be adjusted to accommodate the change, although this is only necessary for amounts over 1 tablespoon.

LEFT: Left to right: margarine, butter, lard

ABOVE: Left to right: dark brown sugar; demerara sugar, light brown sugar; granulated sugar, caster sugar

SWEETENERS

Sugars and liquid sweeteners accelerate the fermentation process by providing the yeast with extra food. Many modern types of yeast no longer need sugar; they are able to use the flour efficiently to provide food. Even so, it is usual to add a small amount of sweetener. This makes the dough more active than if it were left to feed slowly on the natural starches and sugars in the flour. Enriched breads and heavy wholegrain breads need the increased yeast action to help the heavier dough to rise.

Sugar helps delay the staling process in bread because it attracts moisture. It also creates a tender texture. Too much sugar can cause dough to over-rise and collapse. Sweet breads have a moderate sugar level and gain extra sweetness from dried fruits, sweet glazes and icings.

BELOW: Left to right: treacle, golden syrup, molasses, malt extract (syrup), maple syrup, honey

Sweeteners contribute to the color of the bread. A small amount enhances the crust color, giving a golden finish. Some bread machines over-brown sweet doughs, so select a light crust setting or a sweet bread setting, if available, when making sweet yeast cakes.

Any liquid sweetener can be used instead of sugar, but should be counted as part of the total liquid content of the bread. Adjustments may need to be made.

WHITE SUGARS

Granulated sugar can be used for bread making. It is almost pure sucrose and adds little flavor to the finished bread. Do not use confectioners' sugar as the anti-caking agent can affect the flavor. Save confectioners' sugar for glazing and dusting.

BROWN SUGARS

Use light or dark brown, refined or unrefined brown sugar. The darker unrefined sugars will add more flavor, having a higher molasses content. Brown sugars add a touch of color and also increase the acidity, which can be beneficial.

MALT EXTRACT

An extract (syrup) from malted wheat or barley, this has a strong flavor, so use sparingly. It is best used in fruit breads.

HONEY AND MAPLE SYRUP

Honey can be used as a substitute for sugar, but only use two-thirds of the amount suggested for sugar, as it is sweeter. Maple syrup is the reduced sap of the maple tree; use it in place of honey or sugar. It is slightly sweeter than sugar but not as sweet as honey.

MOLASSES, GOLDEN SYRUP AND TREACLE

All these sweeteners are by-products of sugar refining. Molasses is a thick concentrated syrup with a sweet, slightly bitter flavor. It adds a golden color to bread. Golden syrup is light and sweet with a slight butterscotch flavor. Treacle is brownish black and more intensely flavored, and, like molasses, adds a slight bitterness to the bread.

ADDITIONAL INGREDIENTS

MEATS

Meats can be used to flavor bread recipes. The best results often come from using cured meats, such as ham, bacon or salami, and cooked sausages such as pepperoni.

When you use a strongly flavored meat, it is best to chop it finely and add it to the dough during its final kneading. You don't need much—1–2 ounces will be quite sufficient to add extra flavor without over-powering the bread.

Ham and bacon are best added as small pieces, late on in the kneading cycle. Dice ham small. Fry or broil bacon, then crumble them or cut into pieces, or use ready-cut cubes of bacon or pancetta and sauté them first. Make sure the bacon is fully cooked before adding it to the bread dough.

Thinly sliced preserved meats, such as Prosciutto, pastrami, speck, pepperoni and smoked venison can be added as thin strips towards the end of the kneading cycle or incorporated in the dough during shaping, for hand-shaped loaves. Cured and smoked venison marinated in olive oil and herbs gives a basic loaf of bread a wonderful burst of flavor, or you could try adding pastrami to a bread containing rye flour. Strongly flavored meats will make the most impact, but do remember that you need only small amounts.

LEFT: Sausages and bacon are a tasty addition to bread. They should be cooked before adding to a dough.

USING BACON IN A BREAD MACHINE

1 Cut the bacon into thin strips and broil it, or dry-fry in a nonstick frying pan, until it is crisp.

2 Transfer the cooked bacon to a plate lined with paper towels, to blot up excess fat. Let it cool.

3 Add the strips of bacon to the bread machine towards the end of the kneading process or when the machine beeps.

USING MEATS

Some meats are best kept whole or coarsely chopped and used as a filling, as when sausage is layered through a brioche dough, or used as a topping on tray-baked breads and pizzas. There are many different types of salami, flavored with spices such as peppercorns, coriander or paprika, as well as pepperoni and cooked spicy Continental-style sausages, all of which are suitable.

LEFT: From top to bottom: salami, pepperoni, thinly sliced smoked venison, Prosciutto

RIGHT: *From left to right: cottage cheese, mascarpone, fromage frais*

CHEESES

Cheese can be added to a wide variety of breads, to make them more moist and to give them more taste. Some cheeses have powerful flavors that really impact on the bread, while others are much more subtle, and are indistinguishable from the other ingredients except for the richness and tenderness they impart. Soft cheeses such as cottage cheese, mascarpone, fromage frais and ricotta are added in this way as part of the liquid content of the recipe. They contribute little to the overall taste of the bread, but help to create a more tender loaf with a softer crumb.

Grated or chopped hard cheeses can be added at the beginning of kneading so they are totally incorporated in the dough, or else towards the end of kneading, meaning that small amounts can clearly be detected in the bread. Alternatively, the cheese can be sprinkled over the top just before baking, to add color and texture to the crust, or used as a topping or filling, as in pizzas or calzones.

For maximum cheese flavor, use small amounts of strongly flavored cheeses such as extra-mature Cheddar, Parmesan, Pecorino, or blue cheeses such as Roquefort, Gorgonzola, Danish Blue or Stilton.

RIGHT: *Selection of cheeses, clockwise from top left: Cheddar, Emmenthal, feta, Gorgonzola; center: mozzarella*

If the cheese is salty, reduce the amount of added salt, or the action of the yeast will be retarded and the bread may taste unacceptably salty.

Machine-made breads incorporating hard cheeses may not rise as high as ones without, due to the increased richness in the dough, but the texture and flavor are likely to be superb.

USING CHEESE IN A BREAD MACHINE

- Add a soft cheese to the bread pan with the liquids before adding the dry ingredients, unless the instructions for your breadmaking machine state that you should add dry ingredients first.
- Add grated cheese at the beginning of the dough cycle so that it becomes evenly incorporated throughout the cooked bread.

- Add coarsely crumbled cheeses when the machine beeps towards the end of the kneading, so that it retains some of its form and remains in small pockets in the dough.

HERBS AND SPICES

Use herbs and spices as the main flavoring ingredient in bread or to enhance other ingredients.

HERBS

Fresh herbs have the most wonderful aroma, matched only by their flavor in freshly baked breads. Use fresh herbs if possible. Dried herbs that are oily and pungent, such as sage, rosemary and thyme, also work well. Rosemary is especially pungent, so use sparingly. Dried oregano is a fine substitute for fresh. Dried herbs have a more concentrated flavor than fresh; use about a third of the quantity recommended for fresh.

A number of herbs are now available freshly chopped and preserved in oil, which is a good alternative for more delicate herbs such as basil and cilantro which

LEFT: Clockwise from top: basil, thyme, flat-leaf parsley, oregano, cilantro, dill

do not dry well.

Add fresh herbs toward the end of the kneading cycle. Dried herbs can be added with the dry ingredients. Avoid using dried parsley; substitute a different herb instead.

SPICES

Spices are the dried, intensely aromatic, seeds, pods, stems, bark, buds or roots of plants. As with herbs, the fresher they are the more aromatic they will be; the volatile oils fade with age. Use freshly grated black pepper and nutmeg. Cumin, fennel, caraway and cardamom can be bought as whole seeds, and ground in a spice mill, or a coffee mill kept for the purpose, as needed. If you buy ground spices, use them within 6 months.

Add saffron, nutmeg, cinnamon, anise, all-spice and cardamom to sweet or savory breads. Mixed spice and ginger are sweet spices, while juniper berries, cumin, coriander and black onion seeds provide aromatic flavorings for savory breads. A number of whole spices can also be used as toppings for breads.

BELOW: From left to right: Front row: black onion seeds, saffron, fennel, nutmeg; back row: allspice, cinnamon, cumin, ginger

ADDING HERBS AND SPICES

• Frozen chopped herbs are a quick alternative to fresh herbs. Add them to the dough just before the end of the kneading process.
• Add ground spices after the flour, so they do not come into contact with the liquid before mixing.
• Add whole spices along with the dry ingredients if you want them to break down during kneading. If not, add them when the machine beeps, towards the end of kneading.

NUTS

Nuts make a wonderful addition to home-made breads. Their crunchiness combines equally well with the sweet chewiness of dried and semi-dried fruits, and with fresh fruits. They go well with savory additions such as cheese, herbs and spices and they can be used on their own to make rustic-style breads.

Nuts contain natural oils which turn rancid if stored too warm or for too long. Buy in small quantities, store in an air-tight container in a cool place and use them within a few weeks.

Pecans, almonds, macadamia nuts, pistachio nuts and walnuts give wonderful flavor and texture when added to basic breads towards the end of the kneading process. They can be added to teabreads, or used as a decoration on top of sweet breads or yeast cakes. Walnut bread is a

ABOVE: Clockwise from top right: pistachios, pecans, pine nuts, walnuts, slivered almonds, macadamia nuts

rich brown loaf with a soft crunch, perfect with cheeses.

Lightly toast pine nuts, hazelnuts and almonds first to bring out their flavor. Spread the nuts on a baking sheet and place them in an oven preheated to 350°F for 5–8 minutes, or broil until golden. Avoid scorching, and cool before adding them to the bread.

Hazelnuts, almonds and walnuts can be finely ground and used as a nutritious and flavorful flour substitute. Replace up to 15 percent of the flour with the ground nuts. If using hazelnuts, remove the skin first, as it is bitter. This will easily rub off if you toast the nuts in the oven.

Use coconut freshly grated or choose dried, either plain or toasted.

CHESTNUT BREAD

These quantities are for a medium loaf. Increase all ingredients by 25 percent for a large machine; decrease by 25 percent for a small one.

1 Put ½ cup unsweetened chestnut purée in a bowl and stir in scant 1¼ cups water. Mix well. Place in the bread pan. Add the dry ingredients first if necessary.

2 Sprinkle 4 cups white bread flour and ½ cup whole-wheat flour over. Add 2 tablespoons nonfat dry milk, ½ teaspoon ground cloves and 1 teaspoon grated nutmeg. Place 3 tablespoons butter, 1 tablespoon brown sugar and 1 teaspoon salt in separate corners. Make a shallow indentation; add 1½ teaspoons rapid-rise active dry yeast.

3 Set to the basic/normal setting, with raisin setting (if available), light crust. Press Start. Add ¾ cup coarsely chopped walnuts at the beep or after the first kneading. After baking, cool on a wire rack.

VEGETABLES

Raw, canned, dried and freshly cooked vegetables all make perfect additions to savory breads. Making bread also provides a good opportunity to use up any leftover cooked vegetables. Vegetable breads are richer than basic breads, the vegetables contributing flavor and texture to the finished loaves. Many vegetable breads are subtly colored or dotted with attractive flecks.

Fresh vegetables are relatively high in liquid, so if you add them, calculate that about half of their weight will be water

BELOW: Clockwise from top: spinach, green, red and yellow bell peppers, zucchini, sweet potatoes

LEFT: Clockwise from top right: garlic, scallions, chilli peppers, dried sliced onion, onions

and deduct the equivalent amount of liquid from the recipe. Keep an eye on the dough as it mixes and add more flour or liquid as needed.

STARCHY VEGETABLES

Potatoes, sweet potatoes carrots, rutabagas, parsnips and other varieties of starchy vegetables sweeten the bread and contribute a soft texture. You can use leftover mashed or even instant potato, adding 1⅓ –2⅔ cups to a basic bread recipe depending on the size of your machine. Adjust the liquid accordingly.

SPINACH

Fresh spinach leaves need to be blanched briefly in boiling water before being used. After blanching, add them whole with the liquid ingredients at the beginning

PREPARING BELL PEPPERS

1 Cut each pepper into three or four flat pieces, removing the core and seeds. Place in a broiling pan or roasting pan and brush the pieces lightly with olive oil or sunflower oil.

2 Broil until the skins blister and begin to char. Remove each piece as it is cooked and place inside a plastic bag. Seal the bag and let the peppers cool.

3 Peel off and discard the skin, then chop the peppers and add when the bread machine beeps, or 5 minutes before the kneading cycle ends.

LEFT: Fresh or dried mushrooms work well in breads

of the kneading process, and they will mix in and become finely chopped as the cycle progresses. Frozen chopped spinach can be substituted for fresh, but thaw it completely first and reduce the liquid in the recipe to allow for the extra water.

ONIONS, LEEKS AND CHILIES
These vegetables are best if you sauté them first in a little butter or oil, which brings out their flavor. Caramelized onions will add richness and a light golden color to the bread. For speed, you can add dried sliced onions instead of fresh onions, but you may need to add an extra 1 tablespoon or so of liquid.

MUSHROOMS
Dried wild mushrooms can be used in the same way as sun-dried tomatoes to produce a very tasty loaf for serving with soups, casseroles and stews. Strain the soaking water, if you intend to use it in a recipe, to remove any grit.

TOMATOES
Tomatoes are very versatile and give bread a delicious flavor. They can be puréed, canned, fresh or sun-dried. Depending on when you add sun-dried tomatoes they will either remain as pieces, making a bread with interesting flecks of color, or be fully integrated in the dough to provide flavor. To intensify the taste, choose regular sun-dried tomatoes, rather than the ones preserved in oil,

reconstitute them in water, then use the soaking water as the liquid in the recipe. Other tomato products are best added at the beginning of the breadmaking cycle, to ensure a richly colored, full-bodied loaf with a distinct tomato flavor.

OTHER VEGETABLES
Add vegetables such as corn kernels, chopped olives or chopped scallions towards the end of the kneading cycle to ensure that they remain whole. All will impart flavor, color and texture.

Frozen vegetables should be thawed completely before using in the machine. You may need to reduce the liquid quantity in the recipe if you use frozen vegetables instead of fresh. Canned vegetables should be well drained.

CHICKPEAS
The starchiness of chickpeas, like that of potatoes, produces a light bread with good keeping qualities. Add cooked drained chickpeas whole; the machine will reduce them to a pulp very effectively. Chickpeas add a pleasant, nutty flavor to breads.

ADDING VEGETABLES TO BREAD
There are several ways of preparing vegetables ready to add to the machine.

• Add grated raw vegetables such as zucchini, carrots or beets, when you add the water to the pan.

• Sweet potatoes, parsnips, potatoes, winter squashes and pumpkin should be cooked first. Drain, reserving the cooking liquid, and mash them. When cool, add both the cooking liquid and the mashed vegetable to the dough.

• If you want vegetables to remain identifiable in the finished bread add them when the machine beeps for adding extra ingredients or 5 minutes before the end of the kneading cycle, so they stay as slices or small pieces.

FRUIT

Whether you use them fresh, dried or as purées or juices, fruits add complementary flavors to breads and teacakes. The natural sugars help to food the yeast and improve the leavening process, while fruits with natural pectin will improve the keeping quality of baked goods.

DRIED CAKE FRUITS

The familiar dried cake fruits such as sultanas, currants and raisins can easily be incorporated in basic breads, adding their own distinctive flavors. Sprinkle them in gradually, when the machine beeps or towards the end of the kneading cycle.

For added flavor, plump them up in fruit juice or liqueur. You can add up to ⅓ cup of dried fruit for a small bread machine, ⅔ cup for a large machine. If you

BELOW: Clockwise from top left: candied citrus peel, dried pears, dried cranberries, dried prunes, dried mango, and dried figs

ABOVE: Pears, bananas, apples

soak the dried fruit first, use the excess as part of the measured liquid. You may need to add a spoonful or so of extra liquid to a basic bread recipe if you do not soak the fruit first.

RIGHT: Strawberries, raspberries, blueberries

DRIED FRUITS

There is a vast range of dried fruit to choose from, and these are perfect for breads because their flavors are so concentrated. Use combinations of exotic dried fruits, such as papaya, mango, figs and melon. Small dried fruits such as cherries and cranberries can be added whole, while the larger fruits need to be chopped coarsely, as do apricots, pears, dates and peaches. Dried fruits such as pitted prunes can be soaked in sherry or a liqueur, as for cake fruits.

FRESH FRUITS

Berries can be frozen before they are added to the dough to help to keep them intact.

Spread the berries out in a single layer on a baking sheet and freeze them until they are solid. Add to the dough in the machine just before the end of the kneading cycle. You can also use commercially-frozen fruits in this way. When adding juicy fruits, toss them with a little extra flour, to keep the consistency of the bread dough correct. Soft fruits can be added to teabread mixtures too; just fold them in at the end of mixing.

Firm fruits, such as apples or pears, can be added raw, chopped into small chunks. Plums and rhubarb can also be used raw; simply cut them into small pieces. Rhubarb can also be poached first, so that it softens slightly. You can also grate firm fruits, or mash soft ripe fruits such as bananas and pears.

PINEAPPLE AND BANANA BREAD

These ingredient quantities are for a medium bread machine. Increase or decrease by 25 percent as necessary.

1 Pour ¼ cup pineapple juice and ⅞ cup buttermilk into the bread pan. Mash 1 large banana (about 6½ ounces) and add to the pan. Add the dry ingredients first if your machine specifies this.

2 Sprinkle 4 cups unbleached white bread flour and ½ cup whole-wheat flour over, covering the liquid. Place 1 teaspoon salt, 3 tablespoon caster sugar and 3 tablespoon butter in separate corners. Make a shallow indentation in the flour; add 1 teaspoon rapid-rise active dry yeast.

3 Set to the basic/normal setting, with raisin setting (if available), light crust. Press Start. Add ½ cup chopped pineapple chunks at the beep or towards the end of the cycle. Remove from the bread pan and turn out onto a wire rack.

ADDING FRUIT TO BREADS

When you add the fruit and how heavily processed it is will determine whether it remains clearly detectable as whole pieces or blends fully into the dough to impart an even flavor and moistness throughout the bread.

• Add frozen orange concentrate or fruit juice right at the beginning of the mixing process, unless the instructions for your machine state you should add the dry ingredients first.

• Add purées, such as apple, pear or mango, after the water in the recipe has been poured into the bread pan. Alternatively, blend the two together first, then add the mixture to the pan.

BELOW: Fruit juice can replace part of the water quantity in some breads. Left to right: apple juice, pineapple juice, mango juice

• If you wish to add mashed or grated fruits, such as bananas or pears, put them in after the liquids.

• Add fresh or frozen whole fruits, such as berries, when the machine beeps or about 5 minutes before the end of the kneading cycle. Chopped fruits, such as apples and plums, as well as dried fruits, should also be added towards the end of the kneading process.

EQUIPMENT

The accessories required for bread-making are quite simple, the most expensive being the bread machine, which you probably already own. The essential pieces of equipment are largely concerned with accurate measuring; the remaining items are useful for hand-shaped breads.

MEASURING

Items to measure ingredients accurately are vital for making machine-breads.

MEASURING CUPS AND SPOONS

Quantities of dry ingredients, such as flour, sugar, salt and, most importantly, yeast, need to be measured carefully. A set of measuring cups from ¼ to 1 cup and measuring spoons from ¼ teaspoon to 1 tablespoon is ideal. Always level off the ingredient in the cup or spoon for an accurate measure.

MEASURING CUPS FOR LIQUIDS

Heatproof glass cups that are clearly marked are very useful for measuring liquids. Place the measuring cup on a flat surface to ensure accuracy, and check the level of the ingredients by bending down so the measurements are at eye level.

RIGHT: Having a range of different-size glass bowls is useful.

LEFT: Bannetons may be used for final proving before the bread is baked.

LEFT: It is vital that ingredients are measured accurately to when using a bread machine.

MIXING AND RISING

The bread machine will automatically mix dough and make it rise, but there may be some items of equipment you need for hand-shaped breads.

GLASS BOWLS

While most of the mixing will take place inside the machine, you will still need to mix glazes, add extra ingredients, transfer doughs or batters to a large bowl, or use a large bowl as a cover for hand-shaped bread during the final rising period. Glass bowls give all-round visibility and a selection of sizes will prove universally useful around the kitchen.

BELOW: A French baguette tray will give French loaves their traditional shape.

LEFT: Speciality cake pans such as a kugelhopf pan and small brioche molds may be worth acquiring BELOW: Assorted cake pans, fluted loose based tart pan

BANNETON

During the final rising, breads are sometimes supported in cloth-lined baskets, called bannetons. Place baguettes in long bannetons and round loaves in round baskets. Flour the cloth well to prevent the dough from sticking. When the dough has risen you can turn the basket and place the bread directly on a prepared baking sheet.

DISH TOWELS AND PLASTIC WRAP

Use a clean dish towel or plastic wrap to cover the dough during rising. This prevents a dry crust from forming on the dough. Before using, lightly flour the dish towel or oil the plastic wrap to prevent the dough from sticking to the cover.

TIMER

If your bread machine does not have an audible signal to remind you to add extra ingredients, or you want to remember to check the dough partway through the cycle, set a kitchen timer. It is also a good idea to set a timer if the beep of your bread machine is not particularly loud and you are unlikely to be in the kitchen when the signal goes off.

BAKING HAND-SHAPED LOAVES

A variety of pans, trays and other equipment will help you bake breads of interesting shapes or with a crispier crust.

BREAD PANS AND MOLDS

Heavy gauge baking pans and molds are best, because they are less likely to distort in the oven. A number of shapes and sizes are useful. A 2-pound loaf pan measuring $7\frac{1}{4} \times 4\frac{1}{2}$ inches is a good basic size and shape, or try a longer, slightly narrower pan about 9–10 inches long. Both round and square cake pans are used for bread making, to support the dough while it rises. A 6 inches deep cake pan is used for baking panettone. Springform cake pans

RIGHT: Baking trays and loaf pans

BELOW: A peel is useful when making pizzas

with diameters of 8–10 inches make the removal of sweet breads and cakes much easier than when a fixed-bottomed cake pan is used. Square and rectangular pans are perfect for both sweet-and-savory topped breads.

Focaccia or deep-pan pizzas are best cooked in a large, shallow, round cake pan with a diameter of 10–11 inches. A fluted loose-bottomed tart pan and shallow pizza pan are good investments if you cook those types of bread regularly.

Shaped molds are often used for baking speciality breads. A fluted mold with sloping sides is the classic shape for both individual and large Brioche. Kugelhopf is made in a deep fluted pan with a central hole, Savarin in a shallow ring mold and Babas in shallow, individual ring molds.

FRENCH BAGUETTE TRAY

A molded tray, designed to hold two or three loaves, this has a perforated bottom to ensure an even heat while baking. The bread is given its final rising in the tray, which is then placed in the oven for baking. Loaves baked in a tray will have small dimples on the bottom and sides.

BAKING SHEETS

A number of free-form breads need to be transferred to a baking sheet for cooking. A selection of strong, heavy baking sheets is best. Use either totally flat baking sheets, or ones with a lip on one edge only. These make it possible to remove the cooked breads easily.

BAKING STONE

For more rustic bread, sourdoughs, pizza and focaccia, a baking stone or pizza stone helps to ensure a crisp crust.

TERRA-COTTA TILES

Unglazed quarry tiles or terra-cotta tiles can be used instead of a baking stone. The tiles will draw out moisture and help to produce the traditional crisp crust.

PEEL

If you are regularly going to use a baking stone or tiles, a peel (baker's shovel) is a useful piece of equipment. Use it to slide pizzas and bread doughs into the oven, placing them directly on to the preheated surface. Flour the peel generously and place the bread on it for its final rising. Give it a gentle shake just before placing it in the oven to make sure the bottom of the bread doesn't stick to the peel.

WATER SPRAY BOTTLE

Use a water spray bottle to mist the oven when you wish to achieve a crisp crust. A pump-action plastic bottle with a fine spray-head is ideal.

USEFUL TOOLS

This section includes tools for preparing ingredients and for finishing hand-shaped and machine breads.

CUTTERS

Plain cutters are used to cut dough for muffins and rolls. Metal cutters are best as they are not distorted when pressure is applied. A range of cutters 2–4 inches in diameter is most useful.

POTATO PEELER

Use a fixed-blade potato peeler for peeling vegetables and fruit, or removing strips of citrus peel. A swivel-blade peeler is useful for paring very thin layers of citrus skin.

ZESTER

Many sweet breads and cakes include fresh citrus zest and this handy little tool makes light work of preparing it. The zester has a row of holes with cutting edges which shave off thin strips of zest without including the bitter pith that lies just beneath the colored citrus peel. You may then wish to chop the strips into smaller pieces with a very sharp knife.

PASTRY BRUSHES

These are used to apply washes and glazes. Avoid nylon brushes, which will melt if used on hot breads. Brushes made from natural fiber are better.

LEFT: A baking stone, terra-cotta tiles and a water spray all help to produce breads with a crispier crust.

PLASTIC SCRAPER AND SPATULA

Make sure these tools are pliable. Use them to help remove dough that is stuck on the inside of the bread machine pan. The scraper also comes in handy for lifting and turning sticky dough and dividing dough into pieces for shaping into rolls.

KNIVES

You will need a sharp cook's knife for slashing doughs and a smaller paring knife for preparing fruit and vegetables. Use stainless steel for acidic fruits.

SCISSORS AND SCALPEL

Both these items can be used for slashing breads and rolls, to give decorative finishes before baking. A medium-size pair of scissors with thin, pointed blades is perfect. If you use a scalpel, replace the blade regularly, as it must be sharp.

ROLLING PINS

Some breads and buns need to be rolled out for shaping. Cylindrical wooden pins are best. Use a heavy rolling pin about 18 inches long for breads and a smaller one for individual rolls, buns and pastries. A child's toy rolling pin can be very useful for small items.

LEFT: Selection of rolling pins

ABOVE: From left to right: spatula, cook's knife, vegetable knife, scalpel and scissors

THERMOMETERS

All ovens cook with slightly different heat intensities. An oven thermometer will enable you to establish how your oven cooks so you can make any necessary adjustments to recipes.

The time-honored way of testing if a loaf of bread is cooked through is to tap it on the bottom to determine if it sounds hollow.

A much more scientific method is to insert a thermometer into the center of a hand-shaped loaf and check the internal temperature. It should be 375–383°F.

SIEVES

A large sieve is essential for sifting flours together, and it is also handy to have a small sieve for sifting ingredients such as nonfat dry milk, confectioners' sugar and ground spices. Use a plastic sieve for confectioners' sugar, so as not to discolor the sugar.

COOLING AND SLICING

Cooling a bread properly gives a crispier crust. The bread is then ready to eat.

OVEN MITTS

A thick pair of oven mitts or gloves is essential for lifting the bread pan from the machine or breads from the oven, because the metal items will be very hot.

WIRE RACK

The hot cooked bread should be turned out onto a wire rack and set aside to cool before storing or slicing.

BREAD KNIFE AND BOARD

To preserve the delicate crumb structure, bread should be cut with a sharp knife that has a long serrated blade. Cut the bread on a wooden board to prevent damaging the serrated knife.

ABOVE: Oven mitts, and a wire rack for cooling bread

THE RECIPES

With the help of your bread machine you can create a vast array of distinctive breads, both sweet and savory. The machine-baked breads have three sets of ingredients—for small, medium and large bread machines—as the quantities are crucial for success. Other breads can be mixed in any machine, shaped by hand then baked in an oven. Fresh bread tastes delicious and fills the kitchen with a wonderful aroma; now making it has never been easier.

BASIC BREADS

These recipes are the everyday breads that you will want to make time and again. They are some of the easiest breads to make in your machine; perfect for serving toasted with butter and jam or for use in sandwiches. The range of breads includes whole wheat, multi-grain and rye breads, and those flavored and enriched with milk, buttermilk, eggs, potato or rice. If you haven't made bread in your machine before, this is the place to start.

WHITE BREAD

This is a simple all-purpose white bread recipe, which makes the perfect basis for experimenting. Try using different brands of flours and be prepared to make minor alterations to quantities if necessary, to find the optimum recipe for your machine.

SMALL
scant 1¼ cups water
3¼ cups unbleached white bread flour
1½ teaspoons salt
1 tablespoon granulated sugar
2 tablespoons butter
1 teaspoon rapid-rise active dry yeast
unbleached white bread flour, for dusting

MEDIUM
generous 1½ cups water
4½ cups unbleached white bread flour
1½ teaspoons salt
1 tablespoon granulated sugar
2 tablespoons butter
1 teaspoon rapid-rise active dry yeast
unbleached white bread flour, for dusting

LARGE
generous 2 cups water
6 cups unbleached white bread flour
2 teaspoons salt
1½ tablespoons granulated sugar
3 tablespoons butter
1½ teaspoons rapid-rise active dry yeast
unbleached white bread flour, for dusting

MAKES 1 LOAF

1 Pour the water into the bread machine pan. However, if the instructions for your machine specify that the yeast is to be placed in the pan first, reverse the order in which you add the liquid and dry ingredients.

2 Sprinkle the flour over, ensuring that it covers the water. Add the salt, sugar and butter in separate corners of the bread pan. Make a shallow indentation in the center of the flour (but not down as far as the liquid) and add the yeast.

COOK'S TIP
To give the crust a richer golden appearance, add nonfat dry milk to the flour. For a small loaf, you will need 1 tablespoon; for a medium loaf 1½ tablespoons and for a large loaf 2 tablespoons.

3 Set the bread machine to the basic/normal setting, medium crust. Press Start.

4 Remove the bread at the end of the baking cycle and turn out onto a wire rack to cool.

EGG-ENRICHED WHITE LOAF

Adding egg to a basic white loaf gives a richer flavor and creamier crumb, as well as a golden finish to the crust.

1 Put the eggs in a measuring cup and add sufficient water to make a generous 1 cup, 1⅓ cups or scant 1⅞ cups, according to the size of loaf selected.

2 Mix lightly and pour into the bread machine pan. If your instructions specify that the yeast is to be placed in the pan first, reverse the order in which you add the liquid and the dry ingredients.

SMALL
1 egg
water, see method
3¼ cups unbleached white
bread flour
1½ teaspoons granulated sugar
1½ teaspoons salt
1½ tablespoons butter
¾ teaspoon rapid-rise active dry yeast

MEDIUM
1 egg plus 1 egg yolk
water, see method
4½ cups unbleached white
bread flour
2 teaspoons granulated sugar
1½ teaspoons salt
2 tablespoons butter
1 teaspoon rapid-rise active dry yeast

LARGE
2 eggs
water, see method
6 cups unbleached white bread flour
1 tablespoon granulated sugar
2 teaspoons salt
2 tablespoons butter
1½ teaspoons rapid-rise
active dry yeast

MAKES 1 LOAF

3 Sprinkle the flour over, covering the water. Add the sugar, salt and butter in separate corners of the pan. Make a shallow indentation in the center of the flour and add the yeast.

4 Set the machine to the basic/normal setting, medium crust. Press Start. At the end of the baking cycle, turn out onto a wire rack to cool.

BUTTERMILK BREAD

Buttermilk adds a pleasant, slightly sour note to the flavor of this bread. It also gives the bread a good light texture and a golden brown crust. Buttermilk bread tastes especially delicious when toasted and simply spread with a little butter.

SMALL
1 cup buttermilk
¼ cup water
1 tablespoon honey
1 tablespoon sunflower oil
2¼ cups unbleached white bread flour
generous 1 cup whole-wheat bread flour
1½ teaspoons salt
1 teaspoon rapid-rise active dry yeast

MEDIUM
1¼ cups buttermilk
6 tablespoons water
1½ tablespoons honey
1½ tablespoons sunflower oil
3 cups unbleached white bread flour
1⅓ cup whole-wheat bread flour
1½ teaspoons salt
1½ teaspoons rapid-rise active dry yeast

LARGE
scant 1⅝ cups buttermilk
½ cup water
2 tablespoons honey
2 tablespoons sunflower oil
4¼ cups unbleached white bread flour
1¾ cups whole-wheat bread flour
2 teaspoons salt
2 teaspoons rapid-rise active dry yeast

MAKES 1 LOAF

COOK'S TIP
Traditional buttermilk is a by-product of butter making and is the fairly thin liquid left after the fat has been made into butter. Commercial buttermilk is pasteurized and mixed with a special culture which causes it to ferment, resulting in the characteristic slightly sour flavor. If you run short of buttermilk, using a low-fat yogurt and 1–2 teaspoons lemon juice is an acceptable alternative.

1 Pour the buttermilk, water, honey and oil into the bread machine pan. If your instructions specify that the yeast is to be placed in the pan first, reverse the order of the liquid and dry ingredients.

2 Sprinkle both the white and whole-wheat flours over, ensuring that the water is completely covered. Add the salt in one corner of the bread pan. Make a shallow indentation in the center of the flour (but not down as far as the liquid) and add the yeast.

3 Set the bread machine to the basic/normal setting, medium crust. Press Start.

4 Remove the bread from the pan at the end of the baking cycle and turn out onto a wire rack to cool.

LIGHT WHOLE-WHEAT BREAD

—

A tasty, light whole-wheat loaf that can be cooked on the quicker basic or normal setting.

1 Pour the water into the bread machine pan. If the instructions for your bread machine specify that the yeast is to be placed in the pan first, reverse the order in which you add the liquid and dry ingredients to the pan.

2 Sprinkle each type of flour over in turn, ensuring that the water is covered. Add the salt, sugar and butter in separate corners of the bread pan. Make a shallow indentation in the center of the flour and add the yeast.

SMALL
1½ cups water
2¼ cups whole-wheat
bread flour
generous 1 cup white bread flour
1½ teaspoons salt
1½ teaspoons granulated sugar
1½ tablespoons butter
1 teaspoon rapid-rise active dry yeast

MEDIUM
1¾ cups water
3 cups whole-wheat
bread flour
1⅓ cups white bread flour
2 teaspoons salt
2 teaspoons granulated sugar
2 tablespoons butter
1½ teaspoons rapid-rise
active dry yeast

LARGE
scant 2 cups water
4¼ cups whole-wheat bread flour
1¾ cups white bread flour
2 teaspoons salt
1 tablespoon granulated sugar
2 tablespoons butter
2 teaspoons rapid-rise
active dry yeast

MAKES 1 LOAF

VARIATION
This is a fairly light brown loaf as it contains a mixture of white and whole-wheat bread flour. Another option for a lighter brown bread is to replace the whole-wheat bread flour with brown bread flour. This contains less bran and wheat germ than whole-wheat flour, so produces a slightly lighter bread.

3 Set the bread machine to the basic/normal setting, medium crust. Press Start.

4 Remove the bread at the end of the baking cycle and turn out onto a wire rack to cool.

CORNMEAL BREAD

Cornmeal adds a sweet flavor and crumbly texture to this scrumptuous bread. Use a finely ground organic meal. The coarsely ground meal used for polenta makes a good topping.

SMALL
⅔ cup water
6 tablespoons milk
1 tablespoon corn oil
2½ cups unbleached white
bread flour
scant 1 cup cornmeal
1 teaspoon salt
1½ teaspoons light brown sugar
1 teaspoon rapid-rise active dry yeast
water, for glazing
polenta, for sprinkling

MEDIUM
scant 1 cup water
7 tablespoons milk
1½ tablespoons corn oil
3 cups unbleached white bread flour
1¼ cups cornmeal
1 teaspoon salt
2 teaspoons light brown sugar
1 teaspoon rapid-rise active dry yeast
water, for glazing
polenta, for sprinkling

LARGE
generous 1¼ cups water
⅔ cup milk
2 tablespoons corn oil
4 cups unbleached white bread flour
2 cups cornmeal
1½ teaspoons salt
1 tablespoon light brown sugar
1½ teaspoons rapid-rise
active dry yeast
water, for glazing
polenta, for sprinkling

MAKES 1 LOAF

COOK'S TIP
This bread is best cooked
on a rapid setting, even though
the inclusion of cornmeal will
result in a slightly
shallow loaf.

1 Pour the water, milk and corn oil into the pan. Reverse the order in which you add the wet and dry ingredients if the instructions to your machine specify this.

2 Add the flour and the cornmeal, covering the water. Place the salt and sugar in separate corners. Make a shallow indentation in the flour; add the yeast.

3 Set the bread machine to the rapid/ quick setting, medium crust. Press Start. Just before the baking cycle commences brush the top of the loaf with water and sprinkle with polenta.

4 Remove the bread at the end of the baking cycle and turn out onto a wire rack to cool.

ANADAMA BREAD

This traditional New England bread is made with a mixture of white and whole-wheat flours and polenta, which is a coarse cornmeal. The molasses sweetens the bread and gives it a rich color.

1 Pour the water, molasses and lemon juice into the bread machine pan. If the instructions for your machine specify that the yeast is to be placed in the pan first, reverse the order in which you add the liquid and dry ingredients.

2 Sprinkle both types of flour over, then the polenta, so that the water is completely covered. Add the salt and butter in separate corners of the bread pan. Make a shallow indentation in the center of the flour and add the yeast.

SMALL
1 cup water
3 tablespoons molasses
1 teaspoon lemon juice
2½ cups unbleached white bread flour
generous ½ cup whole-wheat bread flour
⅓ cup polenta
1½ teaspoons salt
2 tablespoons butter
1 teaspoon rapid-rise active dry yeast

MEDIUM
generous 1¼ cups water
4 tablespoons molasses
1 teaspoon lemon juice
generous 3 cups unbleached white bread flour
¾ cup whole-wheat bread flour
generous ½ cup polenta
2 teaspoons salt
3 tablespoons butter
1 teaspoon rapid-rise active dry yeast

LARGE
1½ cups water
5 tablespoons molasses
2 teaspoons lemon juice
4¼ cups unbleached white bread flour
scant 1 cup whole-wheat bread flour
¾ cup polenta
2½ teaspoons salt
¼ cup butter
2 teaspoons rapid-rise active dry yeast

MAKES 1 LOAF

COOK'S TIP
Check the moistness of the dough after a couple of minutes' kneading. If it is too dry, add a little water.

3 Set the bread machine to the basic/normal setting, medium crust. Press Start.

4 Remove the bread at the end of the baking cycle and turn out onto a wire rack to cool.

FARMHOUSE LOAF

The flour-dusted split top gives a charmingly rustic look to this tasty whole-wheat-enriched white loaf.

SMALL
scant 1⅛ cups water
3 cups unbleached white bread flour,
plus extra for dusting
¼ cup whole-wheat bread flour
1 tablespoon nonfat dry milk
1½ teaspoons salt
1½ teaspoons granulated sugar
1 tablespoon butter
¾ teaspoon rapid-rise active dry yeast
water, for glazing

MEDIUM
generous 1⅓ cups water
3¾ cups unbleached white bread
flour, plus extra for dusting
¾ cup whole-wheat bread flour
1½ tablespoons nonfat dry milk
1½ teaspoons salt
1½ teaspoons granulated sugar
2 tablespoons butter
1 teaspoon rapid-rise active dry yeast
water, for glazing

LARGE
generous 2 cups water
5¼ cups unbleached white bread flour,
plus extra for dusting
¾ cup whole-wheat bread flour
2 tablespoons nonfat dry milk
2 teaspoons salt
2 teaspoons granulated sugar
2 tablespoons butter
1½ teaspoons rapid-rise
active dry yeast
water, for glazing

MAKES 1 LOAF

1 Pour the water into the bread pan. If the instructions for your machine specify that the yeast is to be placed in the pan first, reverse the order in which you add the liquid and dry ingredients.

2 Sprinkle both the flours over, covering the water completely. Add the milk. Add the salt, sugar and butter in separate corners of the bread pan. Make a shallow indentation in the center of the flour (but not down as far as the liquid) and then add the yeast.

3 Set the bread machine to the basic/normal setting, and select medium crust. Press Start.

4 Ten minutes before the baking time begins, brush the top of the loaf with water and dust with a little white bread flour. Slash the top of the bread with a sharp knife.

5 Remove the bread at the end of the baking cycle and turn out onto a wire rack to cool.

COOK'S TIP
Try this rustic bread using multi-grain flour instead of whole-wheat bread flour for added texture.

MULTI-GRAIN BREAD

Multi-grain flour is a blend. It contains malted wheat grain,
which gives a crunchy texture to this loaf.

1 Add the water to the bread machine pan. If the instructions for your machine specify that the yeast is to be placed in the pan first, simply reverse the order in which you add the liquid and dry ingredients to the pan.

2 Sprinkle the flour over, ensuring that it covers the water. Add the salt, sugar and butter in separate corners of the bread pan. Make a shallow indentation in the center of the flour (but not down as far as the liquid) and add the yeast.

3 Set the bread machine to the whole-wheat or multi-grain setting, medium crust. Press Start.

4 Remove the bread at the end of the baking cycle and turn out onto a wire rack to cool.

COOK'S TIP
This bread tastes especially good toasted and served with homemade jam.

SMALL
generous 1 cup water
3¼ cups multi-grain bread flour
1 teaspoon salt
2 teaspoons granulated sugar
1½ tablespoons butter
½ teaspoons rapid-rise active dry yeast

MEDIUM
1½ cups water
4½ cups multi-grain bread flour
1½ teaspoons salt
1 tablespoon granulated sugar
2 tablespoons butter
1½ teaspoons rapid-rise active dry yeast

LARGE
generous 1⅔ cups water
6 cups multi-grain bread flour
2 teaspoons salt
1 tablespoon granulated sugar
2 tablespoons butter
1½ teaspoons rapid-rise active dry yeast

MAKES 1 LOAF

MALTED LOAF

A malt and golden raisin loaf makes the perfect breakfast or afternoon treat.
Serve it sliced and generously spread with butter.

SMALL
1¼ cups water
1 tablespoon golden syrup or
corn syrup
1½ tablespoons barley malt syrup
3 cups unbleached white bread flour
1½ tablespoons nonfat dry milk
½ teaspoon salt
3 tablespoons butter
½ teaspoon rapid-rise active dry yeast
½ cup golden raisins

MEDIUM
1½ cups water
1½ tablespoons golden syrup
or corn syrup
2 tablespoons barley malt syrup
4½ cups unbleached white
bread flour
2 tablespoons nonfat dry milk
1 teaspoon salt
¼ cup butter
1 teaspoon rapid-rise active dry yeast
generous ½ cup golden raisins

LARGE
generous 1¾ cups water
2 tablespoons golden syrup
or corn syrup
3 tablespoons barley malt syrup
6 cups unbleached white bread flour
2 tablespoons nonfat dry milk
1 teaspoon salt
5 tablespoons butter
1½ teaspoons rapid-rise active dry yeast
generous ⅔ cup golden raisins

MAKES 1 LOAF

1 Pour the water, golden syrup and malt syrup into the bread machine pan. If the instructions for your machine specify that the yeast is to be placed in the pan first, reverse the order in which you add the liquid and dry ingredients.

2 Sprinkle the flour over, ensuring that it covers the liquid. Add the milk. Place the salt and butter in separate corners of the bread pan. Make a shallow indentation in the center of the flour and add the yeast.

3 Set the bread machine to the basic/normal setting, with raisin setting (if available), medium crust. Press Start. Add the golden raisins when the machine beeps or after the first kneading.

4 Remove at the end of the baking cycle and turn out onto a wire rack. If desired, glaze the bread after cooking. Dissolve 1 tablespoon sugar in 1 tablespoon of skim milk and brush over the top crust.

LIGHT RYE AND CARAWAY BREAD

Rye flour adds a distinctive, slightly sour flavor to bread. Rye breads can be dense, so the flour is usually mixed with wheat flour to lighten the texture.

1 Add the water, lemon juice and oil to the bread pan. If your instructions specify that the yeast is to be placed in the pan first, reverse the order in which you add the liquid and dry ingredients.

2 Sprinkle the rye flour and the white bread flour over, ensuring they cover the water. Add the nonfat dry milk and caraway seeds. Add the salt and sugar in separate corners of the bread pan. Make a shallow indentation in the center of the flour, but not down as far as the liquid, and add the yeast.

3 Set the bread machine to the basic/normal setting, medium crust. Press Start.

4 Remove the bread from the pan at the end of the cycle and transfer to a wire rack to cool.

SMALL
scant 1 cup water
1 teaspoon lemon juice
1 tablespoon sunflower oil
¾ cup rye flour
2½ cups unbleached white bread flour
1 tablespoon nonfat dry milk
1 teaspoon caraway seeds
1 teaspoon salt
2 teaspoons light brown sugar
¾ teaspoon rapid-rise active dry yeast

MEDIUM
1¼ cups water
2 teaspoons lemon juice
1½ tablespoons sunflower oil
generous 1 cup rye flour
3¼ cups unbleached white bread flour
1½ tablespoons nonfat dry milk
1½ teaspoons caraway seeds
1½ teaspoons salt
1 tablespoon light brown sugar
1 teaspoon rapid-rise active dry yeast

LARGE
scant 1⅝ cups water
2 teaspoons lemon juice
2 tablespoons sunflower oil
generous 1½ cups rye flour
4½ cups unbleached white bread flour
2 tablespoons nonfat dry milk
2 teaspoons caraway seeds
2 teaspoons salt
4 teaspoons light brown sugar
1½ teaspoons rapid-rise
active dry yeast

MAKES 1 LOAF

FRENCH BREAD

French bread traditionally has a crisp crust and light, chewy crumb. Use the special French bread setting on your bread machine to help to achieve this unique texture.

SMALL
MAKES 1 LOAF
⅔ *cup water*
2 cups unbleached white bread flour
1 teaspoon salt
*1½ teaspoons rapid-rsie
active dry yeust*

MEDIUM
MAKES 2–3 LOAVES
1⅓ cups water
4 cups unbleached white bread flour
1½ teaspoons salt
*1½ teaspoons rapid-rsie
active dry yeast*

LARGE
MAKES 3–4 LOAVES
2⅛ cups water
6 cups unbleached white bread flour
2 teaspoons salt
*2 teaspoons rapid-rsie
active dry yeast*

1 Add the water to the bread machine pan. If the instructions for your machine specify that the yeast is to be placed in the pan first, simply reverse the order in which you add the liquid and dry ingredients to the pan.

2 Sprinkle the flour over, to cover the water. Add the salt in a corner. Make an indentation in the center of the flour and add the yeast. Use the French bread setting (see Cook's Tip). Press Start.

3 When the dough cycle has finished, remove the dough from the machine, place it on a lightly floured surface and punch it down. Divide it into two or three equal portions if using the medium quantities or three or four portions if using the large quantities.

4 On a floured surface shape each piece of dough into a ball, then roll out to a rectangle measuring 7-8 × 3 inches. Fold one-third up lengthwise and one-third down, then press. Repeat twice more, letting the dough rest between foldings to avoid tearing.

5 Gently roll and stretch each piece to an 11–13-inch loaf, depending on whether you aim to make smaller or larger loaves. Place each loaf in a floured banneton or between the folds of a floured and pleated dish towel, so that the French bread shape is maintained during rising.

6 Cover with lightly oiled plastic wrap and leave in a warm place for 30–45 minutes. Preheat the oven to 450°F.

7 Roll the loaf or loaves on to a baking sheet, spacing them well part. Slash the tops several times with a sharp knife. Place at the top of the oven, spray the inside of the oven with water and bake for 15–20 minutes, or until golden. Transfer to a wire rack to cool.

COOK'S TIP
Use the French bread baking setting if you do not have a French bread dough setting. Remove the dough before the final rising stage and shape as directed.

ITALIAN BREADSTICKS

These crisp breadsticks will keep for a couple of days if stored in an airtight container. If you like, you can refresh them in a hot oven for a few minutes before serving. The dough can be made in any breadmaking machine, regardless of capacity.

1 Pour the water and olive oil into the bread machine pan. If the instructions for your machine specify that the yeast is to be placed in the pan first, reverse the order in which you add the liquid and dry ingredients.

2 Sprinkle over the flour, ensuring that it covers the water completely. Add the salt in one corner of the pan. Make a shallow indentation in the center of the flour (but not down as far as the liquid) and add the yeast.

3 Set the bread machine to the dough setting; use basic dough setting (if available). Press Start.

4 Lightly oil two baking sheets. Preheat the oven to 400°F.

5 When the dough cycle has finished, remove the dough from the machine, place it on a lightly floured surface and punch it down. Roll it out to a rectangle measuring 9 × 8 inches.

6 Cut into three 8-inch long strips. Cut each strip widthwise into ten. Roll and stretch each piece to 12 inches.

7 Roll the breadsticks in poppy seeds or sea salt if you like. Space well apart on the baking sheets. Brush lightly with olive oil, cover with plastic wrap and set aside in a warm place for 10–15 minutes.

8 Bake for 15–20 minutes, or until golden, turning once. Transfer to a wire rack to cool.

⅞ cup water
3 tablespoons olive oil, plus extra
for brushing
3 cups unbleached white bread flour
1½ teaspoons salt
1½ teaspoons rapid-rise active
dry yeast
poppy seeds and coarse sea salt,
for coating (optional)

MAKES 30

COOK'S TIP
If you are rolling the breadsticks in sea salt, don't use too much. Crush the sea salt slightly if the crystals are large.

RICE BREAD

Rice is an unusual ingredient, but makes delicious bread that is moist, flavorful and with an interesting texture. The perfect vehicle for leftover cooked rice, it tastes so good that it's worth cooking some specially.

SMALL
generous 1 cup water
1 egg
3 cups unbleached white bread flour
1 cup cooked long-grain white rice,
well drained
1 tablespoon nonfat dry milk
1 teaspoon salt
1½ teaspoons granulated sugar
1 tablespoon butter
1 teaspoon rapid-rise active dry yeast

MEDIUM
generous 1¼ cups water
1 egg
3¾ cups unbleached white
bread flour
1¼ cups cooked long-grain white rice,
well drained
1½ tablespoons nonfat dry milk
1½ teaspoons salt
2 teaspoons granulated sugar
1 tablespoon butter
1 teaspoon rapid-rise active dry yeast

LARGE
1½ cups water
1 egg
5 cups unbleached white bread flour
1¾ cups cooked long-grain white rice,
well drained
2 tablespoons nonfat dry milk
2 teaspoons salt
1 tablespoon granulated sugar
1½ tablespoons butter
2 teaspoons rapid-rise active
dry yeast

MAKES 1 LOAF

1 Pour the water into the bread machine pan, then add the egg. There is no need to beat the egg before you add it as the machine will mix all of the ingredients together thoroughly. If the instructions for your bread machine specify that the yeast is to be placed in the pan first, simply reverse the order in which you add the liquid and dry ingredients.

2 Sprinkle the flour over, ensuring that it covers the water. Add the rice and milk. Add the salt, sugar and butter in separate corners of the bread pan. Make an indentation in the center of the flour and add the yeast.

3 Set the bread machine to the basic/normal setting, medium crust. Press Start.

4 Remove the bread at the end of the baking cycle and turn out onto a wire rack to cool.

COOK'S TIPS
Make sure the rice is cold before using it in this bread. It is important to drain it very well, or the bread dough may become too moist. Watch the dough as it mixes and add a little more flour if necessary.

POTATO BREAD

This golden crusty loaf has a moist soft center and is perfect for sandwiches. Use the water in which the potatoes have been cooked to make this bread. If you haven't got enough, make up the remainder with tap water.

1 Pour the water and sunflower oil into the bread machine pan. However, if the instructions for your machine specify that the yeast is to be placed in the pan first, reverse the order in which you add the liquid and dry ingredients.

2 Sprinkle the flour over, ensuring that it covers the water. Add the mashed potato and milk. Add the salt and sugar in separate corners of the bread pan. Make a shallow indentation in the center of the flour (but not down as far as the liquid) and add the yeast.

3 Set the bread machine to the basic/normal setting, medium crust. Press Start. To glaze the loaf, brush the top with milk either at the beginning of the cooking time or halfway through.

4 Remove the bread at the end of the baking cycle and turn out onto a wire rack to cool.

SMALL
⅞ cup potato cooking water, at room temperature
2 tablespoons sunflower oil
3¼ cups unbleached white bread flour
1½ cups cold cooked mashed potato
1 tablespoon nonfat dry milk
1 teaspoon salt
1½ teaspoons granulated sugar
1 teaspoon rapid-rise active dry yeast
milk, for glazing

MEDIUM
scant 1 cup potato cooking water, at room temperature
3 tablespoons sunflower oil
4½ cups unbleached white bread flour
2 cups cold cooked mashed potato
1½ tablespoons nonfat dry milk
1½ teaspoons salt
2 teaspoons granulated sugar
1½ teaspoons rapid-rise active dry yeast
milk, for glazing

LARGE
scant 1½ cups potato cooking water, at room temperature
¼ cup sunflower oil
6 cups unbleached white bread flour
2⅔ cups cold cooked mashed potato
2 tablespoons nonfat dry milk
2 teaspoons salt
1 tablespoon granulated sugar
1½ teaspoons rapid-rise active dry yeast
milk, for glazing

MAKES 1 LOAF

COOK'S TIP

If using leftover potatoes mashed with milk and butter you may need to reduce the liquid a little. If making the mashed potato, use 6 ounces, 7 ounces or 10 ounces raw potatoes, depending on machine size.

SPECIALITY GRAINS

This selection of recipes includes classic flavors from around the world, producing loaves with a variety of textures and flavors. Gluten is an essential part of the structure of bread, to ensure an open, light crumb and good texture. Most grains other than wheat have little or no gluten, so millet, buckwheat, barley and rye have been blended with wheat flours to provide rich, nutty-flavored loaves that can be successfully baked in your bread machine.

MUESLI AND DATE BREAD

This makes the perfect breakfast or brunch bread. Try making it with your own favorite unsweetened muesli.

scant 1⅛ cups water
2 tablespoons sunflower oil
1 tablespoon honey
*2⅔ cups unbleached white
bread flour*
¾ cup whole-wheat bread flour
*generous 1½ cups unsweetened fruit
and nut muesli*
3 tablespoons nonfat dry milk
1½ teaspoons salt
*1½ teaspoons rapid-rise active
dry yeast*
scant ½ cup pitted dates, chopped

MAKES 1 LOAF

1 Pour the water, oil and honey into the bread pan. Reverse the order in which you add the wet and dry ingredients if necessary. Sprinkle the flours over, covering the water completely. Add the muesli and milk, then the salt, in a corner of the pan. Make a small indentation in the flour; add the yeast.

2 Set the bread machine to the dough setting; use basic raisin dough setting (if available). Press Start. Add the dates when the machine beeps or during the last 5 minutes of kneading. Lightly oil a baking sheet.

3 When the dough cycle has finished, remove the dough from the machine and place it on a surface lightly dusted with whole-wheat flour. Punch it down gently.

4 Shape the dough into a plump round and place it on the prepared baking sheet. Using a sharp knife make three cuts on the top about ½ inch deep, to divide the bread into six sections.

5 Cover the loaf with oiled plastic wrap and set aside to rise for 30–45 minutes, or until it has almost doubled in size.

6 Preheat the oven to 400°F. Bake the loaf for 30–35 minutes until it is golden and hollow sounding. Transfer it to a wire rack to cool.

COOK'S TIP
The amount of water required may vary with the type of muesli used. Add another 1 tablespoon water if the dough is too firm.

BARLEY-ENRICHED FARMHOUSE LOAF

Barley adds a very distinctive, earthy, slightly nutty flavor to this crusty white loaf.

1⅛ cups water
3 tablespoons heavy cream
*3½ cups unbleached white
bread flour*
1 cup barley flour
2 teaspoons granulated sugar
2 teaspoons salt
1½ teaspoons rapid-rise active dry yeast
*2 tablespoons pumpkin or
sunflower seeds*
flour, for dusting

MAKES 1 LOAF

1 Pour the water and cream into the pan. Reverse the order in which you add the liquid and dry ingredients if necessary. Sprinkle both types of flour over, covering the water completely.

2 Add the sugar and salt, placing them in separate corners of the pan. Make a shallow indentation in the center of the flour and add the yeast.

3 Set the bread machine to the dough setting; use basic raisin dough setting (if available). Press Start. Add the pumpkin or sunflower seeds when the machine beeps or during the last 5 minutes of kneading. Lightly oil a 2-pound loaf pan measuring 7¼ × 4½ inches.

4 When the dough cycle has finished, remove the dough from the machine and place on a lightly floured surface. Punch down gently. Shape the dough into a rectangle, making the longer side the same length as the pan.

5 Roll the dough up lengthwise, and tuck the ends under. Place it in the prepared pan, with the seam underneath. Cover with lightly oiled plastic wrap and let rise for 30–45 minutes, or until the dough reaches the top of the pan.

6 Dust the loaf with flour then make a deep lengthwise cut along the top. Let rest for 10 minutes. Preheat the oven to 425°F.

7 Bake the loaf for 15 minutes, then reduce the oven temperature to 400°F and bake for 20–25 minutes more, or until the bread is golden and sounds hollow when tapped on the bottom. Transfer it to a wire rack to cool.

BRAN AND YOGURT BREAD

This soft-textured yogurt bread is enriched with bran. It is high in fibrer and makes wonderful toast.

SMALL
1 cup water
generous ½ cup
strained, plain yogurt
1 tablespoon sunflower oil
1 tablespoon molasses
1¾ cups unbleached white
bread flour
1⅓ cups whole-wheat
bread flour
⅓ cup wheat bran
1 teaspoon salt
¾ teaspoon rapid-rise active dry yeast

MEDIUM
1¼ cups water
¾ cup strained, plain yogurt
1½ tablespoons sunflower oil
2 tablespoons molasses
2⅓ cups unbleached white
bread flour
1¾ cups whole-wheat
bread flour
½ cup wheat bran
1½ teaspoons salt
1 teaspoon rapid-rise active dry yeast

LARGE
1⅓ cups water
scant 1 cup strained, plain yogurt
2 tablespoons sunflower oil
2 tablespoons molasses
3¼ cups unbleached white
bread flour
2¼ cups whole-wheat
bread flour
⅔ cup wheat bran
2 teaspoons salt
1½ teaspoons rapid-rise active dry yeast

MAKES 1 LOAF

1 Pour the water, yogurt, oil and molasses into the bread machine pan. If the instructions for your machine specify that the yeast is to be placed in the pan first, reverse the order in which you add the liquid and dry ingredients.

2 Sprinkle both the white and the whole-wheat flours over, ensuring that the liquid mixture is completely covered. Add the wheat bran and salt, then make a small indentation in the center of the dry ingredients (but not down as far as the liquid) and add the yeast.

3 Set the bread machine to the basic/normal setting, medium crust. Press Start.

4 Remove the bread from the pan at the end of the baking cycle and turn out onto a wire rack to cool. Serve when still just warm, if desired.

COOK'S TIP
Molasses is added to this bread to give added flavor and color. You can use corn syrup or golden syrup instead, to lessen the flavor, if desired.

POLENTA AND WHOLE-WHEAT LOAF

Polenta adds an interesting grainy quality to the texture of this rich whole-wheat bread, which is perfect for everyday use.

1 Add the water and honey to the pan. If necessary, reverse the order in which you add the liquid and dry ingredients. Sprinkle over the polenta and flours, ensuring that the liquid is covered.

2 Add the salt and butter in separate corners of the pan. Make a shallow indentation in the center of the flour (but not down as far as the liquid) and add the yeast.

3 Set the machine to the whole-wheat setting, medium crust. Press Start.

COOK'S TIP
This bread is perfect for breakfast and it may be baked using the automatic delay timer. The small quantity of butter should be fine overnight, but if you wish, substitute vegetable oil and adjust the liquid accordingly.

SMALL
1⅛ cups water
2 tablespoons honey
2 tablespoons polenta
¼ cup unbleached white bread flour
scant 3 cups whole-wheat bread flour
1 teaspoon salt
1½ tablespoons butter
¾ teaspoon rapid-rise active
dry yeast

MEDIUM
1¼ cups water
3 tablespoons honey
scant ½ cup polenta
½ cup unbleached white bread flour
3½ cups whole-wheat
bread flour
1½ teaspoons salt
2 tablespoons butter
1½ teaspoons rapid-rise active
dry yeast

LARGE
1½ cups water
4 tablespoons honey
scant ¾ cup polenta
¾ cup unbleached white bread flour
4¾ cups whole-wheat bread flour
2 teaspoons salt
3 tablespoons butter
2 teaspoon rapid-rise active
dry yeast

MAKES 1 LOAF

4 Remove the loaf from the bread pan at the end of the baking cycle and turn out onto a wire rack to cool.

TOASTED MILLET AND RYE BREAD

1⅓ cups water
½ cup rye flour
4 cups unbleached white bread flour
¼ cup millet flakes
1 tablespoon light brown sugar
1 teaspoon salt
2 tablespoons butter
1 teaspoon rapid-rise active dry yeast
⅓ cup millet seeds
millet flour, for dusting

MAKES 1 LOAF

COOK'S TIP
Before adding, toast the millet seeds under a preheated broiler to enhance their distinctive sweet flavor.

The dough for this delectable loaf is made in the bread machine, but it is shaped by hand before being baked in the oven.

1 Pour the water into the bread pan. If the instructions for your bread machine specify that the yeast is to be placed in the pan first, reverse the order in which you add the liquid and dry ingredients.

2 Sprinkle both types of flour over, then add the millet flakes, ensuring that the water is completely covered. Add the sugar, salt and butter, placing them in separate corners. Make an indentation in the center of the flour (but not down as far as the liquid) and add the yeast.

3 Set the bread machine to the dough setting; use basic raisin dough setting (if available). Press Start. Add the millet seeds when the machine beeps or during the last 5 minutes of kneading. Lightly flour a baking sheet.

4 When the dough cycle has finished, punch the dough down gently on a lightly floured surface.

5 Shape the dough into a rectangle. Roll it up lengthwise, then shape it into a thick baton with square ends. Place it on the prepared baking sheet, making sure that the seam is underneath. Cover it with lightly oiled plastic wrap and let rise in a warm place for 30–45 minutes, or until almost doubled in size.

6 Remove the plastic wrap and dust the top of the loaf with the millet flour. Using a sharp knife, make slanting cuts in alternate directions along the top of the loaf. Let it stand for about 10 minutes. Meanwhile, preheat the oven to 425°F.

7 Bake the loaf for 25–30 minutes, or until golden and hollow-sounding. Turn out onto a wire rack to cool.

BUCKWHEAT AND WALNUT BREAD

Buckwheat flour is made from toasted buckwheat groats. It has a distinctive earthy taste, perfectly mellowed when blended with white flour and walnuts in this compact bread, flavored with molasses.

1 Pour the water, molasses and walnut or olive oil into the bread pan. If the instructions for your machine specify that the yeast is to be placed in the pan first, reverse the order in which you add the liquid and dry ingredients.

2 Sprinkle the flours over, covering the liquid. Add the milk. Place the salt and sugar in separate corners. Make a shallow indentation in the center of the flour (but not down as far as the liquid) and add the easy-blend dried yeast.

SMALL
scant 1⅛ cups water
2 teaspoons molasses
1½ tablespoons walnut or olive oil
2¾ cups unbleached white
bread flour
½ cup buckwheat flour
1 tablespoon nonfat dry milk
1 teaspoon salt
½ teaspoon granulated sugar
1 teaspoon rapid-rise active dry yeast
⅓ cup walnut pieces

MEDIUM
3 teaspoons molasses
1⅓ cups water
2 tablespoons walnut or olive oil
3¾ cups unbleached white
bread flour
¾ cup buckwheat flour
1½ tablespoons nonfat dry milk
1½ teaspoons salt
¾ teaspoon granulated sugar
1 teaspoon rapid-rise active dry yeast
½ cup walnut pieces

LARGE
generous 1¾ cups water
4 teaspoons molasses
3 tablespoons walnut or olive oil
5 cups unbleached white bread flour
1 cup buckwheat flour
2 tablespoons nonfat dry milk
2 teaspoons salt
1 teaspoon granulated sugar
1½ teaspoons rapid-rise active
dry yeast
¾ cup walnut pieces

MAKES 1 LOAF

3 Set the bread machine to the basic/normal setting; use raisin setting (if available), medium crust. Press Start. Add the walnut pieces to the dough when the machine beeps or after the first kneading.

4 Remove the buckwheat and walnut bread from the machine pan at the end of the baking cycle and turn out onto a wire rack to cool.

WILD RICE, OAT AND POLENTA BREAD

Coarse-textured polenta, rolled oats and nutty-tasting wild rice blend
perfectly to make this delightful, nourishing bread.
The dark, slender grains of wild rice add beautiful flecks of color that
are revealed when this bread is split open.

¼ cup wild rice
1¼ cups water
2 tablespoons sunflower oil
scant 3 cups unbleached white
bread flour
½ cup whole-wheat bread flour
½ cup polenta
½ cup rolled oats
2 tablespoons nonfat dry milk
2 tablespoons golden syrup or corn syrup
2 teaspoons salt
1 teaspoon rapid-rise active dry yeast

MAKES 1 LOAF

COOK'S TIP

This bread is perfect for using up any
leftover wild rice you may have. You
will need 1 cup cooked wild rice.

1 Cook the wild rice in boiling salted
water according to the instructions on
the package.

2 Pour the water and the sunflower oil
into the bread machine pan. If the
instructions for your machine specify
that the yeast is to be placed in the pan
first, reverse the order in which you add
the liquid and dry ingredients.

3 Sprinkle the white and the whole-
wheat flours over, then add the polenta,
rolled oats and evaporated nonfat
milk, ensuring that the water is
completely covered.

4 Add the golden syrup and the salt,
placing them in separate corners of the
bread pan. Make a shallow indentation
in the center of the flour mixture (but
not down as far as the liquid) and add
the yeast.

5 Set the bread machine to the dough
setting; use basic raisin dough setting
(if available). Press Start.

6 Add the cooked wild rice when the
machine beeps or during the last
5 minutes of kneading. Lightly oil a
9 × 5-inch loaf pan.

7 When the dough cycle has finished,
remove the dough from the bread
machine pan and place it on a surface
that has been lightly floured. Punch the
dough down gently.

8 Divide the dough into six equal pieces.
In turn, shape each piece of dough into
an oblong mini loaf, about 5 inches in
length. Then place the six dough shapes
widthwise, side by side, in the prepared
loaf pan.

9 Cover the dough with lightly oiled
plastic wrap and set aside to rise in a
warm place for about 30–45 minutes, or
until the dough almost reaches the top
of the pan. Meanwhile preheat the oven
to 425°F.

10 Bake the loaf for 30–35 minutes, or
until it is golden and sounds hollow
when tapped on the bottom. Turn out
onto a wire rack to cool.

VARIATIONS

This bread can also be made with
other varieties of rice. Long-grain
brown rice and white rice are both
good, and they are also much faster to
cook than wild rice.
If you like, use the wild or red
Camargue rice. This variety takes
about an hour to cook, but the vivid
red color of the rice will give unusual
and very attractive flecks of color
in the bread.

FOUR SEED BREAD

This light whole-wheat and millet bread has added bite, thanks to a variety of tasty seeds, all readily available from your local health-food store.

1¼ cups water
2 tablespoons extra virgin olive oil
3½ cups unbleached white
bread flour
½ cup millet flour
½ cup whole-wheat bread flour
1 tablespoon granulated sugar
2 teaspoons salt
1 teaspoon rapid-rise active dry yeast
2 tablespoons pumpkin seeds
2 tablespoons sunflower seeds
1½ tablespoons flax seed
1½ tablespoons sesame seeds,
lightly toasted

FOR THE TOPPING
1 tablespoon milk
2 tablespoons golden flax seed

MAKES 1 LOAF

1 Pour the water and oil into the bread pan. Reverse the order in which you add the wet and dry ingredients if your machine specifies this.

2 Sprinkle all three types of flour over, ensuring that the water is completely covered. Add the sugar and salt in separate corners of the bread pan.

3 Make a shallow indentation in the center of the flour and add the yeast. Set the bread machine to the dough setting; use raisin dough setting (if available). Press Start. Add the seeds when the machine beeps to add extra ingredients or during the last 5 minutes of kneading.

4 When the dough cycle has finished, place the dough on a lightly floured surface and punch down gently.

5 Lightly oil a baking sheet. Shape the dough into a round flat loaf. Make a hole in the center with your finger. Gradually enlarge the cavity, turning the dough, until you have a ring. Place the ring on the baking sheet. Cover it with lightly oiled plastic wrap and let it rise in a warm place for 30–45 minutes, or until the dough has doubled in size.

6 Meanwhile, preheat the oven to 400°F. Brush the top of the bread with milk and sprinkle it with the golden flax seed. Make slashes around the loaf, radiating outward.

7 Bake for 30–35 minutes, or until golden and hollow-sounding. Turn out onto a wire rack to cool.

HAZELNUT AND FIG BREAD

This healthy, high-fiber bread is flavored with figs and hazelnuts.

1 Pour the water and the lemon juice into the bread machine pan. If the instructions for your machine specify that the yeast is to be placed in the pan first, reverse the order in which you add the liquid and dry ingredients.

2 Sprinkle the flours over, then the wheat germ, covering the water. Add the milk. Add the salt, sugar and butter in separate corners. Make an indentation in the flour; add the yeast.

3 Set the bread machine to the basic/normal setting; use raisin setting (if available), medium crust. Press Start. Coarsely chop the dried figs. Add the hazelnuts and the figs to the bread pan when the machine beeps or after the first kneading has finished.

4 Remove the bread at the end of the baking cycle and turn out onto a wire rack to allow to cool.

SMALL
1⅛ cups water
1 teaspoon lemon juice
2½ cups unbleached white
bread flour
¾ cup whole-wheat bread flour
3 tablespoons toasted wheat germ
1 tablespoon nonfat dry milk
1 teaspoon salt
2 teaspoons granulated sugar
1½ tablespoons butter
1 teaspoon rapid-rise active dry yeast
3 tablespoons dried figs
3 tablespoons peeled hazelnuts,
roasted and chopped

MEDIUM
1⅓ cups water
1½ teaspoons lemon juice
3 cups unbleached white bread flour
scant 1 cup whole-wheat
bread flour
4 tablespoons toasted wheat germ
2 tablespoons nonfat dry milk
1½ teaspoons salt
1 tablespoon granulated sugar
2 tablespoons butter
1½ teaspoons rapid-rise active
dry yeast
¼ cup dried figs
⅓ cup peeled hazelnuts, roasted
and chopped

LARGE
scant 2 cups water
2 teaspoons lemon juice
4½ cups unbleached white
bread flour
1 cup whole-wheat bread flour
5 tablespoons toasted wheat germ
3 tablespoons nonfat dry milk
2 teaspoons salt
4 teaspoons granulated sugar
3 tablespoons butter
1½ teaspoons rapid-rise active
dry yeast
⅓ cup dried figs
½ cup peeled hazelnuts, roasted
and chopped

MAKES 1 LOAF

SPELT AND BULGHUR WHEAT BREAD

Two unusual grains are used here. Spelt is a variety of wheat that is not widely grown, but is ground by some millers. Cracked wheat or bulgur is the cracked wheat berry, which has been softened by steaming. It contributes crunch while the spelt flour adds a nutty flavour.

SMALL
½ cup water
7 tablespoons buttermilk
1 teaspoon lemon juice
2¼ cups unbleached white bread flour
scant 1 cup spelt flour
2 tablespoons bulghur wheat
1 teaspoon salt
2 teaspoons granulated sugar
1 teaspoon rapid-rise active dry yeast

MEDIUM
1 cup water
generous ½ cup buttermilk
1½ teaspoons lemon juice
3 cups unbleached white bread flour
1⅓ cups spelt flour
3 tablespoons bulghur wheat
1½ teaspoons salt
1 tablespoon granulated sugar
1½ teaspoons rapid-rise active dry yeast

LARGE
1¼ cups water
⅝ cup buttermilk
2 teaspoons lemon juice
3¾ cups unbleached white bread flour
1¾ cups spelt flour
4 tablespoons bulghur wheat
2 teaspoons salt
4 teaspoons granulated sugar
2 teaspoons rapid-rise active dry yeast

MAKES 1 LOAF

VARIATION
The buttermilk adds a characteristic slightly sour note to this bread. You can replace it with low-fat plain yogurt or low-fat milk for a less pronounced tangy flavor.

1 Pour the water, buttermilk and lemon juice into the bread machine pan. If the instructions for your machine specify that the yeast is to be placed in the pan first, reverse the order in which you add the liquid and dry ingredients.

2 Sprinkle over both types of flour, then the bulghur wheat, ensuring that the liquid is completely covered. Add the salt and sugar, placing them in separate corners of the bread pan.

3 Make a shallow indentation in the center of the flour (but not down as far as the liquid) and add the yeast.

4 Set the bread machine to the basic/normal setting, medium crust. Press Start.

5 Remove the bread at the end of the baking cycle and turn out onto a wire rack to allow to cool.

MULTI-GRAIN BREAD

This healthy, mixed grain bread owes its wonderfully rich flavor to honey and malt extract.

1 Add the water, honey and malt extract to the pan. If your machine's instructions specify that the yeast is to be placed in the pan first, reverse the order in which you add the liquid and dry ingredients.

2 Sprinkle all four types of flour over, ensuring that the liquid is completely covered. Add the rolled oats and milk.

3 Place the salt and butter in separate corners of the bread machine pan. Make a shallow indentation in the center of the flour (but not down as far as the liquid) and add the yeast.

4 Set the bread machine to the whole wheat setting, medium crust. Press Start. Remove the bread at the end of the baking cycle and turn out onto a wire rack to allow to cool.

SMALL
1¼ cups water
1 tablespoon honey
1½ teaspoons malt extract
1 cup multi-grain flour
½ cup rye flour
¾ cup unbleached white bread flour
1¼ cups whole-wheat
bread flour
1 tablespoon rolled oats
1 tablespoon nonfat dry milk
1 teaspoon salt
1½ tablespoons butter
¾ teaspoon rapid-rise active
dry yeast

MEDIUM
1½ cups water
2 tablespoons honey
1 tablespoon malt extract
1¼ cups multi-grain flour
¾ cup rye flour
¾ cup unbleached white bread flour
1¾ cups whole-wheat
bread flour
2 tablespoons rolled oats
2 tablespoons nonfat dry milk
1½ teaspoons salt
2 tablespoons butter
1 teaspoon rapid-rise active dry yeast

LARGE
1¾ cups water
2 tablespoons honey
1½ tablespoons malt extract
1¾ cups multi-grain flour
1 cup rye flour
1 cup unbleached white bread flour
2 cups whole-wheat
bread flour
3 tablespoons rolled oats
3 tablespoons nonfat dry milk
2 teaspoons salt
3 tablespoons butter
1½ teaspoons rapid-rise active
dry yeast

MAKES 1 LOAF

RUSSIAN BLACK BREAD

European rye breads often include cocoa and coffee to add color to this dark traditionally dense, chewy bread. Slice it thinly, serve it with cold meats or pâtés or use it as the basis of an open sandwich.

SMALL

1⅛ cups water
2 tablespoons sunflower oil
2 tablespoons molasses
1 cup rye flour
½ cup whole-wheat bread flour
1½ cups unbleached white bread flour
2 tablespoons oat bran
½ cup dried bread crumbs
1 tablespoon cocoa powder
2 tablespoons instant coffee granules
1½ teaspoons caraway seeds
1 teaspoon salt
1 teaspoon rapid-rise active dry yeast

MEDIUM

generous 1½ cups water
2 tablespoons sunflower oil
2½ tablespoons molasses
1¼ cups rye flour
¾ cup whole-wheat bread flour
2¼ cups unbleached white bread flour
3 tablespoons oat bran
¾ cup dried bread crumbs
1½ tablespoons cocoa powder
2½ tablespoons instant coffee granules
1½ teaspoons caraway seeds
1½ teaspoons salt
1½ teaspoon rapid-rise active dry yeast

LARGE

generous 1⅔ cups water
3 tablespoons sunflower oil
3 tablespoons molasses
1¾ cups rye flour
scant 1 cup whole-wheat bread flour
generous 2½ cups unbleached white bread flour
4 tablespoons oat bran
scant 1 cup dried bread crumbs
2 tablespoons cocoa powder
3 tablespoons instant coffee granules
2 teaspoons caraway seeds
2 teaspoons salt
2 teaspoons rapid-rise active dry yeast

MAKES 1 LOAF

1 Pour the water, sunflower oil and molasses into the bread machine pan. If the instructions for your machine specify that the yeast is to be placed in the bread pan first, then simply reverse the order in which you add the liquid and dry ingredients.

2 Sprinkle the rye, whole-wheat and white flours over, then the oat bran and bread crumbs, ensuring that the water is completely covered. Add the cocoa powder, coffee granules, caraway seeds and salt. Make a shallow indentation in the center of the flour (but not down as far as the liquid underneath) and add the yeast.

3 Set the bread machine to the whole wheat setting, medium crust, and then press Start.

4 Remove the bread at the end of the baking cycle and turn out onto a wire rack to cool.

MAPLE AND OATMEAL LOAF

Rolled oats and oat bran add texture to this wholesome bread, which is suffused with the delectable flavor of maple syrup.

SMALL
1 cup water
1 tablespoon maple syrup
3¾ cups unbleached white
bread flour
½ cup whole-wheat bread flour
¼ cup rolled oats
1 tablespoon oat bran
1 teaspoon salt
1 teaspoon granulated sugar
2 tablespoons butter
1 teaspoon rapid-rise active dry yeast

MEDIUM
1⅓ cups water
2 tablespoons maple syrup
3¼ cups unbleached white
bread flour
¾ cup whole-wheat bread flour
½ cup rolled oats
2 tablespoons oat bran
1 teaspoon salt
1 teaspoon granulated sugar
3 tablespoons butter
1 teaspoon rapid-rise active dry yeast

LARGE
1¾ cups water
3 tablespoons maple syrup
4½ cups unbleached white
bread flour
1 cup whole-wheat bread flour
⅔ cup rolled oats
3 tablespoons oat bran
1½ teaspoons salt
1½ teaspoons granulated sugar
¼ cup butter
1½ teaspoons rapid-rise active dry yeast

MAKES 1 LOAF

1 Pour the water into the bread machine pan and then add the maple syrup. If the instructions for your machine specify that the yeast is to be placed in the pan first, reverse the order in which you add the liquid and dry ingredients.

2 Sprinkle both the white and whole-wheat flours over, then the rolled oats and oat bran, ensuring that the water is completely covered.

3 Add the salt, sugar and butter, placing them in separate corners of the bread pan. Make a shallow indentation in the center of the flour (but not down as far as the liquid) and add the yeast.

4 Set the bread machine to the basic/normal setting, medium crust. Press Start.

5 Remove the bread at the end of the baking cycle and turn out onto a wire rack to cool.

COOK'S TIP
Use 100 percent pure maple syrup. Less expensive products are often blended with cane or corn syrup, which does not have the smooth rich flavor of the real thing.

PARTYBROT

These traditional Swiss-German rolls are baked as one, in a round pan.
As the name suggests, partybrot is perfect for entertaining.

FOR THE MILK ROLLS
scant ⅔ cup milk
2 cups unbleached white bread flour
1½ teaspoons granulated sugar
1 teaspoon salt
1 tablespoon butter
½ teaspoon rapid-rise active dry yeast

FOR THE WHOLE-WHEAT ROLLS
¾ cup water
1½ cups whole-wheat
bread flour
¾ cup unbleached white bread flour
1½ teaspoons granulated sugar
1 teaspoon salt
2 tablespoons butter
½ teaspoon rapid-rise active dry yeast

FOR THE TOPPING
1 egg yolk, mixed with 1 tablespoon
cold water
1 tablespoon rolled oats or
cracked wheat
1 teaspoon poppy seeds

MAKES 19 ROLLS

1 Pour the milk for making the milk rolls into the bread machine pan. However, if the instructions for your bread machine specify that the yeast is to be placed in the pan first, simply reverse the order in which you add the liquid and dry ingredients.

2 Sprinkle the white bread flour over, making sure that it covers the milk completely. Add the sugar, salt and butter, placing them in separate corners of the bread pan.

3 Make a shallow indentation in the center of the flour (but not down as far as the liquid underneath) and add the yeast.

4 Set the bread machine to the dough setting; use basic dough setting (if available). Press Start.

5 Lightly oil a 10-inch springform cake pan, and a large mixing bowl. When the dough cycle has finished, remove the dough from the machine and place it in the mixing bowl.

6 Cover the dough with oiled plastic wrap and put it in the refrigerator while you make the whole-wheat dough. Follow the instructions for the milk roll dough, but use water instead of milk.

7 Remove the milk roll dough from the refrigerator 20 minutes before the end of the whole-wheat dough cycle. When the whole-wheat dough is ready, remove it from the machine and place on a lightly floured surface. Punch it down. Do the same with the milk roll dough.

8 Divide the milk roll dough into nine pieces and the whole-wheat dough into 10. Shape each piece of dough into a small round ball.

9 Place 12 balls, evenly spaced, around the outer edge of the prepared cake pan, alternating milk dough with whole-wheat.

10 Add an inner circle with six more balls and place the remaining ball of whole-wheat dough in the center.

11 Cover the pan with lightly oiled plastic wrap and set the rolls aside to rise in a warm place for 30–45 minutes, or until they have doubled in size. Meanwhile, preheat the oven to 400°F.

12 Brush the whole-wheat rolls with the egg yolk and water glaze. Sprinkle with rolled oats or cracked wheat. Glaze the white rolls and sprinkle with poppy seeds. Bake for 35–40 minutes, or until the partybrot is golden. Leave for 5 minutes to cool in the pan, then turn out onto a wire rack. Serve warm or cold.

FLATBREADS AND PIZZAS

Flatbreads are fun to bake and make delicious meal accompaniments. Naan, often flavored with coriander or black onion seeds, is typical of Indian flatbread, whilst Lavash, Pita and Pide are traditional Middle Eastern specialties. Italy is famous for Foccacia, pizzas, and Calzone, while the French version of pizza is the Pissaladière. All of these breads can be made in your machine using the "dough only" setting and then hand-shaped and oven-baked.

GARLIC AND CORIANDER NAAN

7 tablespoons water
4 tablespoons strained, plain yogurt
2½ cups unbleached white
bread flour
1 garlic clove, finely chopped
1 teaspoon black onion seeds
1 teaspoon ground coriander
1 teaspoon salt
2 teaspoons honey
1 tablespoon melted ghee or butter,
plus 2–3 tablespoons melted ghee or
butter, for brushing
1 teaspoon rapid-rise active dry yeast
1 tablespoon chopped fresh cilantro

MAKES 3

VARIATION
For a basic naan omit the coriander, garlic and black onion seeds. Include a little ground black pepper or ground chile for a slightly piquant note.

Indian restaurants the world over have introduced us to several differently flavored examples of this leavened flatbread, and this version is particularly tasty and will become a great favorite. The bread is traditionally made in a tandoor oven, but this method has been developed to give almost identical results.

1 Pour the water and yogurt into the bread machine pan. If the instructions for your bread machine specify that the yeast is to be placed in the pan first, then simply reverse the order in which you add the liquid and dry ingredients.

2 Sprinkle the flour over, ensuring that it covers the liquid completely. Add the garlic, black onion seeds and ground coriander. Add the salt, honey and the 1 tablespoon melted ghee or butter in separate corners of the bread pan.

3 Make a shallow indentation in the center of the flour (but not down as far as the liquid) and add the yeast.

4 Set the bread machine to the dough setting, use basic or pizza dough setting (if available). Press Start.

5 When the dough cycle has finished, preheat the oven to its highest setting. Place three baking sheets in the oven to heat. Remove the dough from the bread machine and place it on a lightly floured surface.

6 Punch the naan dough down gently and then knead in the chopped fresh cilantro. Divide the dough into three equal pieces.

6 Shape each piece into a ball and cover two of the pieces with oiled plastic wrap. Roll out the remaining piece of dough into a large teardrop shape, making it ¼–½ inch thick. Cover with oiled plastic wrap while you roll out the remaining two pieces of dough to make two more naan.

7 Preheat the broiler to its highest setting. Place the naan on the preheated baking sheets and then bake them for 4–5 minutes, until puffed up. Remove the baking sheets from the oven and place them under the hot broiler for a few seconds, until the naan start to brown and blister.

8 Brush the naan with melted ghee or butter and serve warm.

CARTA DI MUSICA

This crunchy, crisp bread looks like sheets of music manuscript paper, which is how it came by its name. It originated in Sardinia and can be found throughout southern Italy, where it is eaten not only as a bread, but as a substitute for pasta in lasagne. It also makes a good pizza crust.

1¼ cups water
4 cups unbleached white bread flour
1½ teaspoons salt
1 teaspoon granulated sugar
1 teaspoon rapid-rise active dry yeast

MAKES 8

COOK'S TIP
Cutting the partially cooked breads in half is quite tricky. You may find it easier to divide the dough into six or eight pieces, and roll these as thinly as possible before baking. The cutting stage can then be avoided.

5 Now roll out the other three pieces. If the dough starts to tear, cover it with oiled plastic wrap and let it rest for 2–3 minutes.

6 When all the dough has been rolled out, cover with oiled plastic wrap and let rest on the floured surface for 10–15 minutes. Preheat the oven to 450°F. Place two baking sheets in the oven to heat.

7 Keeping the other dough rounds covered, place one round on each baking sheet. Bake for 5 minutes, or until puffed up.

1 Pour the water into the bread machine pan. If the instructions specify that the yeast should be placed in the pan first, simply reverse the order in which you add the liquid and dry ingredients to the pan.

2 Sprinkle the white bread flour over, ensuring that it covers the water. Add the salt in one corner of the bread pan and the sugar in another corner. Make a shallow indentation in the center of the flour (but not down as far as the liquid) and add the yeast.

3 Set the bread machine to the dough setting; use basic dough setting (if available). Press Start.

4 When the dough cycle has finished, remove the dough from the machine and place it on a lightly floured surface. Punch it down gently and divide it into four equal pieces. Shape each piece of dough into a ball, then roll a piece out until about ⅛-inch thick.

8 Remove from the oven and cut each round in half horizontally to make two thinner breads. Place these cut-side up on the baking sheets, return them to the oven and bake for 5–8 minutes more, until crisp. Turn out onto a wire rack and cook the remaining breads.

generous 1 cup water
3 tablespoons strained, plain yogurt
3 cups unbleached white bread flour
1 cup whole-wheat bread flour
1 teaspoon salt
1 teaspoon rapid-rise active dry yeast

FOR THE TOPPING
2 tablespoons milk
2 tablespoons millet seeds

MAKES 10

VARIATION
Instead of making individual lavash you could divide the dough into five or six pieces and make large lavash. Serve these on a platter in the center of the table and invite guests to break off pieces as required.

LAVASH
—

These Middle Eastern flatbreads puff up slightly during cooking, to make a bread that is crispy, but not as dry and crisp as a cracker. Serve warm straight from the oven or cold, with a little butter, if wished.

1 Pour the water and yogurt into the bread machine pan. If the instructions for your machine specify that the yeast is to be placed in the pan first, reverse the order in which you add the liquid and dry ingredients.

2 Sprinkle both types of flour over, ensuring that the liquid is completely covered. Add the salt in one corner of the bread pan. Make an indentation in the center of the flour; add the yeast.

3 Set the bread machine to the dough setting; use basic or pizza dough setting (if available). Press Start.

4 When the dough cycle has finished, place the dough on a lightly floured surface. Punch it down gently and divide it into 10 equal pieces.

5 Shape each piece into a ball, then flatten into a disc with your hand. Cover with oiled plastic wrap; set aside to rest for 5 minutes. Preheat the oven to 450°F. Place three or four baking sheets in the oven.

6 Roll each ball of dough out very thinly, then stretch it over the backs of your hands, to make the lavash. If the dough starts to tear, let it rest for a few minutes after rolling. Stack the lavash between layers of oiled plastic wrap and cover to keep moist.

7 Place as many lavash as will fit comfortably on each baking sheet, brush with milk and sprinkle with millet seeds. Bake for 5–8 minutes, or until puffed and starting to brown. Transfer to a wire rack and cook the remaining lavash.

---

scant 1 cup water
1 tablespoon olive oil
3 cups unbleached white bread flour,
plus extra for sprinkling
1½ teaspoons salt
1 teaspoon granulated sugar
1 teaspoon rapid-rise active dry yeast

MAKES 6–10

1 Pour the water and oil into the bread machine pan. If your instructions specify that the yeast is to be placed in the pan first, reverse the order in which you add the liquid and dry ingredients. Add the flour, ensuring it covers the water.

2 Add the salt and sugar in separate corners of the pan. Make a shallow indentation in the center of the flour and add the yeast. Set the bread machine to the dough setting; use basic or pizza dough setting (if available). Press Start.

PITA BREADS
—

These well-known flat breads are easy to make and extremely versatile. Serve them warm with dips or soups, or split them in half and stuff the pockets with your favorite vegetable, meat or cheese filling.

3 When the dough cycle has finished, remove the dough from the machine. Place it on a lightly floured surface and punch it down gently.

4 Divide the dough into six or ten equal-size pieces, depending on whether you want large or small pita breads. Shape each piece into a ball.

5 Cover the balls of dough with oiled plastic wrap and let them rest for about 10 minutes. Preheat the oven to 450°F. Then place three baking sheets in the oven to heat.

6 Flatten each piece of dough slightly, and then roll out into an oval or round, about ¼ inch thick.

7 Lightly sprinkle each pita with flour. Cover with oiled plastic wrap and let rest for 10 minutes.

8 Place the pitas on the baking sheets and bake for 5–6 minutes, or until they are puffed up and lightly browned. Transfer the pita breads on to wire racks to cool.

MOROCCAN KSRA

*This leavened flatbread is made with semolina and spiced with aniseed.
It is the traditional accompaniment to tagine, a spicy Moroccan stew, but is
equally good with salad, cheeses or dips. It can be served warm or cold.*

*⅞ cup water
2¼ cups unbleached white
bread flour
¾ cup semolina
1 teaspoon aniseed
1½ teaspoons salt
½ teaspoon granulated sugar
1 teaspoon rapid-rise active dry yeast
olive oil, for brushing
sesame seeds, for sprinkling*

MAKES 2

1 Pour the water into the machine pan.
Reverse the order in which you add the
wet and dry ingredients if necessary.

2 Add the flour, semolina and aniseed,
covering the water. Place the salt and
sugar in separate corners. Make an
indentation in the flour; add the yeast.
Set the machine to the dough setting;
use the basic dough setting if available.

3 Press Start on your bread machine,
then lightly flour two baking sheets.
When the cycle has finished, place the
dough on a lightly floured surface.

4 Punch the dough down gently, shape
into two balls, then flatten into ¾ inch
thick disks. Place each dough disk on a
baking sheet.

5 Cover the dough disks with oiled
plastic wrap and set aside to rise for
30 minutes, or until doubled in bulk.

6 Preheat the oven to 400°F. Brush the
top of each piece of dough with olive oil
and sprinkle with sesame seeds. Prick
the surface with a skewer.

7 Bake for about 20–25 minutes, or until
the ksra are golden and sound hollow
when tapped underneath. Turn out
onto a wire rack to cool.

VARIATION
Replace up to half the white bread
flour with whole-wheat bread flour for
a nuttier flavor.

PIDE

*A traditional Turkish ridged flatbread, this is often baked plain, but can also
be sprinkled with aromatic black nigella seeds, which taste rather like
oregano. If you can't find nigella seeds, use poppy seeds.*

*generous 1 cup water
2 tablespoons olive oil
4 cups unbleached white bread flour
1 teaspoon salt
1 teaspoon sugar
1 teaspoon rapid-rise active dry yeast
1 egg yolk mixed with
2 teaspoons water, for glazing
nigella or poppy seeds, for sprinkling*

MAKES 3

1 Pour the water and olive oil into the
bread machine pan. If the instructions
for your machine specify that the yeast
is to be placed in the pan first, reverse
the order in which you add the liquid
and dry ingredients.

2 Sprinkle the flour over, ensuring that
it covers the liquid. Add the salt in one
corner of the bread pan and the sugar in
another corner. Make an indentation in
the center of the flour; add the yeast.

3 Set the bread machine to the dough
setting; use basic dough setting (if
available). Press Start.

4 When the dough cycle has finished,
remove the pide dough from the bread
machine and place it on a surface
lightly dusted with flour. Punch the
dough down gently and divide it into
three equal-size pieces. Shape each
piece of dough into a ball.

5 Roll each ball of dough into a round,
about 6 inches in diameter. Cover with
oiled plastic wrap and let rise for
20 minutes. Meanwhile, preheat the
oven to 450°F.

6 Using your fingers, ridge the bread,
while enlarging it until it is ¼ inch thick.
Start from the top of the round, pressing
your fingers down and away from you,
into the bread. Repeat a second row
beneath the first row, and continue
down the bread.

7 Turn the bread by 90 degrees and
repeat the pressing to give a criss-cross
ridged effect. Place the pide on floured
baking sheets, brush with egg glaze and
sprinkle with nigella or poppy seeds.
Bake for 9–10 minutes, or until puffy
and golden. Serve immediately.

OLIVE FOUGASSE

scant 1 cup water
1 tablespoon olive oil, plus extra
for brushing
3 cups unbleached white bread flour
1 teaspoon salt
1 teaspoon granulated sugar
1 teaspoon rapid-rise active dry yeast
½ cup pitted black
olives, chopped

MAKES 1 FOUGASSE

A French hearth bread, fougasse is traditionally baked on the floor of the hot bread oven, just after the fire has been raked out. It can be left plain or flavored with olives, herbs, nuts or cheese.

1 Pour the water and the olive oil into the bread machine pan. Reverse the order in which you add the wet and dry ingredients if necessary.

2 Sprinkle the flour over, ensuring that it covers the liquid. Add the salt in one corner of the bread pan and the sugar in another corner. Make a shallow indentation in the center of the flour (but not down as far as the liquid) and add the yeast.

3 Set the bread machine to the dough setting; use basic or pizza dough setting (if available). Press Start. When the cycle has finished, remove the dough from the machine and place it on a lightly floured surface.

4 Punch the dough down gently and flatten it slightly. Sprinkle over the olives and fold over the dough two or three times to incorporate them.

5 Flatten the dough and roll it into an oblong, about 12 inches long. With a sharp knife make four or five parallel cuts diagonally through the body of the dough, but leaving the edges intact. Gently stretch the fougasse dough so that it resembles a ladder.

6 Lightly oil a baking sheet, then place the shaped dough on it. Cover with oiled plastic wrap and let rise in a warm place for about 30 minutes, or until the dough has nearly doubled in bulk.

7 Preheat the oven to 425°F. Brush the top of the fougasse with olive oil, place in the oven and bake about for 20–25 minutes, or until the bread is golden. Turn out onto a wire rack to cool.

ONION FOCACCIA

Focaccia, with its characteristic texture and dimpled surface, has become hugely popular in recent years. This version has a delectable red onion and fresh sage topping.

scant 1 cup water
1 tablespoon olive oil
3 cups unbleached white bread flour
½ teaspoon salt
1 teaspoon granulated sugar
1 teaspoon rapid-rise active dry yeast
1 tablespoon chopped fresh sage
1 tablespoon chopped red onion

FOR THE TOPPING
2 tablespoons olive oil
½ red onion, thinly sliced
5 fresh sage leaves
2 teaspoons coarse sea salt
coarsely ground black pepper

MAKES 1 FOCACCIA

7 Meanwhile, preheat the oven to 400°F. Uncover the risen focaccia, and, using your fingertips, poke the dough to make deep dimples over the surface. Cover and let rise for 10–15 minutes, or until the dough has doubled in bulk.

1 Pour the water and oil into the bread pan. Reverse the order in which you add the wet and dry ingredients if necessary.

2 Sprinkle the flour over, ensuring that it covers the liquid. Add the salt and sugar in separate corners. Make a shallow indentation in the flour and add the yeast.

3 Set the bread machine to the dough setting. If your machine has a choice of settings use the basic or pizza dough setting. Press Start.

4 Lightly oil a 10–11-inch shallow round cake pan or pizza pan. When the cycle has finished, remove the dough from the pan and place it on a surface lightly dusted with flour.

5 Punch the dough down and flatten it slightly. Sprinkle over the sage and red onion and knead gently to incorporate.

6 Shape the dough into a ball, flatten it, then roll it into a round of about 10–11 inches. Place in the prepared pan. Cover with oiled plastic wrap and let rise in a warm place for 20 minutes.

8 Drizzle the olive oil over and sprinkle with the onion, sage leaves, sea salt and black pepper. Bake for 20–25 minutes, or until golden. Turn out onto a wire rack to cool slightly. Serve warm.

TOMATO AND PROSCIUTTO PIZZA

This combination of fresh plum tomatoes, sun-dried tomatoes, garlic and prosciutto with three cheeses is truly mouthwatering. Pizzas provide the perfect opportunity for exercising your individuality, so experiment with different topping ingredients if you prefer.

SMALL AND MEDIUM
MAKES ONE 12 INCH PIZZA
⅝ cup water
1 tablespoon extra virgin olive oil
2 cups unbleached white bread flour
1 teaspoon salt
¼ teaspoon granulated sugar
½ teaspoon rapid-rise active dry yeast

FOR THE FILLING
3 tablespoons sun-dried tomato paste
5½ ounces mozzarella cheese, sliced
4 fresh plum tomatoes, about
14 ounces, roughly chopped
1 small yellow bell pepper, halved,
seeded and cut into thin strips
2 ounces prosciutto, torn into pieces
8 fresh basil leaves
4 large garlic cloves, halved
2 ounces feta cheese, crumbled
2 tablespoons extra virgin olive oil
2 tablespoons freshly grated
Parmesan cheese
salt and freshly ground black pepper

LARGE
MAKES TWO 12 INCH PIZZAS
1¼ cups water
2 tablespoons extra virgin olive oil
4 cups unbleached white bread flour
1½ teaspoons salt
½ teaspoon granulated sugar
1 teaspoon rapid-rise active dry yeast

FOR THE FILLING
6 tablespoons sun-dried tomato paste
11 ounces mozzarella cheese, sliced
8 fresh plum tomatoes, about
1¾ pounds, roughly chopped
1 large yellow bell pepper, halved,
seeded and cut into thin strips
4 ounces prosciutto, torn into pieces
16 fresh basil leaves
8 large garlic cloves, halved
4 ounces feta cheese, crumbled
3 tablespoons extra virgin olive oil
4 tablespoons freshly grated
Parmesan cheese
salt and freshly ground
black pepper

1 Pour the water and olive oil into the bread machine pan. If the instructions for your machine specify that the yeast is to be placed in the pan first, reverse the order in which you add the liquid and dry ingredients.

2 Sprinkle over the flour, ensuring that it covers the liquid. Add the salt in one corner of the bread pan and the sugar in another corner. Make a shallow indentation in the center of the flour, then add the yeast.

3 Set the bread machine to the dough setting; use basic or pizza dough setting (if available). Press Start. Lightly oil one or two pizza pans or baking sheets.

4 When the dough cycle has finished, remove the dough from the machine and place it on a lightly floured surface. Punch it down gently. If making the larger quantity divide the dough into two equal pieces. Preheat the oven to 425°F.

5 Roll out the pizza dough into one or two 12-inch rounds. Place in the prepared pan(s) or on the baking sheet(s). Spread the sun-dried tomato paste over the pizza crust(s) and arrange two-thirds of the mozzarella slices on top.

6 Scatter with the chopped tomatoes, pepper strips, prosciutto, whole basil leaves, garlic, remaining mozzarella and feta. Drizzle the olive oil over and sprinkle with the Parmesan. Season with salt and pepper. Bake the pizza for 15–20 minutes, or until golden and sizzling. Serve immediately.

VARIATION
This topping lends itself particularly well to the nutty flavor of a whole-wheat pizza crust. Replace half the unbleached white bread flour with whole-wheat bread flour. You may need to add a little more water as whole-wheat flour absorbs more liquid.

PISSALADIÈRE

This French version of an Italian pizza is typical of Niçoise dishes, with anchovies and olives providing the distinctive flavor typical of the region.

7 tablespoons water
1 egg
2 cups unbleached white bread flour
1 teaspoon salt
2 tablespoons butter
1 teaspoon rapid-rise active dry yeast

FOR THE FILLING
¼ cup olive oil
1¼ pounds onions, thinly sliced
1 tablespoon Dijon mustard
3–4 tomatoes, about 10 ounces,
peeled and sliced
2 teaspoons chopped fresh basil
12 drained canned anchovies
12 black olives
salt and freshly ground black pepper

SERVES 6

1 Pour the water and egg into the bread machine pan. If the instructions for your machine specify that the yeast is to be placed in the pan first, then reverse the order in which you add the liquid and the dry ingredients.

2 Sprinkle the white bread flour over, ensuring that it completely covers the water and the egg. Add the salt in one corner of the pan and the butter in another corner. Make a shallow indentation in the center of the flour (but not down as far as the liquid) and add the yeast.

3 Set the bread machine to the dough setting; use basic or pizza dough setting (if available). Press Start. Then lightly oil an 11 × 8-inch jelly roll pan that is about ½ inch deep.

4 Make the filling. Heat the olive oil in a large frying pan and cook the onions over a low heat for about 20 minutes, until very soft. Set aside to cool.

5 When the dough cycle has finished, remove the dough from the machine and place it on a lightly floured surface. Punch it down gently, then roll it out to a rectangle measuring about 12 × 9 inches. Place in the prepared pan, and press outward and upward, so that the dough covers the bottom and sides.

6 Spread the mustard over the dough. Arrange the tomato slices on top. Season the onions with salt, pepper and basil and spread the mixture over the tomatoes.

7 Arrange the anchovies in a lattice and dot with the black olives. Cover with oiled plastic wrap and let rise for 10–15 minutes. Meanwhile preheat the oven to 400°F. Bake the pissaladière for 25–30 minutes, or until the crust is cooked and golden around the edges. Serve hot or warm.

SICILIAN SFINCIONE

Sfincione is the Sicilian equivalent of pizza. The Sicilians insist they were making these tasty snacks long before pizzas were made in mainland Italy.

1 Pour the water and oil into the bread pan. If your instructions specify that the yeast is to be placed in the bread pan first, reverse the order in which you add the liquid and the dry ingredients.

2 Sprinkle the flour over, ensuring that it covers the liquid. Add the salt in one corner of the bread pan and the sugar in another corner. Make a shallow indentation in the center of the flour; add the yeast.

3 Set the bread machine to the dough setting; use basic or pizza dough setting (if available). Press Start. Then lightly oil two baking sheets.

4 Make the topping. Peel and chop the tomatoes. Put in a bowl, add the garlic and 1 tablespoon of the olive oil and toss together. Heat the sunflower oil in a small pan and sauté the onions until softened. Set aside to cool.

5 When the dough cycle has finished, remove the dough from the machine and place it on a lightly floured surface. Punch it down gently and divide it into four equal pieces.

6 Roll each piece of dough out to a round, each about 6–7 inches in diameter. Space the rounds well apart on the prepared baking sheets, then push up the dough edges on each to make a thin rim. Cover the sfincione with oiled plastic wrap and let rise for 10 minutes. Meanwhile, preheat the oven to 425°F.

7 Sprinkle the topping over the crusts, ending with the Pecorino. Season, then drizzle with the remaining olive oil.

8 Bake near the top of the oven for 15–20 minutes or until the crust of each sfincione is cooked. Serve immediately.

⅞ cup water
2 tablespoons extra virgin olive oil
3 cups unbleached white bread flour
1½ teaspoons salt
½ teaspoon granulated sugar
1 teaspoon rapid-rise active dry yeast

FOR THE TOPPING
6 tomatoes
2 garlic cloves, chopped
3 tablespoons olive oil
1 tablespoon sunflower oil
2 onions, chopped
8 pitted black olives, chopped
2 teaspoons dried oregano
6 tablespoons freshly grated Pecorino cheese
salt and freshly ground black pepper

MAKES 4

CALZONE

Calzone is an enclosed pizza, with the filling inside. It originated in Naples and was originally made from a rectangular piece of pizza dough, unlike the modern version, which looks like a large Cornish pasty.

generous ½ cup water
2 tablespoons extra virgin olive oil,
plus extra for brushing
2 cups unbleached white bread flour
1 teaspoon salt
½ teaspoon granulated sugar
1 teaspoon rapid-rise active dry yeast

FOR THE FILLING
3 ounces salami, in one piece
½ cup drained sun-dried tomatoes in olive oil, chopped
⅔ cup mozzarella cheese, cut into small cubes
⅔ cup freshly grated Parmesan cheese
2 ounces Gorgonzola cheese, cut into small cubes
scant ½ cup ricotta cheese
3 tablespoons chopped fresh basil
2 egg yolks
salt and freshly ground black pepper

MAKES 2

1 Pour the water and olive oil into the bread pan. Reverse the order in which you add the liquid and dry ingredients if this is necessary for your machine. Sprinkle the white bread flour over, ensuring that it covers the liquid.

VARIATIONS
The ingredients for the filling can be varied, depending on what you have in the refrigerator and to suit personal tastes. Replace the salami with ham or sautéed mushrooms. Add a freshly chopped chile for a more piquant version. Make four individual calzones instead of two large ones.

2 Add the salt and sugar in separate corners of the bread pan. Make a shallow indentation in the center of the flour (but not down as far as the liquid) and add the yeast.

3 Set the bread machine to the dough setting; use basic or pizza dough setting (if available). Press Start.

4 To make the topping, cut the salami into ¼-inch dice. Put the dice in a bowl and add the sun-dried tomatoes, mozzarella, Parmesan, Gorgonzola and ricotta cheeses, basil and egg yolks. Mix well and season to taste with salt and plenty of ground black pepper. Lightly oil a large baking sheet.

5 When the cycle has finished, remove the calzone dough from the bread pan and place it on a lightly floured surface. Punch it down gently then divide the dough into two equal pieces. Roll out each piece of dough into a flat round, about ¼ inch thick. Preheat the oven to 425°F.

COOK'S TIP
Calzone can be made in advance, ready for baking. Make the dough, then transfer to a bowl, cover with oiled plastic wrap and store in the refrigerator for up to 4 hours. Knock back if the dough starts to rise to the top of the bowl. Bring back to room temperature, then continue with the shaping and filling. If preferred, shape and fill up to 2 hours before baking. Place the calzone in the refrigerator until you are ready to bake them.

6 Divide the filling between the two pieces of dough, placing it on one half only, in each case. Leave a ½ inch border of the dough all round.

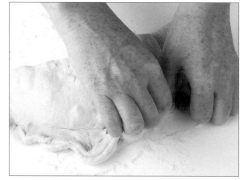

7 Dampen the edges of each dough round with water, fold the remaining dough over the filling and then crimp the edges of each calzone with your fingers to seal securely.

8 Place the calzone on the baking sheet, brush with olive oil and bake for 20 minutes, or until golden and well risen.

SOURDOUGHS AND STARTER DOUGH BREADS

Breads made with starters acquire their wonderful textures and flavors from the multiple ferments and starter doughs. The bread machine provides the perfect environment to nurture these doughs. This section also includes a recipe for bread made with fresh yeast.

FRENCH COURONNE

This crown-shaped loaf is made with a chef starter, which is fermented for at least 2 days and up to a week; the longer it is left the more it will develop the characteristic sourdough flavor.

FOR THE CHEF
⅛ teaspoon rapid-rise active dry yeast
½ cup organic white
bread flour
3 tablespoons water

FOR THE 1ST REFRESHMENT
3½ tablespoons water
1 cup organic white
bread flour

FOR THE LEVAIN
½ cup water
1 cup unbleached white bread flour

FOR THE COURONNE DOUGH
generous 1 cup cold water
scant 3 cups unbleached white
bread flour, plus extra
for dusting
1½ teaspoons salt
1 teaspoon granulated sugar
½ teaspoon rapid-rise active
dry yeast

MAKES 1 LOAF

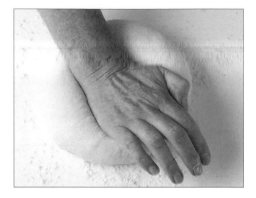

1 Mix the yeast and organic white bread flour for the chef in a small bowl. Add the water and gradually mix to a stiff dough with a metal spoon. Cover the bowl with oiled plastic wrap and set aside in a warm place for 2–3 days.

2 Break open the crust on the chef – the middle should be aerated and sweet smelling. Mix in the water and flour for the first refreshment, stirring to form a fairly stiff dough. Replace the plastic wrap cover and set aside for a further 2 days in a warm place.

3 Transfer the chef to the machine pan. If the instructions for your machine specify that the yeast is to be placed in the pan first, reverse the order in which you add the liquid and dry ingredients.

4 Add the water for the levain. Sprinkle over the flour, ensuring that it covers the water. Set the bread machine to the dough setting; use basic dough setting (if available). Press Start.

5 When the dough cycle has finished, switch the machine off, leaving the levain inside. Do not lift the lid. Leave the levain for 8 hours. If you need the machine, transfer the levain to a bowl, cover it with a damp dish towel and leave it at room temperature.

6 Take the bread pan out of the machine. Remove about half of the levain from the pan. If the levain is in a bowl, put scant 1 cup of it back in the pan. Reserve the spare levain to replenish and use for your next loaf of bread. Meanwhile pour the water for the dough into the bread pan. Sprinkle over the flour. Add the salt and sugar, placing them in separate corners of the bread pan. Make a shallow indentation in the center of the flour and add the yeast.

7 Set the bread machine to the dough setting; use basic dough setting (if available). Press Start. Lightly oil a baking sheet.

8 When the dough cycle has finished, remove the dough from the machine and place it on a lightly floured surface. Punch it down gently, then shape it into a ball and make a hole in the center with the heel of your hand. Gradually enlarge this cavity, using your fingertips and turning the dough, then use both hands to stretch the dough gently into a large doughnut shape. The cavity should measure 5–6 inches across.

9 Place the shaped dough on the prepared baking sheet. Fit a small bowl into the center to prevent the dough from filling in the hole when it rises. Cover it with lightly oiled plastic wrap and leave it in a warm place for an hour, or until almost doubled in size.

10 Preheat the oven to 450°F. Dust the loaf with flour and make four slashes at equal intervals around the couronne. Bake for 35–40 minutes, or until the bread is golden and sounds hollow when tapped on its bottom. Turn out onto a wire rack to cool.

HONEY AND BEER RYE BREAD

The flavor of this rye bread is enhanced by leaving the sourdough starter to develop over 3 days as a prelude to making the dough.

FOR THE STARTER
¾ cup milk
1 cup rye flour
¾ teaspoon rapid-rise active dry yeast

FOR THE DOUGH
scant ¾ cup flat beer
*scant 2¾ cups unbleached white
bread flour*
¾ cup rye flour
1 tablespoon honey
1½ teaspoons salt
½ teaspoon rapid-rise active dry yeast
whole-wheat flour, for dusting

MAKES 1 LOAF

1 Mix the milk, flour and yeast for the starter in a large bowl. Stir, then cover with a damp dish towel. Rest in a warm place for 3 days; stir once a day.

2 Make the dough. Pour the starter into the bread machine pan and add the beer. If the instructions for your machine specify that the yeast is to be placed in the pan first, simply reverse the order in which you add the liquid and dry ingredients.

3 Sprinkle both types of flour over, ensuring that the beer is completely covered. Add the honey and salt, placing them in separate corners of the bread pan. Make a shallow indentation in the center of the flour (but not down as far as the liquid) and add the yeast.

4 Set the bread machine to the dough setting; use basic dough setting (if available). Press Start. Lightly oil a 6½-inch square pan that is fairly deep.

5 When the dough cycle has finished, remove the dough from the machine and place it on a lightly floured surface. Punch it down gently.

6 Roll the dough into a rectangle about ¾ inch thick. It needs to be the same width as the pan and three times as long. Fold the bottom third of the dough up and the top third down, then seal the edges with the rolling pin.

7 Place the folded dough in the prepared pan, cover it with lightly oiled plastic wrap and leave in a warm place for 45–60 minutes, or until the dough has risen almost to the top of the pan.

8 Meanwhile, preheat the oven to 425°F. Dust the top of the loaf with a little whole-wheat flour.

9 Using a sharp knife, slash the loaf with four long cuts. Repeat with five cuts in the opposite direction to give a cross-hatched effect.

10 Bake the bread for 30–35 minutes, or until it sounds hollow when tapped on the bottom. Turn out onto a wire rack to cool slightly before serving.

PANE ALL'OLIO

*Italians love to use olive oil in cooking, as this bread amply proves.
The combined flavors of the olive oil and the biga starter give a rich,
earthy and yeasty flavor to the bread.*

FOR THE BIGA
7 tablespoons water
1½ cups white bread flour
1 teaspoon rapid-rise active dry yeast

FOR THE DOUGH
6 tablespoons water
4 tablespoons extra virgin olive oil
2 cups unbleached white bread flour,
plus extra for dusting
2 teaspoons salt
1 teaspoon granulated sugar

MAKES 1 LOAF

COOK'S TIP
If you haven't got a baking stone, you
can use unglazed terracotta tiles.
Place several tiles edge to edge,
ensuring that the air can flow around
the outside edges.

1 Pour the water for the biga into the
bread machine pan. If the instructions
for your machine specify that the yeast
is to be placed in the pan first, reverse
the order in which you add the liquid
and dry ingredients.

2 Sprinkle the flour over, covering the
water. Make a shallow indentation in the
center of the flour and add the yeast.

3 Set the machine to the dough setting;
use basic dough setting (if available).
Press Start. When the dough cycle has
finished, switch the machine off, but
leave the biga inside, with the lid closed,
for 8 hours. If you need the machine
during this time, transfer the biga to a
bowl, cover it with a damp dish towel
and leave it at room temperature.

4 Remove the bread pan from the
machine. Break the biga into three or
four pieces. If you took it out of the
bread pan, put it back.

5 Pour in the water and olive oil for the
dough. Sprinkle the flour over, covering
the liquid. Add the salt and sugar in
separate corners of the bread pan.

6 Set the bread machine to the dough
setting; use basic dough setting (if
available). Press Start. Lightly flour a
peel (baker's shovel) or baking sheet.

7 When the dough cycle has finished,
place the dough on a lightly floured
surface. Punch it down gently, then
shape it into a plump round.

8 Using the palms of your hands, gently
roll the dough backward and forward,
concentrating on the ends, until it forms
a tapered, torpedo-shaped loaf about
12 inches long. Place the loaf on the
prepared peel or baking sheet and cover
it with lightly oiled plastic wrap. Let it
rise in a warm place for 45–60 minutes,
or until the dough has almost doubled
in size.

9 Meanwhile, place a baking stone on a
shelf about a third of the way up from
the bottom of the oven. Preheat the
oven to 450°F. Dust the top of the bread
lightly with flour and slash it along its
length. Transfer the bread to the hot
baking stone.

10 Mist the inside of the oven with
water. Bake the loaf for 15 minutes,
misting the oven again after 2 minutes
and then after 4 minutes. Reduce the
oven temperature to 375°F and bake the
loaf for 20–25 minutes more, or until it
is golden all over and the bread sounds
hollow when tapped on the bottom.
Turn out onto a wire rack before serving
warm or cooled.

PAIN DE CAMPAGNE

This rustic-style French bread is made using a poolish or sponge. The fermentation period is fairly short, which makes for a loaf which is not as sour as some breads of this type. It is also lighter and slightly less chewy.

FOR THE POOLISH
⅞ *cup water*
1½ *cups unbleached white
bread flour*
½ *cup whole-wheat bread flour*
¼ *teaspoon rapid-rise active dry yeast*

FOR THE DOUGH
½ *cup water*
2 *cups unbleached white bread flour;
plus extra for dusting*
½ *cup whole-wheat bread flour*
¼ *cup rye flour*
1½ *teaspoons salt*
½ *teaspoon granulated sugar*
½ *teaspoon rapid-rise active dry yeast*

MAKES 1 LOAF

1 Pour the water for the poolish into the bread machine pan. If the instructions for your machine specify that the yeast is to be placed in the pan first, reverse the order in which you add the liquid and dry ingredients.

2 Sprinkle both types of flour over, ensuring that the water is completely covered. Make a shallow indentation in the center of the flour; add the yeast. Set the bread machine to the dough setting; use basic dough setting (if available). Press Start.

3 When the dough cycle has finished, switch the machine off, but leave the poolish inside, with the lid closed, for 2 to 8 hours, depending on how sour you like your bread to taste.

4 Remove the bread pan from the machine. Pour in the water for the dough. Sprinkle each type of flour over, then add the salt and sugar in separate corners. Make a shallow indentation in the center of the flour; add the yeast. Set the bread machine to the dough setting. If your machine has a choice of settings, use the basic dough setting. Press Start.

5 When the dough cycle has finished, place the dough on a lightly floured surface. Punch it down gently, then shape it into a plump, round ball. Place on a lightly oiled baking sheet.

6 Cover with a large glass bowl or lightly oiled plastic wrap and let rise in a warm place for 30–45 minutes, or until the dough has almost doubled in bulk. Preheat the oven to 425°F.

7 Dust the top of the loaf with flour. Cut three parallel slashes across the loaf, then cut three more slashes at right angles to the first set.

8 Transfer the baking sheet to a rack near the bottom of the oven and bake the bread for 40 minutes, or until it is golden and sounds hollow when tapped on the bottom. Turn out onto a wire rack.

CIABATTA

This popular flat loaf is irregularly shaped and typically has large air holes in the crumb. The dough for this bread is extremely wet. Do not be tempted to add more flour—it's meant to be that way.

FOR THE BIGA
⅞ cup water
1½ cups unbleached white
bread flour
½ teaspoon rapid-rise active dry yeast

FOR THE CIABATTA DOUGH
⅞ cup water
2 tablespoons milk
2 tablespoons extra virgin olive oil
scant 3 cups unbleached white bread
flour, plus extra for dusting
1½ teaspoons salt
½ teaspoon granulated sugar
¼ teaspoon rapid-rise active dry yeast

MAKES 2 LOAVES

1 Pour the water for the biga into the bread pan. If necessary, reverse the order in which you add the liquid and dry ingredients. Sprinkle the flour over, covering the water. Make an indentation in the center of the flour; add the yeast.

2 Set the bread machine to the dough setting; use basic dough setting (if available). Press Start. Mix for 5 minutes, then switch off the machine.

3 Leave the biga in the bread machine, or place in a large mixing bowl covered with lightly oiled plastic wrap, overnight or for at least 12 hours, until the dough has risen and is just starting to collapse.

4 Return the biga to the pan, if necessary. Add the water, milk and oil for the ciabatta dough. Sprinkle the flour over. Add the salt and sugar in separate corners. Make a shallow indentation in the center of the flour and add the yeast.

5 Set the bread machine to the dough setting; use the basic dough setting (if available). Press Start.

6 When the cycle has finished, transfer the dough to a bowl and cover with oiled plastic wrap. Let rise for about 1 hour, until the dough has tripled in size. Sprinkle two baking sheets with flour.

7 Using a spoon or a dough scraper, divide the dough into two portions. Carefully tip one portion of the dough onto one of the prepared baking sheets, trying to avoid knocking the air out of the dough. Using well-floured hands shape the dough into a rectangular loaf about 1 inch thick, pulling and stretching as necessary. Repeat with the remaining piece of dough.

8 Sprinkle both loaves with flour. Leave them, uncovered, in a warm place for about 20–30 minutes. The dough will spread and rise. Meanwhile, preheat the oven to 425°F.

9 Bake the ciabatta for 25–30 minutes, or until both loaves have risen, are light golden in color and sound hollow when tapped on the bottom. Transfer them to a wire rack to cool before serving with butter, or olive oil for dipping.

PAIN DE SEIGLE

Based on a rye starter, this is typical of the breads eaten in the Pyrenees.
Serve it thickly buttered – it makes the perfect accompaniment for shellfish.

FOR THE CHEF
⅞ cup water
1½ cups rye flour
¼ teaspoon rapid-rise active dry yeast

FOR THE 1ST REFRESHMENT
¼ cup + 1 tablespoon water
½ cup flour

FOR THE 2ND REFRESHMENT
1 tablespoon water
½ cup flour

FOR THE BREAD DOUGH
1 tablespoon water
2 cups unbleached white bread flour
2 teaspoons salt
1 teaspoon honey
½ teaspoon rapid-rise active dry yeast
unbleached white bread flour,
for dusting

MAKES 1 LOAF

1 Pour the water for the chef into the bread machine pan. If the instructions for your machine specify that the yeast is to be placed in the pan first, reverse the order in which you add the liquid and dry ingredients.

2 Sprinkle the rye flour over, ensuring that it covers the water completely. Make a shallow indentation in the center of the flour (but not down as far as the liquid) and add the yeast. Set the bread machine to the dough setting; use basic dough setting (if available). Press Start. Mix the dough for about 10 minutes, and then switch off the bread machine.

3 Let the chef ferment in the machine, with the lid closed, for about 24 hours. If you need the machine, transfer the chef to a bowl, cover it with a damp dish towel and then set aside at room temperature.

4 Remove the bread pan from the machine. Return the chef to the bread pan, if necessary, and add the water and flour for the first refreshment. Set the bread machine to the dough setting, press Start and mix for 10 minutes. Switch off the machine and leave the dough inside for a further 24 hours.

5 Add the water and flour for the second refreshment. Mix as for the first refreshment, but this time leave the dough in the machine for only 8 hours.

6 Add the water for the bread dough to the mixture in the bread machine pan. Sprinkle over the flour. Place the salt and honey in separate corners of the bread pan. Make a shallow indentation in the center of the flour and add the yeast. Set the bread machine to the dough setting; use basic dough setting (if available). Press Start. Lightly flour a baking sheet.

COOK'S TIP
When shaping the loaf into a twist make sure that you continue to twist it in the same direction after you have turned the dough round to finish shaping the loaf.

7 When the dough cycle has finished, place the dough on a lightly floured surface. Punch it down gently, then divide the dough into two equal pieces. Roll each piece of dough into a rope about 18 inches long.

8 Place the two ropes side by side. Starting at the center, place one piece of dough over the other. Continue twisting in this fashion until you reach the end of the rope. Turn the dough around and twist the other ends. Dampen the ends with water; tuck them under to seal.

9 Place the twist on the baking sheet, cover with oiled plastic wrap and let rise in a warm place for 45 minutes, or until almost doubled in size.

10 Preheat the oven to 425°F. Dust the top of the loaf lightly with flour and bake for 40 minutes, or until the bread is golden and sounds hollow when tapped on the bottom. Switch off the oven, but leave the loaf inside, with the door slightly ajar, for 5 minutes. Turn out onto a wire rack to cool.

SAVORY BREADS

Adding flavorings to a basic dough provides many new ideas. Herbs, such as rosemary, dill and sage, along with garlic and onion will fill the kitchen with delicious scents. Cottage cheese and feta give loaves a subtle flavor, while Gorgonzola, Parmesan and mascarpone are combined with chives to give a rich loaf with a wonderful aroma. Sausages, smoked venison, salami and pancetta are just a few of the meats you can add to savory breads.

scant 1 cup water
3 cups unbleached white bread flour
¼ cup whole-wheat bread flour
1 tablespoon nonfat dry milk
1 teaspoon salt
1¼ teaspoons granulated sugar
1 teaspoon rapid-rise active dry yeast
scant ½ cup well drained, pitted black olives, chopped
2 ounces feta cheese, crumbled
1 tablespoon olive oil, for brushing

MAKES 1 LOAF

COOK'S TIP
Depending on the moisture content of the olives and cheese you may need to add a tablespoon or two of flour to the bread dough when adding these extra ingredients.

FETA CHEESE AND BLACK OLIVE LOAF

Conjuring up memories of holidays in Greece, this bread has a delicious flavor, thanks to the Mediterranean ingredients.

1 Pour the water into the bread pan. If necessary, reverse the order in which you add the liquid and dry ingredients. Sprinkle the flours over, covering the water completely. Add the milk. Place the salt and sugar in separate corners of the bread pan. Make an indentation in the flour; add the yeast.

2 Set the bread machine to the dough setting; use basic raisin dough setting (if available). Press Start. Lightly oil a 7–8-inch deep round cake pan.

3 Add the olives and feta cheese when the bread machine beeps or 5 minutes before the end of the kneading cycle. Once the dough cycle has finished, place the dough on a lightly floured surface and punch down gently.

4 Shape the dough into a plump ball, the same diameter as the pan. Place in the prepared pan, cover with oiled plastic wrap and let rise for 30–45 minutes. Preheat the oven to 400°F.

5 Remove the plastic wrap and brush the olive oil over the top of the loaf. Bake for 35–40 minutes, or until golden. Turn the bread out onto a wire rack to cool.

---

6 tablespoons water
1 egg
2 cups unbleached white bread flour
1 teaspoon salt
2 tablespoons butter
1 teaspoon rapid-rise active dry yeast

FOR THE FILLING
4–5 leeks
2 tablespoons sunflower oil
3 ounces sliced pancetta or bacon, cut into strips
⅝ cup sour cream
5 tablespoons milk
2 eggs, lightly beaten
1 tablespoon chopped fresh basil leaves
salt and freshly ground black pepper

MAKES 1 LOAF

1 Pour the water and egg into the bread machine pan. Reverse wet and dry ingredients if necessary.

LEEK AND PANCETTA TRAY BREAD

What could be more delicious than this rich yeast dough, topped with leeks and pancetta in a sour cream custard? Serve it sliced, with a simple salad of dressed greens, for a tasty supper or lunchtime treat.

2 Sprinkle the flour over, ensuring that it covers the water and egg. Place the salt and butter in separate corners of the bread pan. Make a shallow indentation in the center of the flour (but not down as far as the liquid) and add the yeast.

3 Set the bread machine to the dough setting; use basic or pizza dough setting (if available). Press Start. Then lightly oil a 8 × 12-inch jelly roll pan that is about ½ inch deep.

4 Slice the leeks thinly. Heat the sunflower oil in a large frying pan and cook the leeks over a low heat for about 5 minutes, until they have softened slightly but not browned. Set them aside to cool.

5 When the dough cycle has finished, place the dough on a lightly floured surface. Punch it down gently, then roll it out to a rectangle measuring about 9 × 13 inches. Place in the prepared pan and press the edges outward and upward, so that the dough covers the bottom and sides evenly. Preheat the oven to 375°F.

6 Scatter the leeks over the dough. Arrange the pancetta slices on top. Mix the sour cream, milk and eggs together. Add the basil and season with salt and ground black pepper. Pour the mixture over the leeks.

7 Bake for 30–35 minutes, or until the filling has set and the crust is golden around the edges. Serve hot or warm.

GRAINY MUSTARD AND BEER LOAF

For a ploughman's lunch par excellence, serve this wonderful bread with cheese and pickles.

SMALL

*1 cup
flat beer
1 tablespoon vegetable oil
2 tablespoons wholegrain mustard
2¼ cups unbleached white
bread flour
generous 1 cup whole-wheat
bread flour
1 tablespoon nonfat dry milk
1 teaspoon salt
1½ teaspoons granulated sugar
1 teaspoon rapid-rise active dry yeast*

MEDIUM

*1¼ cups flat beer
1 tablespoon vegetable oil
3 tablespoons wholegrain mustard
3 cups unbleached white bread flour
1⅓ cups whole-wheat
bread flour
1½ tablespoons nonfat dry milk
1½ teaspoons salt
2 teaspoon granulated sugar
1 teaspoon rapid-rise active dry yeast*

LARGE

*generous 1½ cups
flat beer
2 tablespoons vegetable oil
4 tablespoons wholegrain mustard
4¼ cups unbleached white
bread flour
1¾ cups whole-wheat
bread flour
2 tablespoons nonfat dry milk
1½ teaspoons salt
1 tablespoon granulated sugar
1½ teaspoons rapid-rise active
dry yeast*

MAKES 1 LOAF

1 Pour the beer and oil into the bread machine pan. Add the mustard. If the instructions for your machine specify that the yeast is to be placed in the pan first, reverse the order in which you add the liquid and dry ingredients.

2 Sprinkle the white and whole-wheat flours over, ensuring that the liquid is completely covered. Add the milk Add the salt and sugar, placing them in separate corners of the bread pan. Make a shallow indentation in the center of the flour (but not down as far as the liquid) and add the yeast.

3 Set the bread machine to the basic/normal setting, medium crust. Press Start.

4 Remove the bread at the end of the baking cycle and turn out onto a wire rack to cool.

COOK'S TIP
Use pale ale for a more subtle taste or brown ale if you prefer a stronger flavor to your bread. Open at least 1 hour before using, to make sure it is flat.

COTTAGE CHEESE-PEPPERONI LOAF

Cottage cheese gives this bread an interesting texture. It is quite filling, and has a delicious, spicy taste, thanks to the pepperoni and oregano. Serve it with vegetable soups or salad.

1 Place the cottage cheese in the bread machine pan and pour in the water and extra virgin olive oil. If the instructions for your bread machine specify that the yeast is to be placed in the bread pan first, then simply reverse the order in which you add the liquid and dry ingredients.

2 Sprinkle the flour over, ensuring that it covers the water. Add the oregano. Add the salt and sugar in separate corners of the bread pan. Make a shallow indentation in the center of the flour (but not down as far as the liquid) and add the yeast.

3 Set the bread machine to the basic/normal setting, with raisin setting (if available), medium crust. Press Start. Add the pepperoni and scallion when the machine beeps or sprinkle them over the dough 5 minutes before the end of the kneading cycle.

4 Remove the bread at the end of the baking cycle and turn out onto a wire rack to cool.

SMALL
scant ½ cup cottage cheese
¾ cup water
1 tablespoon extra virgin olive oil
3¼ cups unbleached white
bread flour
1 teaspoon dried oregano
1 teaspoon salt
1½ teaspoons granulated sugar
1 teaspoon rapid-rise active dry yeast
1 ounce pepperoni, cut into
¼-inch chunks
1 scallion, chopped

MEDIUM
¾ cup cottage cheese
1 cup water
1½ tablespoons extra virgin olive oil
4½ cups unbleached white
bread flour
1½ teaspoons dried oregano
1 teaspoon salt
2 teaspoons granulated sugar
1½ teaspoons rapid-rise active dry yeast
2 ounces pepperoni, cut into
¼-inch chunks
2 scallions, chopped

LARGE
1 cup cottage cheese
1¼ cups water
2 tablespoons extra virgin olive oil
6 cups unbleached white bread flour
2 teaspoons dried oregano
1½ teaspoons salt
1 tablespoon granulated sugar
1½ teaspoons rapid-rise active
dry yeast
3 ounces pepperoni, cut into
¼-inch chunks
3 scallions, chopped

MAKES 1 LOAF

COOK'S TIP
Extra ingredients are usually added toward the end of the kneading cycle, and some machines will alert you to this by means of a beep or buzzing noise. Consult the manual for your machine if necessary.

⅞ cup water
3 cups unbleached white bread flour
½ teaspoon granulated sugar
1 teaspoon salt
1 teaspoon rapid-rise active dry yeast

FOR THE FILLING
6 ounces mozzarella cheese, grated or
finely chopped
1 cup freshly grated Parmesan cheese
1 tablespoon chopped fresh
flat-leaf parsley
2 tablespoons fresh basil leaves
1 teaspoon freshly ground
black pepper
1 garlic clove, finely chopped

FOR THE TOPPING
1 tablespoon extra virgin olive oil
4–5 small fresh rosemary sprigs,
woody stems removed

MAKES 1 LOAF

STROMBOLI

This variation on Italian Focaccia takes its name from the volcanic island of Stromboli, near Sicily. The dough is pierced to allow the filling to "erupt" through the holes during baking. This bread can be served warm or cold.

1 Pour the water into the machine pan. Reverse the order in which you add the wet and dry ingredients if necessary. Sprinkle the flour over, ensuring that it covers the water. Add the sugar and salt in separate corners of the pan. Make a shallow indentation in the center of the flour and add the yeast.

2 Set the bread machine to the dough setting; use basic dough setting (if available). Press Start.

3 Lightly oil a baking sheet. When the dough cycle has ended, remove the dough and place on a lightly floured surface. Punch it down gently. Roll the dough out into a rectangle measuring 12 × 9 inches. Cover with oiled plastic wrap and let rest for 5 minutes.

4 Sprinkle the cheeses over leaving a ½ inch border along each edge. Add the parsley, basil, pepper and garlic.

5 Starting from a shorter side, roll up the dough, jelly roll fashion, tucking the side edges under to seal. Place the roll, seam down, on the baking sheet. Cover with lightly oiled plastic wrap and leave in a warm place for 30 minutes, or until the dough roll has almost doubled in size.

6 Preheat the oven to 400°F. Brush the top of the bread with olive oil, then use a skewer to prick holes in the bread, from the top right through to the bottom. Sprinkle the rosemary over the bread. Bake for 30–35 minutes, or until the bread is golden. Transfer it to a wire rack.

---

generous ¾ cup water
1 egg
5 tablespoons mascarpone cheese
3½ cups unbleached white
bread flour
½ cup multi-grain flour
2 teaspoons granulated sugar
1 teaspoon salt
1½ teaspoons rapid-rise active
dry yeast
3 ounces Mountain Gorgonzola
cheese, cut into small dice
1 cup freshly grated Parmesan cheese
3 tablespoons snipped fresh chives

FOR THE TOPPING
1 egg yolk
1 tablespoon water
1 tablespoon wheat flakes

MAKES 1 LOAF

THREE CHEESES BREAD

A tempting trio of Italian cheeses—mascarpone, Gorgonzola and Parmesan— are responsible for the marvellous flavor of this round loaf.

1 Place the water, egg and mascarpone in the pan. Reverse the order in which you add the wet and dry ingredients if necessary. Sprinkle both types of flour over, covering the water completely.

2 Add the sugar and salt in separate corners. Make a shallow indentation in the flour; add the yeast. Set the machine to the dough setting; use basic raisin dough setting (if available). Press Start.

3 Add the Gorgonzola, Parmesan and chives as the machine beeps or during the last 5 minutes of kneading. Lightly oil a baking sheet.

4 When the dough cycle has finished, place the dough on a floured surface. Punch down gently, then shape it into a round loaf, about 8 inches in diameter.

5 Cover with oiled plastic wrap; let rise in a warm place for 30–45 minutes. Preheat the oven to 400°F.

6 Mix the egg yolk and water together and brush this glaze over the top of the bread. Sprinkle with wheat flakes. Score the top of the bread into eight equal segments. Bake for 30–35 minutes, or until golden and hollow-sounding. Turn out onto a wire rack to cool.

VENISON TORDU

This pretty twisted bread is punctuated with strips of smoked venison, black pepper and crushed juniper berries. It tastes delicious on its own, perhaps with a glass of red wine. Alternatively, cut the bread into thick slices and serve it with olives and nuts before an Italian meal.

1 cup water
3 cups unbleached white bread flour
1 teaspoon granulated sugar
1 teaspoon salt
1 teaspoon rapid-rise active dry yeast
1½ ounces smoked venison, cut into strips
1 teaspoon freshly ground black pepper
1 teaspoon juniper berries, crushed
unbleached white bread flour, for dusting

MAKES 1 LOAF

1 Pour the water into the bread machine pan. If the instructions for your bread machine specify that the yeast is to be placed in the pan first, simply reverse the order in which you add the liquid and dry ingredients to the pan.

2 Sprinkle the white bread flour over, ensuring that it completely covers the water. Add the sugar and salt, placing them in separate corners of the bread pan. Make a shallow indentation in the center of the flour (but not down as far as the liquid underneath) and add the yeast.

3 Set the bread machine to the dough setting; use basic dough setting (if available). Press Start. Meanwhile, lightly oil a baking sheet.

4 When the dough cycle has finished, remove the dough from the bread machine pan and place it on a lightly floured surface. Punch it down gently. Shape the dough into a ball and flatten the top slightly.

5 Roll the dough out to a round, about ¾ inch thick. Sprinkle the top of the dough with venison strips, black pepper and juniper berries. Leave a ½ inch border around the edge.

6 Fold one side of the dough to the center, then repeat on the other side.

7 Press the folds gently with a rolling pin to seal them, then fold again along the center line.

COOK'S TIP
Try using cured and smoked venison, marinated in olive oil and herbs, for this recipe. The olive oil and herbs add an extra flavor which beautifully complements this bread. Alternatively, sprinkle 1 teaspoon of dried herbs such as rosemary, thyme, sage or oregano over the dough in step 4.

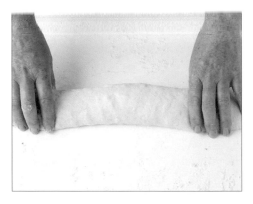

8 Press the seam gently to seal, then roll the dough backwards and forwards to make a loaf about 26 inches long.

9 Using the side of your hand, press across the center of the loaf to make an indentation. Bring both ends towards each other to make an upside down "U" shape and twist together.

10 Place the venison tordu on the prepared baking sheet. Cover with lightly oiled plastic wrap and let rise in a warm place for 30 minutes, or until it has almost doubled in size. Meanwhile, preheat the oven to 425°F. Remove the plastic wrap and dust the top of the twisted loaf with white bread flour.

11 Bake for 25–30 minutes, or until the bread is golden and sounds hollow when tapped on the bottom. Turn out onto a wire rack to cool. Serve freshly baked, while the bread is still slightly warm.

1¼ cups water
2 tablespoons vegetable oil
1 tablespoon tomato paste
4½ cups unbleached white
bread flour
1½ teaspoons paprika
1 teaspoon cayenne pepper
1 teaspoon dried oregano
½ teaspoon freshly ground
black pepper
1 garlic clove, crushed
1½ teaspoons salt
½ teaspoon sugar
1½ teaspoons rapid-rise active
dry yeast
FOR THE GLAZE
1 egg yolk
1 tablespoon water

MAKES 1 LOAF

CAJUN SPICED BRAID

The traditional Louisiana flavors of tomatoes, garlic, spices and hot seasonings make this piquant, spicy loaf irresistible.

1 Pour the water and vegetable oil into the bread machine pan, then add the tomato paste. If the instructions for your machine specify that the yeast is to be placed in the pan first, reverse the order in which you add the liquid and dry ingredients.

2 Sprinkle the flour over, ensuring that it covers the liquid. Add the paprika, cayenne, oregano, black pepper and crushed garlic. Place the salt and sugar in separate corners of the bread pan. Make a shallow indentation in the center of the flour (but not down as far as the liquid) and add the yeast.

3 Set the bread machine to the dough setting; use basic dough setting (if available). Press Start. Lightly oil a baking sheet.

4 Once the dough cycle has finished, place the dough on a floured surface. Punch it down and divide into three.

5 Roll the pieces into ropes, all the same length. Put next to each other. From the center, braid from left to right, working towards yourself. Press the ends together and tuck under.

6 Turn the dough around and braid the remaining ropes, as before. Place on the prepared baking sheet, cover with oiled plastic wrap and leave in a warm place to rise for 30–45 minutes. Meanwhile, preheat the oven to 400°F.

7 Mix the egg yolk and water for the glaze together. Remove the plastic wrap and brush the glaze over the braid. Bake for 30–35 minutes, or until golden.

scant 1 cup water
1 tablespoon olive oil
3 cups unbleached
white flour
½ cup grated aged Cheddar cheese
½ teaspoon salt
1 teaspoon granulated sugar
1 teaspoon rapid-rise active dry yeast
1 teaspoon black peppercorns,
coarsely crushed
2 ounces salami, chopped
milk, for brushing

MAKES 1 LOAF

SALAMI AND PEPPERCORN BREAD

This loaf marbled with salami and black pepper makes a great accompaniment to hot soup. For a quick snack, try it toasted with a cheese topping.

2 Sprinkle the flour over, ensuring that it covers the liquid. Add half the cheese. Add the salt in one corner of the bread pan and the sugar in another corner. Make a shallow indentation in the center of the flour (but not down as far as the liquid) and add the yeast.

3 Set the bread machine to the dough setting; use basic or pizza dough setting (if available). Press Start. Then lightly oil a baking sheet.

4 Once the dough cycle has finished, remove the dough from the machine and place it on a lightly floured surface. Punch it down gently and flatten it slightly. Sprinkle the peppercorns and salami over and knead gently until both are evenly incorporated.

5 Shape into a round loaf; place on the baking sheet. Cover with an oiled bowl and leave in a warm place for 30 minutes. Preheat the oven to 400°F.

6 Uncover the bread, brush it with milk and sprinkle with the remaining cheese. Bake for about 30–35 minutes, or until golden. Turn out onto a wire rack to cool.

1 Pour the water and olive oil into the bread machine pan. If the instructions for your bread machine specify that the yeast is to be placed in the bread pan first, then simply reverse the order in which you add the liquid and dry ingredients.

MARBLED PESTO BREAD

Using ready-made pesto sauce means that this scrumptuous bread is very easy to make. Use a good quality sauce—or, if you have the time, make your own—so that the flavors of garlic, basil, pine nuts and Parmesan cheese can be clearly discerned.

⅝ cup milk

scant ⅔ cup water

2 tablespoons extra virgin olive oil

4 cups unbleached white bread flour

1½ teaspoons granulated sugar

1½ teaspoons salt

1½ teaspoons rapid-rise active dry yeast

7 tablespoons prepared pesto sauce

FOR THE TOPPING

1 tablespoon extra virgin olive oil

2 teaspoons coarse sea salt

MAKES 1 LOAF

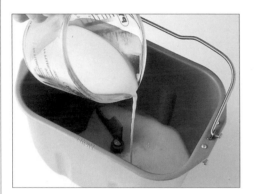

1 Remove the milk from the refrigerator 30 minutes before using, to bring it to room temperature. Pour the water, milk and extra virgin olive oil into the bread machine pan. If the instructions for your bread machine specify that the yeast is to be placed in the pan first, then simply reverse the order in which you add the liquid and dry ingredients.

2 Sprinkle the flour over, ensuring that it covers the liquid mixture completely. Add the sugar and salt, placing them in separate corners of the bread pan.

3 Make a shallow indentation in the center of the flour (but do not go down as far as the liquid) and pour the dried yeast into the hollow.

4 Set the bread machine to the dough setting. If your machine has a choice of settings use the basic dough setting. Press Start. Lightly oil a 10 × 4 inch loaf pan.

5 When the dough cycle has finished, remove the dough from the machine and place it on a lightly floured surface.

6 Punch it down gently, then roll it out to a rectangle about ¾ inch thick and 10 inches long. Cover with oiled plastic wrap and let relax for a few minutes, if the dough proves difficult to roll out.

7 Spread the pesto sauce over the dough. Leave a border of ½ inch along one long edge. Roll up the dough lengthwise, jelly roll fashion, tuck the ends under and place seam down in the prepared pan.

8 Cover with oiled plastic wrap and set aside in a warm place to rise for 45 minutes or until the dough has more than doubled in size and reaches the top of the loaf tin. Meanwhile, preheat the oven to 425°F.

9 Remove the plastic wrap and brush the olive oil over the top of the loaf. Use a sharp knife to score the top with four diagonal cuts. Repeat the cuts in the opposite direction to make a criss-cross pattern. Sprinkle with the sea salt.

10 Bake for 25–30 minutes, or until the bread is golden and sounds hollow when tapped on the bottom. Turn out onto a wire rack to cool.

COOK'S TIP

For a really luxurious twist to this bread, make your own pesto filling. Put 3 ounces basil leaves, 1 clove garlic, 2 tablespoons pine nuts, salt and pepper, and ⅓ cup olive oil in a mortar and crush to a paste with a pestle, or place in a blender and blend until creamy.

Work in 2 ounces freshly grated Parmesan cheese.

Any leftover pesto can be kept for up to 2 weeks in the refrigerator.

SUN-DRIED TOMATO BREAD

The dense texture and highly concentrated flavor of sun-dried tomatoes makes them perfect for flavoring bread dough, and when Parmesan cheese is added, the result is an exceptionally tasty loaf.

SMALL
¼ cup sun-dried tomatoes
⅔ cup water
⅓ cup milk
1 tablespoon extra virgin olive oil
scant 3 cups unbleached
white bread flour
½ cup whole-wheat bread flour
½ cup freshly grated
Parmesan cheese
1 teaspoon salt
1 teaspoon granulated sugar
¾ teaspoon rapid-rise active
dry yeast

MEDIUM
½ cup sun-dried tomatoes
1 cup water
½ cup milk
2 tablespoons extra virgin olive oil
3¾ cups unbleached white
bread flour
¾ cup whole-wheat bread flour
⅔ cup freshly grated
Parmesan cheese
1½ teaspoons salt
2 teaspoons granulated sugar
1 teaspoon rapid-rise active dry yeast

LARGE
¾ cup sun-dried tomatoes
1¼ cups water
⅔ cup milk
3 tablespoons extra virgin olive oil
5 cups unbleached white bread flour
1 cup whole-wheat
bread flour
1 cup freshly grated Parmesan cheese
2 teaspoons salt
2 teaspoons granulated sugar
1½ teaspoons rapid-rise active
dry yeast

MAKES 1 LOAF

1 Place the sun-dried tomatoes in a small bowl and pour over enough warm water to cover them. Let soak for 15 minutes, then place in a sieve that you have placed over a measuring cup. Allow the tomatoes to drain thoroughly, then chop them finely.

2 Check the quantity of tomato water against the amount of water required for the loaf, and add more water if this is necessary. Pour it into the bread machine pan, then add the milk and olive oil. If the instructions for your machine specify that the yeast is to be placed in the pan first, then simply reverse the order in which you add the liquid and dry ingredients.

3 Sprinkle both types of flour over, ensuring that the liquid is completely covered. Sprinkle the Parmesan over, then add the salt and sugar, placing them in separate corners of the bread pan. Make a shallow indentation in the center of the flour (but not down as far as the liquid) and add the yeast.

4 Set the bread machine to the basic/normal setting; use raisin setting (if available), medium crust. Press Start. Add the tomatoes at the beep or during the last 5 minutes of kneading. Remove the bread at the end of the baking cycle and turn out onto a wire rack to cool.

GARLIC AND HERB WALNUT BREAD

Walnut bread is very popular in France. This variation includes both garlic and basil for additional flavor.

1 Pour the milk, water and olive oil into the bread machine pan. If the instructions for your machine specify that the yeast is to be placed in the pan first, reverse the order in which you add the liquid and dry ingredients.

2 Sprinkle the flour over and rolled oats, ensuring that they completely cover the liquid mixture. Add the chopped walnuts, garlic, oregano and basil. Place the salt and sugar in separate corners of the bread machine pan. Make a shallow indentation in the center of the flour (but do not go down as far as the liquid) and add the yeast.

3 Set the bread machine to the basic/normal setting, medium crust. Press Start.

4 Remove the bread at the end of the baking cycle and turn out onto a wire rack to cool.

SMALL
⅓ cup milk
⅓ cup water
2 tablespoons extra virgin olive oil
scant 3 cups unbleached white bread flour
scant ⅓ cup rolled oats
⅓ cup chopped walnuts
1 garlic clove, finely chopped
1 teaspoon dried oregano
1 teaspoon fresh basil, chopped
1 teaspoon salt
1½ teaspoons granulated sugar
½ teaspoon rapid-rise active dry yeast

MEDIUM
generous ¾ cup milk
½ cup water
3 tablespoons extra virgin olive oil
4 cups unbleached white bread flour
½ cup rolled oats
½ cup chopped walnuts
1½ garlic cloves, finely chopped
1½ teaspoons dried oregano
1½ teaspoons fresh basil, chopped
1½ teaspoons salt
2 teaspoons granulated sugar
1 teaspoon rapid-rise active dry yeast

LARGE
1 cup milk
⅝ cup water
4 tablespoons extra virgin olive oil
generous 5¼ cups unbleached white bread flour
scant ⅔ cup rolled oats
generous ½ cup chopped walnuts
2 garlic cloves, finely chopped
1½ teaspoons dried oregano
1½ teaspoons fresh basil, chopped
2 teaspoons salt
2 teaspoons granulated sugar
1½ teaspoons rapid-rise active dry yeast

MAKES 1 LOAF

DILL, ONION AND RYE BREAD

These crusty loaves are perfect partners for your favorite sandwich filling, or can be served solo with pasta, salads and soups.

1¼ cups water
2 tablespoons extra virgin olive oil
scant 1 cup rye flour
generous 3 cups unbleached white
bread flour, plus extra for dusting
2 tablespoons nonfat dry milk
2 teaspoons light brown sugar
1 teaspoon salt
1 teaspoon rapid-rise active dry yeast
1 tablespoon dried dill
1 tablespoon dill seeds
2 tablespoons dried onion

MAKES 2 LOAVES

1 Pour the water and oil into the bread pan. Reverse the order in which you add the wet and dry ingredients if necessary.

2 Sprinkle both types of flour over the water. Add the milk. Place the sugar and salt in separate corners.

3 Make an indentation in the center of the flour; add the yeast. Set the machine to the dough setting; use raisin dough setting (if available). Press Start.

4 Add the dried dill, dill seeds and dried onion as the machine beeps or during the last 5 minutes of kneading. Lightly oil a baking sheet.

5 When the dough cycle has finished, remove the dough from the machine and place it on a lightly floured surface. Punch it down gently.

6 Divide the dough into two equal pieces. Roll out each piece to a disk, about 1 inch thick. Fold one side to the center and press gently with the rolling pin to seal. Repeat with the other side, then fold again along the center line.

7 Press gently along the seam to seal it, then roll backward and forward to make a loaf about 12 inches in length. Make a second loaf with the remaining dough.

8 Place the loaves on the baking sheet, leaving plenty of room for rising. Cover with lightly oiled plastic wrap and leave in a warm place for 30–45 minutes, or until each loaf has almost doubled in size.

9 Remove the plastic wrap and dust the tops of the loaves with flour. Using a sharp knife, make slashes along the top of both of them. Let stand for 10 minutes. Meanwhile, preheat the oven to 425°F.

10 Bake the loaves for 20 minutes, or until they sound hollow when tapped on the bottom. Transfer to a wire rack to cool.

SAGE AND SAUSAGE LOAF

When this tasty loaf is sliced, the sausage filling is revealed. It is perfect for picnics, parties or as a lunchtime meal with salad.

1 tablespoon sunflower oil
7 ounces spicy Mediterranean
sausages
3 eggs
2 tablespoons water
generous 3 cups unbleached white
bread flour
2 tablespoons nonfat dry milk
2 teaspoons granulated sugar
1½ teaspoons salt
¼ cup butter, melted
1 teaspoon rapid-rise active dry yeast
1 teaspoon dried sage

FOR THE GLAZE
1 egg yolk
1 tablespoon water

MAKES 1 LOAF

1 Heat the oil in a heavy frying pan. Add the sausages. Fry them over a medium heat for 7–10 minutes or until cooked, turning frequently. Let cool.

2 Add the eggs and water to the bread pan. Reverse the order in which you add the wet and dry ingredients if necessary.

3 Sprinkle the flour over, covering the liquid. Add the evaporated milk. Place the sugar, salt and butter in separate corners of the pan. Make an indentation in the center of the flour; add the yeast.

4 Set the bread machine to the dough setting; use basic raisin dough setting (if available). Press Start. Add the sage when the machine beeps or during the last 5 minutes of kneading. Lightly oil a 9 × 5 inch loaf pan.

5 When the dough cycle has finished, place the dough on a floured surface. Punch down gently. Roll into a rectangle 1 inch thick and 9 inches long.

6 Place the sausages down the center and roll the dough tightly around them. Place in the pan. Cover with lightly oiled plastic wrap and set aside to rise in a warm place for 30–45 minutes.

7 Preheat the oven to 375°F. To glaze, mix the yolk and water; brush over the bread and bake for 30–35 minutes, or until golden. Turn out onto a wire rack to cool.

MIXED HERB COTTAGE LOAF

There's something very satisfying about the shape of a cottage loaf, and the flavor of fresh herbs—chives, thyme, tarragon and parsley—adds to the appeal. This loaf makes the perfect centerpiece for the table, for guests to help themselves.

1¼ cups water
4 cups unbleached white bread flour,
plus extra for dusting
1½ teaspoons granulated sugar
1½ teaspoons salt
1½ teaspoons rapid-rise active dry yeast
1 tablespoon snipped fresh chives
2 teaspoons chopped fresh thyme
1 tablespoon chopped fresh tarragon
2 tablespoons chopped fresh parsley

FOR THE GLAZE
1 teaspoon salt
1 tablespoon water

MAKES 1 LOAF

1 Pour the water into the bread machine pan. If the operating instructions for your bread machine specify that the yeast is to be placed in the pan first, then simply reverse the order in which you add the water and dry ingredients.

2 Sprinkle the flour over, ensuring that it covers the water completely. Add the granulated sugar and the salt, placing them in separate corners of the bread machine pan. Make a shallow indentation in the center of the flour (but do not go down as far as the water) and add the yeast.

3 Set the bread machine to the dough setting; use basic raisin dough setting (if available). Press Start.

4 Add the chives, thyme, tarragon and parsley when the machine beeps to add extra ingredients, or during the final 5 minutes of kneading. Lightly flour two baking sheets.

5 When the dough cycle has finished, remove the dough from the machine. Place it on a surface that has been lightly floured. Punch the dough down gently and then divide it into two pieces, making one piece twice as large as the other.

6 Take each piece of dough in turn and shape it into a plump ball. Place the balls of dough on the prepared baking sheets and cover each with a lightly oiled mixing bowl.

7 Set aside in a warm place for about 20–30 minutes, or until the dough has almost doubled in size.

8 Cut a cross, about 1½ inches across, in the top of the larger piece of dough. Brush the surface with water and place the smaller round on top.

9 Carefully press the handle of a wooden spoon through the center of both pieces of dough. Cover the loaf with oiled plastic wrap and let it rise for 10 minutes.

10 Meanwhile, preheat the oven to 425°F. Mix the salt and water for the glaze in a bowl, then brush the mixture over the top of the bread.

11 Using a sharp knife, make eight long slashes around the top of the bread and 12 small slashes around the bottom. Dust the top of the bread lightly with white bread flour.

12 Bake for 30–35 minutes, or until the bread is golden and sounds hollow when tapped on the bottom. Turn the loaf out onto a wire rack to cool.

VARIATION
Vary the combination of fresh herbs you use, according to availability and taste. You should aim for just under 5 tablespoons in all, but use more pungent herbs sparingly, so they do not become too overpowering.

VEGETABLE BREADS

The subtle orange hue from pumpkin or carrot, the orangey-red crumb from tomatoes and the amazing colors of spinach or beet bread are only part of the story. Vegetables—grated, puréed, mashed or chopped—can be incorporated into bread doughs to provide wonderfully flavored and colored loaves. Almost any vegetable can be used, often in conjunction with spices, as in Carrot and Fennel Bread, or fresh herbs, as in Fresh Tomato and Basil Loaf.

SPINACH AND PARMESAN BLOOMER

This pretty pale green loaf is flavored with spinach, onion and Parmesan cheese. Whole pine nut are dispersed through the dough of this perfect summertime bread.

1 tablespoon olive oil
1 onion, chopped
4 ounces fresh young spinach leaves
generous ½ cup water
1 egg
4 cups unbleached white bread flour
¼ teaspoon freshly grated nutmeg
⅔ cup freshly grated
Parmesan cheese
1½ teaspoons salt
1 teaspoon granulated sugar
1½ teaspoons rapid-rise active dry yeast
2 tablespoons pine nuts

MAKES 1 LOAF

1 Heat the olive oil in a frying pan, add the chopped onion and sauté until a light golden color. Add the spinach, stir well to combine and cover the pan very tightly. Remove from the heat and let stand for 5 minutes. Then stir again and leave the pan uncovered, to cool.

2 Place the spinach mixture in the bread machine pan. Add the water and egg. If the instructions for your machine specify that the yeast is to be placed in the pan first, then simply reverse the order in which you add the liquid mixture and dry ingredients.

3 Sprinkle the white bread flour over, ensuring that it completely covers the liquid mixture in the bread pan. Sprinkle the grated nutmeg and the Parmesan cheese over the flour.

4 Place the salt and sugar in separate corners of the bread pan. Make a shallow indentation in the center of the flour (but not down as far as the liquid) and add the yeast.

5 Set the bread machine to the dough setting; use basic raisin dough setting (if available). Press Start. Lightly flour two baking sheets.

6 Add the pine nuts to the dough when the machine beeps or during the last 5 minutes of the kneading process.

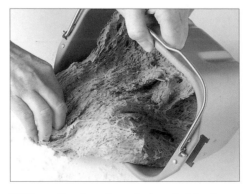

7 When the dough cycle has finished, remove the dough from the machine and place it on a surface that has been lightly floured. Gently punch the dough down, then carefully roll it out to a rectangle about 1 inch thick.

8 Roll up the rectangle of dough from one long side to form a thick baton shape, with a square end.

9 Place the baton on the prepared baking sheet, seam side up, cover it with lightly oiled plastic wrap and set aside to rest for 15 minutes.

10 Turn the bread over and place on the second baking sheet. Plump up the dough by tucking the ends and sides under. Cover it with lightly oiled plastic wrap again and let it rise in a warm place for 30 minutes. Meanwhile preheat the oven to 425°F.

11 Using a sharp knife, slash the top of the bloomer with five diagonal slashes. Bake it for 30–35 minutes, or until it is golden and the bottom sounds hollow when tapped. Turn the bread out onto a wire rack to cool.

VARIATION
Use Swiss chard instead of spinach, if you prefer. Choose young leaves, stripping them off the ribs. If fresh spinach is unavailable you could replace it with defrosted frozen spinach. Make sure any excess water has been squeezed out first, before placing in the bread machine. It may be worth holding a little of the water back and checking the dough as it starts to mix in step 5.

FRESH TOMATO AND BASIL LOAF

Here are some classic Mediterranean flavors incorporated into a bread. Sweet plum tomatoes, onions and fresh basil complement each other in this attractively shaped loaf. Serve to accompany lunch either with butter or with individual bowls of best quality extra virgin olive oil for dipping.

1 tablespoon extra virgin olive oil
1 small onion, chopped
3 plum tomatoes, about 7 ounces, peeled, seeded and chopped
4½ cups unbleached white bread flour
½ teaspoon freshly ground black pepper
1½ teaspoons salt
2 teaspoons granulated sugar
1 teaspoon rapid-rise active dry yeast
1 tablespoon chopped fresh basil

FOR THE GLAZE
1 egg yolk
1 tablespoon water

MAKES 1 LOAF

1 Heat the extra virgin olive oil in a small frying pan or saucepan. Add the chopped onion and fry over a moderate heat for 3–4 minutes, until the onion is light golden in color.

2 Add the plum tomatoes and cook for 2–3 minutes, until slightly softened. Drain through a sieve placed over a measuring cup or bowl, pressing the mixture gently with the back of a spoon to extract the juices.

3 Set the tomato and onion mixture aside. Make the cooking juices up to 1¼ cups with water (but see Variation). Set aside. When the liquid is cold, pour it into the bread machine pan. If the instructions for your machine specify that the yeast is to be placed in the pan first, reverse the order in which you add the liquid and dry ingredients.

4 Sprinkle over the flour, ensuring that it covers the tomato and onion liquid. Add the ground black pepper, then place the salt and sugar in separate corners of the bread machine pan.

5 Make a shallow indentation in the center of the flour (but not down as far as the liquid) and add the yeast.

6 Set the bread machine to the dough setting; use basic dough setting (if available). Press Start. Then lightly oil a 9 × 5-inch bread pan.

7 When the dough cycle has finished, remove the dough from the bread machine and place it on a lightly floured surface. Punch it down gently.

8 Knead in the reserved tomato and onion mixture and the chopped fresh basil. You may need to add a little extra flour if the dough becomes too moist when you have incorporated the vegetable mixture.

9 Flatten the dough and shape it into a 1 inch thick rectangle. Fold the sides to the middle and press down the edge to seal. Make a hollow along the center and fold in half again. Gently roll it into a loaf about 16 inches long.

10 Shape into an "S" shape and place in the prepared tin. Cover with oiled plastic wrap and set aside in a warm place to rise for 30–45 minutes. Meanwhile preheat the oven to 400°F.

11 Make the glaze by mixing the egg yolk and water together. Remove the plastic wrap and brush the glaze over the bread. Bake in the preheated oven for 35–40 minutes, or until golden.

VARIATION
To intensify the tomato flavor of the loaf, substitute 1 tablespoon sun-dried tomato purée for 1 tablespoon of water when you are topping up the cooking juices in step 3.

SWEET POTATO BREAD

Adding sweet potato to the dough creates a loaf with a rich golden crust and the crumb is beautifully moist. Make sure you use the deep yellow sweet potatoes, in preference to the white variety of sweet potatoes, to give the bread a lovely color.

SMALL
6 ounces sweet potatoes, peeled
scant ⅞ cup water
3 cups unbleached white bread flour
2 tablespoons rolled oats
1½ tablespoons nonfat dry milk
1 teaspoon salt
1 tablespoon brown sugar
6 tablespoons butter
1 teaspoon rapid-rise active dry yeast

FOR THE TOPPING
2 teaspoons water
1 teaspoon rolled oats
1 teaspoon wheat grain

MEDIUM
8 ounces sweet potatoes, peeled
scant 1 cup water
4½ cups unbleached white
bread flour
3 tablespoons rolled oats
2 tablespoons nonfat dry milk
1½ teaspoons salt
1½ tablespoons brown sugar
3 tablespoons butter
1½ teaspoons rapid-rise active
dry yeast

FOR THE TOPPING
1 tablespoon water
2 teaspoons rolled oats
2 teaspoons wheat grain

LARGE
12 ounces sweet potatoes, peeled
scant 1⅜ cups water
6 cups unbleached white bread flour
4 tablespoons rolled oats
2 tablespoons nonfat dry milk
1½ teaspoons salt
1½ tablespoons brown sugar
¼ cup butter
1½ teaspoons rapid-rise active
dry yeast

FOR THE TOPPING
1 tablespoon water
1 tablespoon rolled oats
1 tablespoon wheat grain

MAKES 1 LOAF

1 Cook the sweet potato in plenty of boiling water for 40 minutes or until very tender. Drain, and when cool enough to handle, peel off the skin. Place the sweet potato in a large bowl and mash well, but do not add any butter or milk.

2 Pour the water into the bread machine pan. However, if the instructions for your bread machine specify that the yeast is to be placed in the bread pan first, simply reverse the order in which you add the liquid and dry ingredients.

VARIATION
This bread is a good opportunity to use up any leftover sweet potato. If the potato has been mashed with milk and butter you may need to reduce the quantity of liquid a little. Use the following quantities of cooked, mashed sweet potatoes:
small machine: 1½ cups
medium machine: 2 cups large
machine: 2⅔ cups

COOK'S TIP
Rolled oats add a chewy texture and nutty taste to this loaf of bread. Make sure you use the traditional old-fashioned rolled oats, rather than "quick cook" oats.

3 Sprinkle the flour, rolled oats and milk over the water. Weigh and measure the cooked sweet potatoes to ensure the quantity matches the amount given in the variation. Then add the potatoes to the bread pan.

4 Place the salt, sugar and butter in three separate corners of the bread machine pan. Make a shallow indentation in the flour (but not down as far as the liquid underneath) and add the yeast.

5 Set the bread machine to the basic/normal setting, medium crust. Press Start.

6 When the rising cycle is almost complete, just before the bread begins to bake, add the topping: brush the top of the loaf with the water and sprinkle the rolled oats and wheat grain over the top of the bread.

7 Remove the bread at the end of the baking cycle and turn out onto a wire rack to cool.

PARSNIP AND NUTMEG BREAD

The moment you cut into this loaf, the irresistible aroma of nutmeg and parsnips fills the air. Stopping at a single slice is difficult.

SMALL

scant 1⅛ cups water

1½ cups mashed
cooked parsnips

3¼ cups unbleached white
bread flour

1 tablespoon nonfat dry milk

½ teaspoon freshly grated nutmeg

2 tablespoons butter

1 teaspoon salt

1 teaspoon granulated sugar

1 teaspoon rapid-rise active dry yeast

MEDIUM

scant 1¼ cups water

2 cups mashed
cooked parsnips

4½ cups unbleached white
bread flour

2 tablespoons nonfat dry milk

1 teaspoon freshly grated nutmeg

3 tablespoons butter

1½ teaspoons salt

1½ teaspoons granulated sugar

1½ teaspoons rapid-rise active
dry yeast

LARGE

scant 1½ cups water

2⅔ cups mashed
cooked parsnips

6 cups unbleached white bread flour

3 tablespoons nonfat dry milk

1 teaspoon freshly grated nutmeg

¼ cup butter

2 teaspoons salt

2 teaspoons granulated sugar

1½ teaspoons rapid-rise active
dry yeast

MAKES 1 LOAF

1 Pour the water into the bread machine pan and add the mashed parsnips. If the instructions for your machine specify that the yeast is to be placed in the pan first, reverse the order in which you add the liquid mixture and dry ingredients.

2 Sprinkle the flour over, ensuring it covers the ingredients already placed in the pan. Add the milk and freshly grated nutmeg. Place the butter, salt and sugar in separate corners of the bread machine pan. Make a shallow indentation in the center of the flour (but do not go down as far as the liquid) and add the yeast.

3 Set the bread machine to the basic/normal setting, medium crust. Press Start.

4 Remove the bread at the end of the baking cycle and turn out onto a wire rack to cool.

COOK'S TIP
Drain the parsnips thoroughly before mashing so that the dough does not become too wet. Let the mashed parsnips cool completely before adding them to the bread.

BEET BREAD

This spectacular bread takes on the color of the beet juice. It is also flecked with beet flesh, which gives the finished loaf a slightly sweet flavor and delightful consistency.

SMALL
¾ cup water
1 cup grated raw beet
2 scallions, chopped
3¼ cups unbleached white
bread flour
1 tablespoon butter
1½ teaspoons salt
1 teaspoon granulated sugar
1 teaspoon rapid-rise active dry yeast

MEDIUM
¾ cup water
1½ cups grated raw beets
3 scallions, chopped
4½ cups unbleached white
bread flour
2 tablespoons butter
2 teaspoons salt
1 teaspoon granulated sugar
1 teaspoon rapid-rise active dry yeast

LARGE
1¼ cups water
2 cups grated raw beet
4 scallions, chopped
6 cups unbleached white bread flour
3 tablespoons butter
2 teaspoons salt
1½ teaspoons granulated sugar
1½ teaspoons rapid-rise active
dry yeast

MAKES 1 LOAF

3 Sprinkle the flour over the beets and water, ensuring it covers them both. Add the butter, salt and sugar in separate corners of the bread pan. Make a shallow indentation in the center of the flour (but not down as far as the liquid) and add the yeast.

4 Set the bread machine to the basic/ normal setting, medium crust. Press Start. If you like, slash the top of the loaf with diagonal slashes just before the baking cycle starts.

5 Remove the bread at the end of the baking cycle and turn out onto a wire rack to cool.

1 Pour the water into the bread pan. Sprinkle the grated beets over. If the instructions for your machine specify that the yeast is to be placed in the pan first, reverse the order in which you add the liquid mixture and dry ingredients.

2 Add the chopped scallions. However, if your bread machine offers you the option of adding any extra ingredients during the kneading cycle, set the scallions aside so that you may add them later on.

BUBBLE CORN BREAD

This recipe brings together two traditional American breads—corn bread and bubble loaf. It has the flavor of corn and is spiked with hot chile. Chunks or "bubbles" of bread can easily be pulled from the bread for easy eating.

⅜ cup milk
½ cup water
1 egg
3½ cups unbleached white bread flour
scant 1 cup yellow cornmeal
1 teaspoon granulated sugar
1 teaspoon salt
1½ teaspoons rapid-rise active dry yeast
1 tablespoon chopped fresh green chile
⅔ cup drained canned corn kernels
2 tablespoons butter

MAKES 1 LOAF

1 Pour the milk and water into the bread pan. Add the egg. Reverse the order in which you add the liquid and dry ingredients, if necessary. Sprinkle the flour and cornmeal over, covering the liquid. Add the sugar and salt in separate corners. Make a shallow indentation in the flour; add the yeast.

2 Set the bread machine to the dough setting; use basic raisin dough setting (if available). Press Start. Add the chile and corn when the machine beeps or during the last 5 minutes of kneading. Lightly oil a baking sheet.

3 When the dough cycle has finished, remove the dough and gently punch it down, then cut it into 20 equal pieces. Shape into balls.

4 Arrange half of the dough balls in the bottom of a 8½-inch nonstick springform cake pan, spacing them slightly apart. Place the remaining balls of dough on top so that they cover the spaces.

5 Cover the pan with oiled plastic wrap and let rise in a warm place for about 30–45 minutes, or until the dough has almost doubled in bulk. Meanwhile preheat the oven to 400°F.

6 Melt the butter in a small saucepan. Drizzle it over the top of the risen loaf. Bake the bread for 30–35 minutes, or until golden and well risen. Turn the bread out onto a wire rack to cool. Serve warm or cold.

MIXED PEPPER BREAD

Colorful and full of flavor, this bread looks good when sliced, as the pretty pepper studs can be seen to advantage. Add orange pepper too, if you like.

½ red bell pepper, cored and seeded
½ green bell pepper, cored and seeded
½ yellow bell pepper, cored and seeded
⅞ cup milk
½ cup water
4½ cups unbleached white bread flour
2 teaspoons granulated sugar
1½ teaspoons salt
1½ teaspoons rapid-rise active dry yeast
milk, for brushing
1 teaspoon cumin seeds

MAKES 1 LOAF

1 Cut the peppers into fine dice. Pour the milk and water into the bread pan. Reverse the order in which you add the wet and dry ingredients if necessary.

2 Sprinkle the flour over, ensuring that it covers the liquid. Add the sugar and salt in separate corners of the pan.

3 Make a shallow indentation in the center of the flour and add the yeast. Set the bread machine to the dough setting; use basic raisin dough setting (if available). Press Start. Lightly oil a baking sheet.

4 Add the mixed peppers when the machine beeps or during the last 5 minutes of kneading.

5 When the dough cycle has finished, remove the dough from the machine and place it on a lightly floured surface. Gently punch it down and shape it into a round, plump ball. Roll gently into an oval. Place on the prepared baking sheet, cover with oiled plastic wrap and let rise for 30–45 minutes, or until doubled in bulk.

6 Preheat the oven to 400°F. Brush the loaf top with the milk and sprinkle with the cumin seeds. Use a sharp knife to cut a lengthwise slash.

7 Bake for 35–40 minutes, or until the bread is golden and the bottom sounds hollow when tapped. Turn the bread out onto a wire rack to cool.

SUN-DRIED TOMATO AND PORCINI LOAF

The powerful concentrated flavors of mushrooms and sun-dried tomatoes exude from this Mediterranean-style bread.

SMALL
⅛ ounce dried porcini mushrooms
1 cup warm water
3¼ cups unbleached white
bread flour
1½ teaspoons salt
1 tablespoon granulated sugar
2 tablespoons butter
1 teaspoon rapid-rise active dry yeast
¼ cup well-drained sun-dried
tomatoes in olive oil

MEDIUM
½ ounce dried porcini mushrooms
1½ cups warm water
4½ cups unbleached white
bread flour
1½ teaspoons salt
1 tablespoon granulated sugar
2 tablespoons butter
1 teaspoon rapid-rise active dry yeast
⅓ cup well-drained sun-dried
tomatoes in olive oil

LARGE
1 ounce dried porcini mushrooms
2 cups warm water
6 cups unbleached white bread flour
2 teaspoons salt
1½ tablespoons granulated sugar
3 tablespoons butter
1½ teaspoons rapid-rise active
dry yeast
½ cup well-drained sun-dried
tomatoes in olive oil

MAKES 1 LOAF

1 Place the dried mushrooms in a small bowl and pour the warm water over. Let soak for about 30 minutes. Pour the mushrooms into a sieve placed over a bowl. Drain thoroughly, reserving the soaking liquid. Set the mushrooms aside. Make up the soaking liquid to scant 1 cup, generous 1⅓ cups or generous 1⅔ cups, depending on the size of loaf you are making.

2 Pour the liquid into the bread pan. If necessary, reverse the order in which you add the liquid and dry ingredients.

3 Sprinkle the flour over, covering the water. Add the salt, sugar and butter, placing them in separate corners.

COOK'S TIP
Add a tablespoon or two of extra flour if the dough is too soft after adding the mushrooms and tomatoes.

4 Make an indentation in the flour; add the yeast. Set the bread machine to the basic/normal setting; use raisin setting (if available), medium crust. Press Start.

5 Chop the reserved mushrooms and the tomatoes. Add them to the dough when the machine beeps, or during the last 5 minutes of the kneading cycle.

6 Remove the bread at the end of the baking cycle and turn out onto a wire rack to cool.

GOLDEN PUMPKIN BREAD

The pumpkin purée gives this loaf a rich golden crumb, a soft crust and a beautifully moist light texture, as well as a delightfully sweet-savory flavor. It is perfect for serving with soups and casseroles.

1 Mash the pumpkin and put it in the bread machine pan. Add the buttermilk, water and oil. If the instructions for your machine specify that the yeast is to be placed in the pan first, reverse the order in which you add the liquid mixture and dry ingredients.

2 Sprinkle over the flour and cornmeal, ensuring that the liquid is completely covered. Add the golden syrup and salt in separate corners of the bread machine pan. Make a shallow indentation in the center of the flour (but not down as far as the liquid) and add the yeast.

SMALL
¾ cup cooked pumpkin, cooled
6 tablespoons buttermilk
½ cup water
1 tablespoon extra virgin olive oil
scant 3 cups unbleached white
bread flour
½ cup cornmeal
1 tablespoon golden syrup
or corn syrup
1 teaspoon salt
¾ teaspoon rapid-rise active dry yeast
1 tablespoon pumpkin seeds

MEDIUM
⅞ cup cooked pumpkin, cooled
scant ½ cup buttermilk
½ cup water
2 tablespoons extra virgin olive oil
3¾ cups unbleached white
bread flour
¾ cup cornmeal
1½ tablespoons golden syrup
or corn syrup
1½ teaspoons salt
1 teaspoon rapid-rise active dry yeast
1½ tablespoons pumpkin seeds

LARGE
1 cup cooked pumpkin, cooled
⅔ cup buttermilk
⅔ cup water
3 tablespoons extra virgin olive oil
5 cups unbleached white bread flour
scant 1 cup cornmeal
2 tablespoons golden syrup
2 teaspoons salt
1½ teaspoons rapid-rise active dry yeast
2 tablespoons pumpkin seeds

MAKES 1 LOAF

3 Set the bread machine to the basic/normal setting; use raisin setting (if available), medium crust. Press Start. Add the pumpkin seeds when the machine beeps, or during the last 5 minutes of kneading.

4 Remove at the end of the baking cycle. Turn out onto a wire rack to cool.

POTATO AND SAFFRON BREAD

A dough that includes potato produces a moist loaf with a springy texture and good keeping qualities. Saffron adds an aromatic flavor and rich golden color to this bread.

1 large potato, about 8 ounces, peeled
1 teaspoon saffron threads
1 egg
4 cups unbleached white bread flour
2 tablespoons nonfat dry milk
2 tablespoons butter
1 tablespoon honey
1½ teaspoons salt
1½ teaspoons rapid-rise active dry yeast

MAKES 1 LOAF

COOK'S TIP
If you have time, soak the saffron for 3–4 hours. The longer it soaks, the better the color and flavor will be.

1 Place the potato in a pan of boiling water, reduce the heat and simmer until tender. Drain the potato, reserving ⅞ cup of the cooking water in a cup. Add the saffron threads to the hot water; let stand for 30 minutes. Mash the potato (without adding butter or milk) and let cool.

2 Add the saffron water to the bread pan. Add the mashed potato and the egg. Reverse the order in which you add the wet and dry ingredients if necessary.

3 Sprinkle the flour over, ensuring that it covers the ingredients already placed in the pan. Spoon over the evaporated milk. Add the butter, honey and salt in separate corners of the bread pan. Make a shallow indentation in the center of the flour (but not down as far as the liquid) and add the yeast.

4 Set the bread machine to the dough setting; use basic dough setting (if available). Press Start. Lightly flour a baking sheet.

5 When the dough cycle has finished, remove the dough from the machine and place on a lightly floured surface. Gently punch it down.

6 Shape the dough into a round, plump ball. Place on the baking sheet, cover with oiled plastic wrap and let rise for 30–45 minutes. Meanwhile preheat the oven to 400°F.

7 Slash the top of the loaf with three or four diagonal cuts, then rotate and repeat to make a criss-cross effect.

8 Bake the bread for 35–40 minutes, or until the bottom sounds hollow when tapped. Turn out onto a wire rack.

CARAMELIZED ONION BREAD

The unmistakable, mouthwatering flavor of golden fried onions is captured in this coburg-shaped bread. Serve with soup, cheeses or salad.

¼ cup butter
2 onions, chopped
1¼ cups water
1 tablespoon honey
4 cups unbleached white bread flour
1½ teaspoons salt
½ teaspoon freshly ground black pepper
1½ teaspoons rapid-rise active dry yeast

MAKES 1 LOAF

1 Melt the butter in a frying pan and sauté the onions over a low heat until golden. Remove the pan from the heat and let the onions cool slightly. Place a sieve over the bread machine pan, then pour the contents of the frying pan into it, so that the juices fall into the pan. Set the onions aside to cool completely.

2 Add the water and honey to the bread pan. Reverse the order in which you add the wet and dry ingredients if necessary. Sprinkle the flour over, covering the liquid. Place the honey, salt and pepper in separate corners. Make an indentation in the center, of the flour add the yeast.

3 Set the bread machine to the dough setting; use basic raisin dough setting (if available). Press Start. Add the onions when the machine beeps or in the last 5 minutes of kneading. Lightly flour a baking sheet.

4 When the cycle has finished, remove the dough from the bread pan and place on a lightly floured surface.

5 Punch down gently; shape into a ball. Place on the baking sheet and cover with oiled plastic wrap. Let rise for about 45 minutes. Preheat the oven to 400°F. Slash a ½-inch deep cross in the top of the loaf. Bake for 35–40 minutes. Turn out onto a wire rack.

ROLLS, BUNS AND PASTRIES

These hand-shaped delights include the French Ham and Cheese Croissants, Swedish Saffron Braids and fruit-filled Danish Pastries. Chelsea Buns, Yorkshire Teacakes and Pikelets are British classics, while Parker House Rolls and Doughnuts are traditional American offerings. Savory rolls using mixed grains and onions, herb and ricotta-flavored knots or Cashew and Olive Scrolls are just a few of the characterful small breads in this section to enjoy.

CALAS

These tasty morsels are a Creole speciality, made from a rice-based yeast dough which is then deep-fried. They are delicious served warm with coffee or as a breakfast treat.

generous ⅓ cup short-grain rice
1¼ cups milk
⅝ cup water
2 eggs
generous 1 cup unbleached white bread flour
1 teaspoon grated lemon zest
½ teaspoon ground ginger
½ teaspoon freshly grated nutmeg
¼ cup sugar
¼ teaspoon salt
1 teaspoon rapid-rise active dry yeast
oil, for deep-frying
confectioner's sugar, for dusting

MAKES ABOUT 25

1 Place the rice, milk and water in a saucepan and slowly bring to a boil. Lower the heat, cover and simmer for about 20 minutes, stirring occasionally, until the rice is soft and the liquid has been absorbed. Set aside to cool.

2 Add the eggs to the bread machine pan. Reverse the order in which you add the wet and dry ingredients if necessary.

3 Add the rice. Sprinkle the flour over, then the lemon zest, ginger and nutmeg. Add the sugar and salt, placing them in separate corners of the bread pan. Make a small indentation in the center of the flour (but not down as far as the liquid) and add the yeast.

4 Set the bread machine to the dough setting; use basic dough setting (if available). Press Start. When the dough cycle has finished, lift out the pan containing the batter from the machine.

5 Preheat the oven to 275°F. Heat the oil for deep-frying to 350°F or until a cube of dried bread, added to the oil, turns golden in 45 seconds. Add tablespoons of batter a few at a time and fry for 3–4 minutes, turning occasionally, until golden.

6 Use a slotted spoon to remove the calas from the oil and drain on paper towels. Keep them warm in the oven while you cook the remainder. When all the calas have been cooked, dust them with confectioners' sugar and serve warm.

COOK'S TIP
If you are using a large bread machine it is a good idea to make double the quantity of dough. If you use the quantities listed here, it is important to check that all the flour is thoroughly mixed with the liquid.

BREAKFAST PANCAKES

These thick, succulent breakfast pancakes are often served with a sauce made from lingonberries. They are equally delicious served with maple syrup and with strips of crispy bacon.

2 eggs
1¼ cups milk
2 cups unbleached white bread flour
1 teaspoon salt
1 tablespoon granulated sugar
1 tablespoon butter, melted
1 teaspoon rapid-rise active dry yeast
maple syrup or lingon berry sauce, to serve

MAKES ABOUT 15

1 Separate 1 egg and set the white aside. Place the yolk in the bread machine pan and add the whole egg and the milk. If the instructions for your machine specify that the yeast is to be placed in the pan first, reverse the order in which you add the liquid and dry ingredients to the pan.

2 Sprinkle the flour over, ensuring that it covers the liquid. Add the salt, sugar and butter, placing them in separate corners of the bread pan. Make a small indentation in the center of the flour (but not down as far as the liquid) and add the yeast.

3 Set the bread machine to the dough setting; use basic dough setting (if available). Press Start.

4 When the dough cycle has finished pour the batter into a large measuring cup. Whisk the reserved egg white; fold it into the batter. Preheat the oven to 275°F.

5 Lightly oil a large, heavy frying pan or griddle and place over a medium heat. Add about 3 tablespoons batter, letting it spread out to form a pancake about 4 inches wide. If room, make a second pancake alongside the first.

6 Cook each pancake until the surface begins to dry out, then turn over using a spatula and cook the other side for about 1 minute, or until golden.

7 Stack the pancakes between sheets of waxed paper on a warm plate and keep them warm in the oven while you cook the rest of the batter. Serve the pancakes with the syrup or sauce.

WHOLE-WHEAT ENGLISH MUFFINS

1½ cups milk
2 cups unbleached white bread flour
2 cups stoneground whole-wheat
bread flour
1 teaspoon granulated sugar
1½ teaspoons salt
1 tablespoon butter
1½ teaspoons rapid-rise active
dry yeast
rice flour or fine semolina,
for dusting

MAKES 9

COOK'S TIP

If you don't have a griddle, cook the
muffins in a heavy frying pan.
It is important that they cook slowly.

After a long walk on a wintry afternoon, come home to warm muffins,
carefully torn apart and spread thickly with butter.

1 Pour the milk into the bread machine
pan. If the instructions for your bread
machine specify that the yeast is to be
placed in the pan first, then reverse the
order in which you add the liquid and
dry ingredients.

2 Sprinkle each type of flour over in
turn, making sure that the milk is
completely covered. Add the sugar, salt
and butter, placing each of them in
separate corners of the bread pan. Then
make a shallow indentation in the center
of the flour (but do not go down as
far as the liquid underneath) and add
the yeast.

3 Set the machine to the dough setting;
use basic dough setting (if available).
Press Start. Sprinkle a baking sheet
with rice flour or semolina.

4 When the dough cycle has finished,
place the dough on a floured surface.
Punch it down gently. Roll out the
dough until it is about ½ inch thick.

5 Using a floured 3-inch plain cutter, cut
out nine muffins. If you like, you can
re-roll the trimmings, knead them
together and let the dough rest for a few
minutes before rolling it out again and
cutting out an extra muffin or two.

6 Place the muffins on the baking sheet.
Dust with rice flour or semolina. Cover
with oiled plastic wrap and let rise in a
warm place for 20 minutes, or until
almost doubled in size.

7 Heat a griddle over a medium heat.
You should not need any oil if the
griddle is well seasoned; if not, add the
merest trace of oil. Cook the muffins
slowly, three at a time, for about
7 minutes on each side. Serve warm.

PIKELETS

Pikelets are similar to crumpets, and have the same distinctive holey tops, but crumpets are thicker and are cooked inside a ring, which supports them while they set. Serve pikelets warm with preserves and butter. They are also excellent with cream cheese and smoked salmon.

⅝ cup water
⅝ cup milk
1 tablespoon sunflower oil
2 cups unbleached white bread flour
1 teaspoon salt
1 teaspoon caster sugar
1½ teaspoons easy-blend dried yeast
¼ teaspoon baking soda
4 tablespoons water
1 egg white

MAKES ABOUT 20

5 Dissolve the bicarbonate of soda in the remaining water and stir it into the batter. Whisk the egg white in a grease-free bowl until it forms soft peaks, then fold it into the batter.

6 Cover the batter mixture with oiled plastic wrap and let the mixture rise for 30 minutes. Preheat the oven to 275°F.

1 Pour the water into the bread machine pan, then add the milk and sunflower oil. If the instructions for your bread machine specify that the yeast is to be placed in the pan first, reverse the order in which you add the liquid and dry ingredients to the pan.

2 Sprinkle the white bread flour over, ensuring that it covers the liquid completely. Add the salt and sugar, placing them in separate corners of the bread pan. Make a shallow indentation in the center of the flour (but not down as far as the liquid) and add the yeast.

3 Set the bread machine to the dough setting; use basic dough setting (if available). Press Start. Then lightly oil two baking sheets.

4 When the dough cycle has finished, carefully lift the bread pan out of the machine and pour the batter for the pikelets into a large mixing bowl.

7 Lightly grease a griddle and heat it gently. When it is hot, pour generous tablespoonfuls of batter onto the hot surface, spacing them well apart to allow for spreading, and cook until the tops no longer appear wet and have acquired lots of tiny holes.

8 When the bottom of each pikelet is golden, turn it over, using a spatula, and cook until pale golden.

9 Remove the cooked pikelets and layer them in a folded dish towel. Place in the oven to keep them warm while you cook the remaining batter. Serve the pikelets immediately.

generous ½ cup water
2¼ cups unbleached white
bread flour
2 tablespoons nonfat dry milk
1 tablespoon granulated sugar
½ teaspoon salt
⅔ cup butter, softened
1½ teaspoons rapid rise
active dry yeast
8 ounces semisweet chocolate, broken
into pieces

FOR THE GLAZE
1 egg yolk
1 tablespoon milk

MAKES 9

1 Pour the water into the bread machine pan. If the instructions for your bread machine specify that the yeast is to be placed in the pan first, then simply reverse the order in which you add the liquid and dry ingredients.

2 Sprinkle the flour over, then the milk, ensuring that the water is completely covered.

3 Add the sugar, salt and 2 tablespoons of the softened butter, placing them in separate corners of the bread pan. Make a shallow indentation in the center of the flour (but not down as far as the liquid) and add the yeast.

4 Set the bread machine to the dough setting; use basic dough setting (if available). Press Start. Meanwhile shape the remaining softened butter into an oblong-shaped block, about ¾ inch thick.

PETIT PAIN AU CHOCOLAT

A freshly baked petit pain au chocolat is almost impossible to resist, with its buttery, flaky yet crisp pastry concealing a delectable chocolate filling. For a special finish, drizzle melted chocolate over the tops of the freshly baked and cooked pastries.

5 Lightly grease two baking sheets. When the dough cycle has finished, place the dough on a floured surface. Punch down and shape into a ball. Cut a cross halfway through the top of the dough.

6 Roll out around the cross, leaving a risen center. Place the butter in the center. Fold the rolled dough over the butter to enclose; seal the edges.

7 Roll to a rectangle ¾-inch thick, twice as long as wide. Fold the bottom third up and the top down; seal the edges with a rolling pin. Wrap the dough in lightly oiled plastic wrap. Place in the refrigerator and chill for 20 minutes.

8 Do the same again twice more, giving a quarter turn and chilling each time. Chill again for 30 minutes.

9 Roll out the dough to a rectangle measuring 21 × 12 inches. Using a sharp knife, cut the dough into three strips lengthwise and widthwise to make nine 7 × 4-inch rectangles.

10 Divide the chocolate among the three dough rectangles, placing the pieces lengthwise at one short end.

11 Mix the egg yolk and milk for the glaze together. Brush the mixture over the edges of the dough.

12 Roll up each piece of dough to completely enclose the chocolate, then press the edges together to seal.

13 Place the pastries seam side down on the prepared baking sheets. Cover with oiled plastic wrap and let rise in a warm place for about 30 minutes or until doubled in size.

14 Meanwhile, preheat the oven to 400°F. Brush the pastries with the remaining glaze and bake for about 15 minutes, or until golden. Turn out onto a wire rack to cool just slightly and serve warm.

VARIATION
Fill this flaky yeast pastry with a variety of sweet and savory fillings. Try chopped nuts, tossed with a little brown sugar and cinnamon or, for a savory filling, thin strips of cheese, wrapped in ham or mixed with chopped cooked bacon.

MIXED GRAIN ONION ROLLS

*These crunchy rolls, flavored with golden onions, are perfect for snacks,
sandwiches or to serve with soup.*

¼ cup butter
1 large onion, finely chopped
1¼ cups water
2½ cups unbleached white
bread flour
1 cup multi-grain bread flour
¾ cup oat bran
2 teaspoons salt
2 teaspoons honey
1½ teaspoons rapid-rise active dry yeast
cornmeal, for dusting
2 tablespoons millet flakes
1 tablespoon coarse oatmeal
1 tablespoon sunflower seeds

MAKES 12

1 Melt half the butter in a frying pan.
Add the chopped onions and sauté for
8–10 minutes, or until softened and
lightly browned. Set aside to cool.

2 Pour the water into the machine pan.
If the instructions for your machine
state the yeast is to be placed in the
pan first, reverse the order in which
you add the wet and dry ingredients.

3 Sprinkle the white bread flour, multi-
grain flour and oat bran over, ensuring
that the water is completely covered.
Add the salt, honey and remaining butter,
placing them in separate corners of the
bread pan. Make a shallow indentation in
the center of the flour (but not down as
far as the liquid) and add the yeast.

4 Set the bread machine to the dough
setting; use basic raisin dough setting
(if available). Press Start. Lightly oil
two baking sheets and sprinkle them
with cornmeal.

5 Add the millet, coarse oatmeal,
sunflower seeds and cooked onion when
the machine beeps. If your machine
does not have this facility add these
ingredients 5 minutes before the end of
the kneading cycle.

6 When the dough cycle has finished,
remove the dough from the bread
machine and place it on a surface that
has been lightly floured. Punch the
dough down gently, then divide it into
12 equal pieces.

VARIATION
If time is short you can omit the
cutting in step 9 and cook as round
shaped rolls.

7 Shape each piece into a ball, making
sure that that tops are smooth. Flatten
them slightly with the palm of your hand
or a small rolling pin. Place the rolls on
the prepared baking sheets and dust
them with more cornmeal.

8 Cover the rolls with oiled plastic wrap
and leave them in a warm place for
30–45 minutes, or until doubled in
size. Meanwhile, preheat the oven
to 400°F.

9 Using a pair of lightly floured sharp
scissors snip each roll in five places,
cutting inwards from the edge, almost to
the center. Bake for 18–20 minutes, or
until the rolls are golden. Turn them out
onto a wire rack to cool.

PARKER HOUSE ROLLS

These stylish rolls were first made in a hotel in Boston, after which they are named. They are delicious served warm.

1 Pour the milk and egg into the bread machine pan. If the instructions for your bread machine specify that the yeast is to be placed in the pan first, reverse the order in which you add the liquid and dry ingredients.

2 Sprinkle the flour over, ensuring that it covers the liquid. Add the sugar, salt and 2 tablespoons of the melted butter, placing them in separate corners of the bread pan. Make a shallow indentation in the center of the flour (but do not go down as far as the liquid underneath) and add the yeast.

3 Set the machine to the dough setting; use basic dough setting (if available). Press Start. Lightly oil two baking sheets.

4 When the dough cycle has finished, remove the dough from the machine, place it on a lightly floured surface and punch it down gently.

generous ¾ cup milk
1 egg
4 cups unbleached white bread flour
2 teaspoons granulated sugar
1½ teaspoons salt
6 tablespoons butter, melted
1 teaspoon rapid-rise active dry yeast

MAKES 10 ROLLS

COOK'S TIP
If you do not have a small rolling pin—and can't borrow one from a child's cooking set—use a small clean bottle or the rounded handle of a knife to shape the rolls.

5 Roll out to a ½ inch thickness. Use a 3 inch cutter to make ten rounds, then use a small rolling pin to roll or flatten each across the center in one direction, to create a valley about ¼ inch thick.

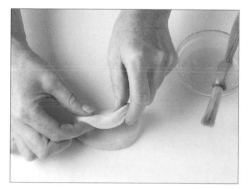

6 Brush with a little remaining melted butter to within ½ inch of the edge. Fold over, ensuring the top piece of dough overlaps the bottom. Press down lightly on the folded edge.

7 Place the rolls on the prepared baking sheets, just overlapping, brush them with more melted butter and cover with oiled plastic wrap. Let rise in a warm place for 30 minutes, or until doubled in size.

8 Preheat the oven to 400°F. Bake the rolls for 15–18 minutes, or until they are golden. Brush the hot rolls with the last of the melted butter and transfer them to a wire rack to cool.

1 egg
7 tablespoons milk
2 cups unbleached white bread flour
1 teaspoon salt
½ teaspoon granulated sugar
¼ cup butter
1 teaspoon rapid-rise active dry yeast
2 tablespoons milk,
for glazing (optional)

MAKES 12

COOK'S TIP
Make double the quantity and freeze
the surplus. You will only need the
same amount of yeast.

1 Pour the egg and milk into the bread
pan. If necessary for your machine,
place the dry ingredients in the pan
before the liquid.

BRIDGE ROLLS

*Milk and egg flavor these small, soft-textured finger rolls. Use them for
canapés or serve them with soup.*

2 Sprinkle the flour over, ensuring
that it covers the liquid. Add the
salt, sugar and butter, placing them
in separate corners of the bread
machine pan. Then make a shallow
indentation in the center of the
flour (but do not go down as far
as the liquid) and add the yeast.

3 Set the bread machine to the dough
setting; use basic dough setting (if
available). Press Start. Lightly oil two
baking sheets.

4 When the dough cycle has finished,
remove the dough from the bread
machine and place it on a lightly floured
surface. Punch it down gently, then
divide it into 12 pieces and cover with a
piece of oiled plastic wrap.

5 Take one piece of dough, leaving the
rest covered, and shape it on the floured
surface into a tapered long roll. Repeat
with the remaining dough until you have
12 evenly shaped rolls.

6 Place six rolls in a row, keeping them
fairly close to each other, on each
baking sheet. Cover with oiled plastic
wrap and set aside in a warm place for
about 30 minutes, or until the rolls have
doubled in size and are touching each
other. Meanwhile, preheat the oven
to 425°F.

7 Brush the bridge rolls with milk, if you
like, and bake them for 15–18 minutes,
or until lightly browned. Transfer the
batch to a wire rack to cool, then
separate into rolls.

WHOLE-WHEAT BAPS

*There's nothing nicer than waking up to the aroma of fresh baked bread.
The whole-wheat flour adds extra flavor to these soft breakfast rolls.*

scant ⅔ cup milk
scant ⅔ cup water
*2 cups stoneground whole-wheat
bread flour, plus extra
for dusting*
2 cups unbleached white bread flour
1½ teaspoons salt
2 teaspoons granulated sugar
1 teaspoon rapid-rise active dry yeast
milk, for glazing

MAKES 10

1 Pour the milk and water into the pan.
Reverse the order in which you add the
wet and dry ingredients if necessary.

2 Sprinkle the flours over, covering the
liquid. Add the salt and sugar in
separate corners. Make a shallow
indentation in the center of the flour
and add the yeast. Set the bread
machine to the dough setting; use basic
dough setting (if available). Press Start.

3 When the dough cycle has finished,
remove the dough from the machine and
place it on a lightly floured surface.
Punch it down gently, then divide it into
ten pieces and cover these with lightly
oiled plastic wrap.

4 Take one piece of dough, leaving the
rest covered, and cup your hands around
it to shape it into a ball. Place it on the
lightly floured surface and roll it into a
flat oval measuring 4 × 3 inches.

5 Repeat with the remaining dough so
that you have ten flat oval dough pieces.
Lightly oil two baking sheets.

6 Place the baps on the prepared baking
sheets. Cover with oiled plastic wrap
and leave to rise in a warm place for
about 30 minutes, or until the baps are
almost doubled in size. Meanwhile,
preheat the oven to 400°F.

7 Using three middle fingers, press each
bap in the center to help disperse any
large air bubbles. Brush with milk and
dust lightly with whole-wheat flour.

8 Bake for 15–20 minutes, or until the
baps are lightly browned. Turn out onto
a wire rack and serve warm.

RICOTTA AND OREGANO KNOTS

The ricotta cheese adds a wonderful moistness to these beautifully shaped rolls. Serve them slightly warm to appreciate fully the flavor of the oregano as your butter melts into the crumb.

4 tablespoons ricotta cheese
scant 1 cup water
4 cups unbleached white bread flour
3 tablespoons nonfat dry milk
2 teaspoons dried oregano
1 teaspoon salt
2 teaspoons granulated sugar
6 tablespoons butter
1 teaspoon rapid-rise active dry yeast

FOR THE TOPPING
1 egg yolk
1 tablespoon water
freshly ground black pepper

MAKES 12

1 Spoon the cheese into the bread machine pan and add the water. Reverse the order in which you add the liquid and dry ingredients if the instructions for your bread machine specify this.

2 Sprinkle over the flour, ensuring that it covers the cheese and water. Add the milk and oregano. Place the salt, sugar and butter in separate corners of the bread pan. Make a shallow indentation in the center of the flour (but not down as far as the liquid) and add the yeast.

3 Set the bread machine to the dough setting; use basic dough setting (if available). Press Start. Lightly oil two baking sheets.

4 When the dough cycle has finished, remove the dough from the machine and place it on a lightly floured surface.

5 Punch the dough down gently, then divide it into 12 pieces and cover these with oiled plastic wrap.

6 Take one piece of dough, leaving the rest covered, and roll it on the floured surface into a rope about 10 inches long. Lift one end of the dough over the other to make a loop. Push the end through the hole in the loop to make a neat knot.

7 Repeat with the remaining dough. Place the knots on the prepared baking sheets, cover them with oiled plastic wrap and let rise in a warm place for about 30 minutes, or until doubled in size. Meanwhile, preheat the oven to 425°F.

8 Mix the egg yolk and water for the topping in a small bowl. Brush the mixture over the rolls. Sprinkle some with freshly ground black pepper and leave the rest plain.

9 Bake for about 15–18 minutes, or until the rolls are golden brown. Turn out onto a wire rack to cool.

WHOLE-WHEAT AND RYE PISTOLETS

A whole-wheat and rye version of this French and Belgian speciality. Unless your bread machine has a program for whole-wheat dough, it is worth the extra effort of the double rising, because this gives a lighter roll with a more developed flavor.

1¼ cups water
2½ cups stoneground whole-wheat bread flour
½ cup unbleached white bread flour, plus extra for dusting
1 cup rye flour
2 tablespoons nonfat dry milk
2 teaspoons salt
2 teaspoons granulated sugar
2 tablespoons butter
1½ teaspoons rapid-rise active dry yeast

FOR THE GLAZE
1 teaspoon salt
1 tablespoon water

MAKES 12

1 Pour the water into the bread pan. If the instructions for your machine specify that the yeast is to be placed in the pan first, reverse the order in which you add the liquid and dry ingredients.

2 Sprinkle all three types of flour over, ensuring that the water is completely covered. Add the milk. Then add the salt, sugar and butter, placing them in separate corners of the bread pan. Make a shallow indentation in the center of the flour (but do not go down as far as the water underneath) and add the yeast.

3 Set the bread machine to the dough setting; use whole-wheat dough setting (if available). If you have only one basic dough setting you may need to repeat the program to allow sufficient time for this heavier dough to rise. Press Start. Lightly oil two baking sheets.

4 When the dough cycle has finished, remove the dough from the bread machine pan and place it on a surface that has been lightly floured. Punch the dough down gently, then divide it into 12 even-size pieces. Cover these with oiled plastic wrap.

5 Leaving the rest of the dough covered, shape one piece into a ball. Roll on the floured surface into an oval. Repeat with the remaining dough.

6 Place the rolls on the prepared baking sheets. Cover them with oiled plastic wrap and leave them in a warm place for about 30–45 minutes, or until almost doubled in size. Meanwhile preheat the oven to 425°F.

7 Mix the salt and water for the glaze and brush the mixture over the rolls. Dust the tops of the rolls with flour.

8 Using the oiled handle of a wooden spoon held horizontally, split each roll almost in half, along its length. Replace the plastic wrap and leave for 10 minutes.

9 Bake the rolls for 15–20 minutes, until the bottoms sound hollow when tapped. Turn out onto a wire rack to cool.

HAM AND CHEESE CROISSANTS

*The crispy layers of yeast pastry melt in your mouth to reveal a cheese and
ham filling. Serve the croissants freshly baked and still warm.*

½ cup milk
2 tablespoons water
1 egg
2½ cups unbleached white bread
flour
½ cup fine French bread flour
1 teaspoon salt
1 tablespoon granulated sugar
2 tablespoons butter, plus
¾ cup butter, softened
1½ teaspoons rapid-rise active dry yeast

FOR THE FILLING
6 ounces Emmenthal or Gruyère
cheese, cut into thin batons
2½ ounces thinly sliced dry cured
smoked ham, torn into small pieces
1 teaspoon paprika

FOR THE GLAZE
1 egg yolk
1 tablespoon milk

MAKES 12

1 Pour the milk, water and egg into the
pan. Reverse the order in which you add
the wet and dry ingredients, if necessary.

2 Sprinkle the flours over. Place the salt,
sugar and 2 tablespoons butter in
separate corners. Add the yeast in an
indentation in the flour. Set the machine
to the dough setting; use basic dough
setting (if available). Press Start. Shape
the softened butter into an oblong block
¾ inch thick.

3 When the dough cycle has finished,
place the dough on a floured surface and
punch down gently. Roll out to a rectangle
slightly wider than the butter block, and
just over twice as long. Place the butter on
one half of the pastry, fold it over and seal
the edges, using a rolling pin.

4 Roll out again into a rectangle ¾-inch
thick, twice as long as it is wide. Fold
the top third down, the bottom third up,
seal, wrap in plastic wrap and chill for
15 minutes. Repeat the rolling, folding
and chilling twice more, giving the
pastry a quarter turn each time. Wrap in
plastic wrap and chill for 30 minutes.

5 Lightly oil two baking sheets. Roll out
the pastry into a rectangle measuring
21 × 12 inches. Cut into two 6-inch
strips. Taking one strip, measure 6 inches
along one long edge and 3 inches along
the opposite long edge. Using the 6-inch
length as the bottom of your first
triangle, cut two diagonal lines to the
3 inches mark opposite, using a sharp
knife. Continue along the strip, cutting
six triangles in all. You will end up
with two scraps of waste pastry, at
either end of the strip. Repeat with
the remaining strip.

6 Place a pastry triangle on the work
surface in front of you, with the pointed
end facing you. Divide the cheese and
ham into 12 portions and put one
portion on the wide end of the triangle.
Hold and gently pull each side point to
stretch the pastry a little, then roll up
the triangle from the filled end with one
hand while pulling the remaining point
gently towards you with the other hand.

7 Curve the ends of the rolled triangle
away from you to make a crescent.
Place this on one of the baking sheets,
with the point underneath. Fill and
shape the remaining croissants. Cover
with oiled plastic wrap and let rise for
30 minutes, until almost doubled in size.
Preheat the oven to 400°F.

8 Mix the egg yolk and milk for the glaze
and brush over the croissants. Bake for
15–20 minutes, until golden. Turn out
onto a wire rack. Serve warm.

SAFFRON BRAIDS

Delicately scented and colored with saffron, these deep-fried braids are favorite coffee-time treats in Scandinavia.

1 Heat the milk until hot but not boiling. Pour over the saffron in a bowl. Leave for 45 minutes or until cold.

2 Pour the saffron milk into the bread machine pan, then add the eggs. If the instructions for your machine specify that the yeast is to be placed in the pan first, reverse the order in which you add the liquid and dry ingredients.

3 Sprinkle the flour over, ensuring that it covers the saffron milk completely. Add the salt, sugar and butter, placing them in separate corners of the bread machine pan. Make a shallow indentation in the center of the flour (but do not go down as far as the liquid) and add the yeast.

4 Set the bread machine to the dough setting; use basic dough setting (if available). Press Start. Lightly oil two baking sheets.

5 When the dough cycle has finished, remove the dough for the saffron braids from the bread machine and place it on a lightly floured surface. Punch it down gently, then divide the dough into eight even-size pieces. Cover these with a piece of oiled plastic wrap.

⅞ cup milk
¾ teaspoon saffron strands
2 eggs
4 cups unbleached white bread flour
½ teaspoon salt
¼ cup granulated sugar
¼ cup butter
1 teaspoon rapid-rise active dry yeast
sunflower oil, for deep-frying
granulated sugar, for sprinkling

MAKES 8

6 Take one piece of dough, leaving the rest covered, and use a sharp knife to divide it into three. Roll out each small piece into a 8-inch rope.

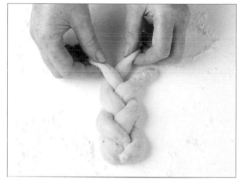

7 Place the ropes next to each other, pinch the ends together and braid them from left to right. When you reach the other end, press the ends together and tuck them under.

8 Repeat with the remaining portions of dough. Place the plaits on the baking sheets. Cover with oiled plastic wrap and set aside in a warm place for 30–45 minutes or until almost doubled in size.

9 Preheat the oil for deep-frying to 360°F or until a cube of dried bread, added to the oil, turns golden brown in 30–60 seconds.

10 Fry the saffron braids two at a time for 4–5 minutes, until they are golden. Drain on paper towels and sprinkle with granulated sugar. Serve warm.

CHINESE-STYLE CHICKEN BUNS

These delectable sesame seeded buns, filled with chicken flavored with ginger and soy sauce, are perfect for picnics.

⅝ cup low-fat milk
2 cups unbleached white bread flour
½ teaspoon salt
½ teaspoon granulated sugar
1 tablespoon butter
1 teaspoon rapid-rise active dry yeast

FOR THE FILLING
2 tablespoons sunflower oil
2-inch piece of fresh
ginger root, grated
2 tablespoons soy sauce
1 tablespoon honey
8 ounces chicken breast
fillets, chopped
3 scallions, chopped
1 tablespoon chopped fresh cilantro
salt and freshly ground black pepper

FOR THE TOPPING
1 egg yolk
1 tablespoon water
sesame seeds

MAKES 8

1 Pour the milk into the bread machine pan. If the instructions for your bread machine specify that the yeast is to be placed in the pan first, simply reverse the order in which you add the liquid and dry ingredients.

2 Sprinkle the flour over, ensuring that the milk is completely covered. Add the salt, sugar and butter, placing them in separate corners of the bread pan. Make a shallow indentation in the center of the flour (but not down as far as the liquid) and add the yeast.

3 Set the bread machine to the dough setting; use basic dough setting (if available). Press Start. Lightly grease a baking sheet.

4 Make the filling. Mix half the oil with the grated ginger, soy sauce and honey. Add the chicken and toss to coat. Cover and set aside for 30 minutes.

5 Heat a nonstick wok or frying pan and add the remaining oil. When it is hot, add the chicken mixture and stir-fry over medium heat for 5–6 minutes. Add the scallions and cook for 2 minutes more, or until the chicken is cooked. Stir in the coriander and seasoning. Set aside to cool.

6 When the dough cycle has finished, remove the dough from the machine and place it on a lightly floured surface. Punch it down gently, then divide it into eight pieces.

7 Roll out each piece of dough to a 5-inch round. Divide the chicken filling among the rounds of dough, placing in the center of each.

8 Beat the egg yolk and water for the topping in a small bowl. Brush a little of the mixture around the edge of each dough round.

9 Bring up the sides of the dough to cover the filling and pinch the edges together to seal. Place the buns seam-side down on the baking sheet.

10 Cover the buns with oiled plastic wrap and let rise in a warm place for about 30 minutes or until almost doubled in size. Meanwhile, preheat the oven to 400°F.

11 Brush the tops of the buns with the remaining egg glaze and sprinkle with the sesame seeds. Bake for about 18–20 minutes, or until the buns are golden brown. Turn out onto a wire rack to cool slightly. If you like, serve immediately, while the buns are hot.

VARIATION
If you have any leftover stir-fried vegetables, use as a filling in place of the chicken filling. To make another vegetarian version of these buns, cut 8 ounces mixed vegetables into small pieces or strips and marinade as for the chicken in step 4. Use vegetables such as carrots, broccoli, leeks, bean-sprouts and peppers.

⅞ cup water
3 tablespoons extra virgin olive oil
3 cups unbleached white bread flour
1 teaspoon salt
½ teaspoon granulated sugar
1 teaspoon rapid-rise active dry yeast

FOR THE TOPPING
2 tablespoons water
1 tablespoon sea salt
1 tablespoon sesame seeds

MAKES ABOUT 70

COOK'S TIP
Make these tasty nibbles up to a day in advance. Re-heat in a moderate oven for a few minutes, to refresh.

1 Pour the water and oil into the pan. If necessary, reverse the order in which you add the liquid and dry ingredients.

SPANISH PICOS

These small bread shapes, dusted with salt and sesame seeds, are often eaten in Spain with pre-dinner drinks, but can also be served as an accompaniment to an appetizer or soup.

2 Sprinkle the flour over, ensuring that it covers the liquid. Add the salt and sugar, placing them in separate corners of the bread pan. Make a shallow indentation in the center of the flour (but not down as far as the liquid) and add the yeast.

3 Set the machine to the dough setting; use basic dough setting (if available). Press Start. Then lightly oil two baking sheets.

4 When the dough cycle has finished, remove the dough from the machine and place it on a lightly floured surface. Punch it down gently, then roll it out to a rectangle measuring 12 × 9 inches. Cut lengthwise into three strips, then cut each strip of dough into 1-inch wide ribbons.

5 Preheat the oven to 400°F. Tie each ribbon into a loose knot and place on the prepared baking sheets, spacing them well apart. Cover with oiled plastic wrap and let rise in a warm place for 10–15 minutes. Leave the picos plain or brush with water and sprinkle with salt or sesame seeds. Bake for 10–15 minutes, or until golden.

CASHEW AND OLIVE SCROLLS

These attractively shaped rolls have a crunchy texture and ooze with the flavors of olives and fresh herbs.

⅝ cup milk
½ cup water
2 tablespoons extra virgin olive oil
4 cups unbleached white bread flour
1 teaspoon salt
½ teaspoon granulated sugar
1½ teaspoons rapid-rise active dry yeast
1 teaspoon finely chopped fresh rosemary or thyme
½ cup salted cashews, finely chopped
½ cup pitted green olives, finely chopped
3 tablespoons freshly grated Parmesan cheese, for sprinkling

MAKES 12

1 Pour the milk, water and oil into the pan. If the instructions for your machine specify that the yeast is to be placed in the pan first, reverse the order in which you add the wet and dry ingredients.

2 Sprinkle the flour over, ensuring that it covers the liquid. Add the salt and sugar, placing them in separate corners of the bread pan. Make a shallow indentation in the center of the flour (but not down as far as the liquid) and add the yeast.

3 Set the machine to the dough setting; use basic raisin dough setting (if available). Press Start. Add the herbs, cashew nuts and olives when the machine beeps. If your machine does not have this facility, then add these ingredients about 5 minutes before the end of the kneading period. Lightly oil two baking sheets.

4 When the dough cycle has finished, remove the dough from the machine and place it on a lightly floured surface. Punch it down gently.

5 Divide the dough into 12 pieces of equal size and cover with oiled plastic wrap. Take one piece of dough, leaving the rest covered. Roll it into a rope about 9 inches long, tapering the ends. Starting from the middle, shape the rope into an "S" shape, curling the ends in to form a neat spiral.

6 Transfer the spiral—or scroll—to a prepared baking sheet. Make 11 more scrolls in the same way. Cover with oiled plastic wrap and let rise in a warm place for 30 minutes, or until doubled in size.

7 Meanwhile, preheat the oven to 400°F. Sprinkle the rolls with Parmesan cheese and bake them for 18–20 minutes, or until risen and golden. Turn out onto a wire rack to cool.

scant 1 cup milk
1 egg
4 cups unbleached white bread flour
1½ teaspoons ground apple pie spice
½ teaspoon ground cinnamon
½ teaspoon salt
¼ cup granulated sugar
¼ cup butter
1½ teaspoons rapid-rise active
dry yeast
scant ½ cup currants
3 tablespoons golden raisins
3 tablespoons mixed candied fruit peel

FOR THE PASTRY CROSSES
½ cup all-purpose flour
2 tablespoons margarine

FOR THE GLAZE
2 tablespoons milk
2 tablespoons granulated sugar

MAKES 12

1 Pour the milk and egg into the bread pan. Reverse the order in which you add the liquid and dry ingredients if your machine requires this.

2 Sprinkle the flour over, ensuring that it covers the liquid. Add the apple pie spice and cinnamon. Place the salt, sugar and butter in separate corners of the pan. Make an indentation in the center of the flour and add the yeast.

COOK'S TIP
If preferred, to make the crosses roll out 2 ounces shortcrust pastry, and cut into narrow strips. Brush the buns with water to attach the crosses.

HOT CROSS BUNS

The traditional cross on these Easter buns probably symbolized the four seasons; it was only later used to mark Good Friday and the Crucifixion.

3 Set the bread machine to the dough setting; use basic raisin dough setting (if available). Press Start. Lightly grease two baking sheets.

4 Add the dried fruit and peel when the machine beeps or 5 minutes before the end of the kneading period.

5 When the dough cycle has finished, remove the dough from the machine and place it on a lightly floured surface. Punch it down gently, then divide it into 12 pieces. Cup each piece between your hands and shape it into a ball. Place on the prepared baking sheets, cover with oiled plastic wrap and let rise for 30–45 minutes or until the dough has almost doubled in size.

6 Meanwhile, preheat the oven to 400°F. Make the pastry for the crosses. In a bowl, rub the flour and margarine together until the mixture resembles fine bread crumbs. Bind with enough water to make a soft pastry that can be piped.

7 Spoon the pastry into a pastry bag fitted with a plain nozzle and pipe a cross on each bun. Bake the buns for 15–18 minutes, or until golden.

8 Meanwhile, heat the milk and sugar for the glaze in a small saucepan. Stir thoroughly until the sugar dissolves. Brush the glaze over the top of the hot buns. Turn out onto a wire rack. Serve warm or cool.

HAMAN'S HATS

These delicate tricorn-shaped pastries are properly known as Hamantaschen and are traditionally eaten at the Jewish festival of Purim. They can be filled with dried fruits or poppy seeds.

1 Pour the milk and egg into the bread machine pan. However, if the instructions for your machine specify that the yeast is to be placed in the bread machine pan first, simply reverse the order in which you add the liquid and dry ingredients to the pan.

2 Sprinkle the flour over, ensuring that it covers the milk and egg mixture. Add the sugar, salt and butter, placing them in separate corners of the bread pan. Make a shallow indentation in the center of the flour (but not down as far as the liquid) and add the yeast.

3 Set the bread machine to the dough setting; use basic dough setting (if available). Press Start. Lightly grease two baking sheets.

4 Make the filling. Put the poppy seeds in a heatproof bowl, pour boiling water over to cover and let cool. Drain thoroughly through a fine sieve. Melt 1 tablespoon of the butter in a small pan, add the poppy seeds and cook, stirring, for 1–2 minutes. Remove from the heat and stir in the ground almonds, honey, mixed peel and golden raisins. Cool.

5 When the dough cycle has finished, place the dough on a lightly floured surface. Punch it down gently and then shape it into a ball.

6 Roll out the pastry to a thickness of about ¼ inch. Cut out 4-inch circles using a plain cutter, re-rolling the trimmings as necessary. Then melt the remaining butter.

7 tablespoons milk
1 egg
2¼ cups unbleached white bread flour
2 tablespoons granulated sugar
½ teaspoon salt
2 tablespoons butter, melted
1 teaspoon rapid-rise active dry yeast
beaten egg, to glaze

FOR THE FILLING
¼ cup poppy seeds
3 tablespoons butter
¼ cup ground almonds
1 tablespoon honey
1 tablespoon chopped mixed peel
1 tablespoon golden raisins, chopped

MAKES 10–12

7 Brush each circle of dough with the melted butter and place a spoonful of filling in the center. Bring up the edges over the filling to make tricorn shapes, leaving a little of the filling showing. Transfer the shaped pastries to the prepared baking sheets, cover them with oiled plastic wrap and let them rise for 30 minutes, or until the hamantaschen are doubled in size.

8 Preheat the oven to 375°F. Brush the pastries with the beaten egg and bake for 15 minutes, or until golden. Turn out onto a wire rack.

VARIATION
For the filling, chopped prunes can be used instead of poppy seeds, or use a mixture of chopped raisins and golden raisins.

CHELSEA BUNS

scant 1 cup milk
1 egg
4½ cups unbleached white
bread flour
½ teaspoon salt
6 tablespoons granulated sugar
¼ cup butter, softened
1 teaspoon rapid-rise (fast-action) dried yeast

FOR THE FILLING
2 tablespoons butter, melted
⅔ cup golden raisins
3 tablespoons chopped candied peel
2 tablespoons currants
2 tablespoons light brown sugar
1 teaspoon ground apple pie spice

FOR THE GLAZE
¼ cup granulated sugar
4 tablespoons water
1 teaspoon orange flower water

MAKES 12 BUNS

Chelsea buns are said to have been invented by the owner of the Chelsea Bun House in London at the end of the 17th century. They make the perfect accompaniment to a cup of coffee or tea. They are so delicious, it is difficult to resist going back for more!

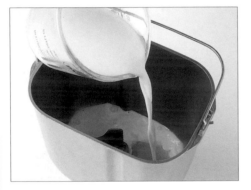

1 Pour the milk into the bread machine pan. Add the egg. If the instructions for your machine specify that the yeast is to be placed in the pan first, reverse the order in which you add the liquid and dry ingredients.

2 Sprinkle the flour over, ensuring that it completely covers the liquid. Add the salt, sugar and butter in three separate corners of the bread machine pan. Make a shallow indentation in the center of the flour (but not down as far as the liquid) and add the yeast.

3 Set the bread machine to the dough setting; use basic dough setting (if available). Press Start.

4 Lightly grease a 9-inch square cake pan. When the dough cycle has finished, remove the dough from the machine and place it on a lightly floured surface.

5 Punch the dough down gently, then roll it out to form a square that is approximately 12 inches.

6 Brush the dough with the melted butter for the filling and sprinkle it with the raisins, candied peel, currants, brown sugar and apple pie spice, leaving a ½ inch border along one edge.

7 Starting at a covered edge, roll the dough up, jelly roll fashion. Press the edges together to seal. Cut the roll into 12 slices and then place these cut side uppermost in the prepared pan.

COOK'S TIP
Use confectioners' sugar instead of sugar and make a thin glaze icing to brush over the freshly baked buns.

8 Cover with oiled plastic wrap. Let rise in a warm place for 30–45 minutes, or until the dough slices have doubled in size. Meanwhile preheat the oven to 400°F.

9 Bake the buns for 15–20 minutes, or until they have risen well and are evenly golden all over. Once they are baked, let them cool slightly in the pan before turning them out onto a wire rack to cool further.

10 Make the glaze. Mix the granulated sugar and water in a small saucepan. Heat, stirring occasionally, until the sugar is completely dissolved. Then boil the mixture rapidly for 1–2 minutes without stirring, until syrupy.

11 Stir the orange flower water into the glaze and brush the mixture over the warm buns. Serve slightly warm.

YORKSHIRE TEACAKES

scant 1¼ cups milk
4 cups unbleached white bread flour
1 teaspoon salt
3 tablespoons granulated sugar
3 tablespoons lard or butter
1 teaspoon rapid-rise active dry yeast
¼ cup currants
⅓ cup golden raisins
milk, for glazing

MAKES 8–10

COOK'S TIP

If you forget to add the fruit when making the dough, don't worry. Just knead it in when you punch the dough down before shaping it.

These fruit-filled tea-time treats are thought to be a refinement of the original medieval manchet or "handbread"—a hand-shaped loaf made without a pan. Serve them split and buttered, either warm from the oven or toasted.

1 Pour the milk into the bread machine pan. If the instructions for your machine specify that the yeast is to be placed in the pan first, then simply reverse the order in which you add the liquid and dry ingredients to the pan.

2 Sprinkle the flour over, ensuring that it covers the milk completely. Add the salt, sugar and lard or butter, placing them in separate corners of the bread machine pan. Make a shallow indentation in the center of the flour (but do not go down as far as the liquid) and add the yeast.

3 Set the bread machine to the dough setting; use basic raisin dough setting (if available). Press Start. Add the currants and golden raisins when the machine beeps. If your machine does not have this facility, simply add the dried fruits 5 minutes before the end of the kneading period.

4 Lightly grease two baking sheets. When the dough cycle has finished, remove the dough from the machine and place it on a lightly floured surface. Punch it down gently.

5 Divide the dough into eight or ten portions, depending on how large you like your Yorkshire teacakes, and shape into balls. Flatten out each ball into a disk about ½ inch thick.

6 Place the disks on the prepared baking sheets, about 1 inch apart. Cover them with oiled plastic wrap and set aside in a warm place for 30–45 minutes, or until they are almost doubled in size. Meanwhile, preheat the oven to 400°F.

7 Brush the top of each teacake with milk, then bake for 15–18 minutes, or until golden. Turn out onto a wire rack to cool slightly.

8 To serve, split open while still warm and spread with butter, or let the buns cool, then split and toast them before adding butter.

DEVONSHIRE SPLITS

A summer afternoon, a scrumptious cream tea; Devonshire splits are an essential part of this British tradition.

⅝ cup milk
2 cups unbleached white bread flour
2 tablespoons granulated sugar
½ teaspoon salt
1 teaspoon rapid-rise active dry yeast
confectioners' sugar, for dusting

FOR THE FILLING
clotted cream or whipped
heavy cream
raspberry or strawberry jam

MAKES 8

5 When the dough cycle has finished, remove the dough from the machine and place it on a lightly floured surface. Punch it down gently, then divide it into eight equal-size portions.

6 Shape each portion of dough into a ball, using cupped hands. Place on the prepared baking sheets, and flatten the top of each ball slightly. Cover with oiled plastic wrap. Let rise for 30–45 minutes or until doubled in size.

7 Meanwhile, preheat the oven to 425°F. Bake the buns for 15–18 minutes, or until they are light golden in color. Turn out onto a wire rack to cool.

8 Split the buns open and fill them with cream and jam. Dust them with confectioners' sugar just before serving.

2 Sprinkle the flour over, ensuring that it covers the liquid completely. Add the granulated sugar and salt, placing them in separate corners of the bread machine pan.

3 Make a shallow indentation in the center of the flour (do not go down as far as the milk underneath) and pour the yeast into the hollow.

1 Pour the milk into the bread pan. If your machine instructions specify it, reverse the order in which you add the liquid and dry ingredients.

4 Set the bread machine to the dough setting; use basic dough setting (if available). Press Start. Lightly grease two baking sheets.

DOUGHNUTS

The main thing to remember about doughnuts is the speed with which they disappear, so make plenty of both the cinnamon-coated rings and the round ones filled with jam.

6 tablespoons water
scant ⅔ cup milk
1 egg
4 cups unbleached white bread flour
¼ cup granulated sugar
1 teaspoon salt
¼ cup butter
1½ teaspoons rapid-rise active dry yeast
oil for deep-frying
granulated sugar, for sprinkling
ground cinnamon, for sprinkling

FOR THE FILLING
3 tablespoons raspberry jam
1 teaspoon lemon juice

MAKES ABOUT 16

1 Pour the water and milk into the bread machine pan. Break in the egg. If the instructions for your bread machine specify that the yeast is to be placed in the pan first, simply reverse the order in which you add the liquid and dry ingredients.

2 Sprinkle the flour over, ensuring that it covers the liquid. Add the sugar, salt and butter, placing them in separate corners of the bread pan. Make a shallow indentation in the center of the flour (but not down as far as the liquid) and add the yeast.

3 Set the bread machine to the dough setting; use basic dough setting (if available). Press Start.

4 When the dough cycle has finished, remove the dough from the machine and place it on a lightly floured surface.

5 Punch the dough down gently and divide it in half. Cover one half with lightly oiled plastic wrap. Divide the remaining piece of dough into eight equal portions.

6 Take each portion in turn and use your hands to roll it into a smooth ball. Lightly oil two baking sheets.

7 Place the eight dough balls on one of the prepared baking sheets. Cover them with oiled plastic wrap and leave in a warm place to rise for about 30 minutes, or until doubled in size.

8 Roll the remaining dough out to a thickness of ½ inch. Cut into circles using a 3-inch plain cutter. Then make the dough circles into rings using a 1½-inch plain cutter.

9 Place the rings on the remaining baking sheet, cover them with oiled plastic wrap and leave them in a warm place for about 30 minutes, or until doubled in size.

10 Heat the oil for deep-frying to 350°F, or until a cube of dried bread, added to the oil, turns golden brown in 30–60 seconds. Add the doughnuts, three or four at a time.

11 Cook the doughnuts for about 4–5 minutes, or until they are golden. Remove from the oil using a slotted spoon and drain on paper towels.

VARIATION
Make oblong shaped doughnuts and split almost in half lengthwise once cold. Fill with whipped cream and your favorite jam.

12 Toss the round doughnuts in sugar and the ring doughnuts in a mixture of sugar and ground cinnamon. Set aside to cool.

13 Heat the jam and lemon juice in a small pan until warm, stirring to combine. Let cool, then spoon the mixture into a pastry bag fitted with a small plain nozzle.

14 When the round doughnuts have cooled, use a skewer to make a small hole in each. Insert the piping nozzle and squeeze a little of the jam mixture into each doughnut.

MARZIPAN AND ALMOND TWISTS

If you like almonds, you'll love these. Amaretto liqueur, marzipan and flaked almonds make up a triple whammy.

6 tablespoons water
1 egg
¼ cup Amaretto liqueur
3 cups unbleached white bread flour
2 tablespoons nonfat dry milk
3 tablespoons granulated sugar
¼ teaspoon salt
¼ cup butter, melted
1½ teaspoons rapid-rise active dry yeast

FOR THE MARZIPAN FILLING AND TOPPING
1 cup ground almonds
½ cup confectioners' sugar
2–3 drops of pure almond extract
1 egg, separated
5 teaspoons water
2 teaspoons milk
flaked almonds, for sprinkling

MAKES 9

1 Pour the water, egg and Amaretto into the bread machine pan. If the instructions for your machine specify that the yeast is to be placed in the pan first, reverse the order in which you add the liquid and dry ingredients.

2 Sprinkle the flour over, ensuring that it covers the liquid. Add the milk. Place the sugar, salt and butter in separate corners of the bread pan. Make a shallow indentation in the center of the flour (but not down as far as the liquid) and pour the yeast into the hollow.

3 Set the bread machine to the dough setting; use basic dough setting (if available). Press Start. Lightly grease two baking sheets and set aside.

4 Make the marzipan filling. Mix the almonds, confectioners' sugar, almond essence, egg white and 3 teaspoons of the water in a bowl and set aside. In a separate bowl, beat the egg yolk with the remaining 2 teaspoons water.

5 When the dough cycle has finished, remove the dough from the machine and place it on a lightly floured surface. Punch it down gently and then roll it out into a 18 × 9 inch rectangle. Cut this in half lengthwise to make two 9-inch squares.

6 Spread the filling over one of the squares to cover it completely. Brush some beaten egg yolk mixture over the remaining square and place it egg-side down on top of the marzipan filling.

7 Cut nine strips, each 1-inch wide. Cut a lengthwise slit near the end of one of the strips. Twist the strip, starting from the uncut end, then pass the end through the slit and seal the ends together, with egg mixture. Repeat with the remaining strips.

8 Place the twists on the prepared baking sheets and cover with oiled plastic wrap. Leave in a warm place to rise for 30 minutes or until doubled in size.

9 Meanwhile, preheat the oven to 400°F. Mix the remaining egg yolk mixture with the milk and brush the mixture over the twists to glaze. Sprinkle with a few flaked almonds and bake for 12–15 minutes, or until golden. Turn out onto a wire rack to cool.

COCONUT MILK SUGAR BUNS

A hint of coconut flavors these spiral-shaped rolls. Serve them warm or cold with butter and preserves.

1 Pour the coconut milk, milk, egg and vanilla extract into the bread machine pan. If the instructions for your bread machine specify that the yeast is to be placed in the pan first, reverse the order in which you add the liquid and dry ingredients to the pan.

2 Sprinkle the flour over, then the coconut, ensuring that the liquid is completely covered. Add the salt, granulated sugar and butter, placing them in separate corners of the bread pan. Make a shallow indentation in the center of the flour (but not down as far as the liquid) and add the yeast.

3 Set the bread machine to the dough setting; use basic dough setting (if available). Press Start. Then lightly oil two baking sheets.

4 When the dough cycle has finished, remove the dough from the machine and place it on a lightly floured surface. Punch it down gently. Divide the dough into 12 equal pieces and cover these with oiled plastic wrap.

5 Take one piece of dough, leaving the rest covered; roll it into a rope about 15 inches long.

½ cup canned coconut milk
½ cup milk
1 egg
½ teaspoon pure vanilla extract
4 cups unbleached white bread flour
⅓ cup dried coconut
½ teaspoon salt
¼ cup granulated sugar
3 tablespoons butter
1 teaspoon rapid-rise active dry yeast

FOR THE TOPPING
¼ cup butter, melted
2 tablespoons demerara sugar

MAKES 12

6 Curl the rope into a loose spiral on one of the prepared baking sheets. Tuck the end under to seal. Repeat with the remaining pieces of dough, spacing the spirals well apart.

7 Cover with oiled plastic wrap and leave to rise in a warm place for 30 minutes, or until doubled in size. Preheat the oven to 425°F.

8 Brush the buns with the melted butter and sprinkle them with the demerara sugar. Bake for 12–15 minutes, or until the buns are golden. Turn out on to a wire rack to cool.

APPLE AND RAISIN DANISH PASTRIES

These Danish pastries are filled with fruit and are beautifully light and flaky,

FOR THE DANISH PASTRY
1 egg
5 tablespoons milk
2 cups unbleached white bread flour
1 tablespoon granulated sugar
½ teaspoon salt
¾ cup butter, softened
1½ teaspoons rapid-rise or fine dry yeast

FOR THE FILLING
2 tablespoons butter
12 ounces cooking apples, diced
1 tablespoon cornstarch
2 tablespoons granulated sugar
2 tablespoons water
1 teaspoon lemon juice
3 tablespoons golden raisins

TO FINISH
1 egg, separated
flaked almonds, for sprinkling

MAKES 12

1 Place the egg and milk in the bread pan. Reverse the order in which you add the liquid and dry ingredients if necessary. Sprinkle the flour over, covering the liquid. Add the sugar, salt and 2 tablespoons of the butter in separate corners of the bread pan.

2 Make a shallow indentation in the center of the flour; add the yeast. Set the bread machine to the dough setting; use basic dough setting (if available). Press Start. Lightly oil two baking sheets.

3 Shape the remaining butter into a block ¾ inch thick. When the dough cycle has finished, remove the prepared dough and place it on a lightly floured surface. Punch it down gently and then roll it out into a rectangle that is slightly wider than the butter block, and just over twice as long.

4 Place the butter on one half, fold the pastry over it, then seal the edges, using a rolling pin. Roll the butter-filled pastry into a rectangle ¾ inch thick, making it twice as long as it is wide. Fold the top third down and the bottom third up, seal the edges, wrap in plastic and chill in the refrigerator for 15 minutes. Repeat the folding and rolling process twice, giving the pastry a quarter turn each time. Wrap in plastic wrap; chill for 20 minutes.

5 Make the filling. Melt the butter in a pan. Toss the apples, cornstarch and sugar in a bowl. Add to the pan and toss.

6 Add the water and lemon juice. Cook over a medium heat for 3–4 minutes, stirring. Stir in the golden raisins.

7 Let the filling cool. Meanwhile, roll out the pastry into a rectangle measuring 16 × 12 inches. Cut into 4-inch squares. Divide the filling among the squares, spreading it over half of each piece of pastry so that when they are folded, they will make rectangles.

8 Brush the pastry edges on each square with the lightly beaten egg white, then fold the pastry over the filling to make a rectangle measuring 4 × 2 inches and press the edges together firmly. Make a few cuts along the long joined edge of each pastry.

9 Place the pastries on the baking sheets, cover them with oiled plastic wrap and let rise for 30 minutes.

10 Preheat the oven to 400°F. Mix the egg yolk with 1 tablespoon water and brush over the pastries. Sprinkle with a few flaked almonds and bake for 15 minutes, or until golden. Transfer to a wire rack to cool.

APRICOT STARS

When apricots are in season, these light pastries can be decorated with them.

1 quantity Danish pastry—see
Apple and Raisin Danish Pastries

FOR THE FILLING
½ cup ground almonds
½ cup confectioners' sugar
1 egg, lightly beaten
12 drained canned apricot halves

FOR THE GLAZE
1 egg yolk
2 tablespoons water
¼ cup apricot jam

MAKES 12

1 Roll out the pastry into a rectangle measuring 16 × 12 inches. Cut into 4 inch squares. On each square, make a 1 inch diagonal cut from each corner toward the center. Mix the ground almonds, confectioners' sugar and egg together. Divide the filling among the pastry squares, placing it in the center.

2 Beat the egg yolk for the glaze with half the water. On each square, fold one corner of each cut section to the center. Secure with the glaze. Place an apricot half, round side up, on top in the center.

3 Lightly oil two baking sheets. Place the pastries on them and cover with oiled plastic wrap. Let them rise for 30 minutes or until doubled in size. Preheat the oven to 400°F.

4 Brush the pastries with the remaining egg glaze and bake them for 15 minutes, until golden. While the stars are cooking, heat the apricot jam in a small saucepan with the remaining water. Transfer the cooked pastries onto a wire rack, brush them with the warm apricot glaze and let cool.

CHERRY TURNOVERS

Danish pastries are filled with a sweet cherry filling spiked with Kirsch.

FOR THE DANISH PASTRY DOUGH
1 egg
2 cups unbleached white bread flour
½ teaspoon ground cinnamon
1 tablespoon granulated sugar
½ teaspoon salt
generous ⅓ cup
butter, softened
1½ teaspoons rapid-rise active dry yeast

FOR THE FILLING AND TOPPING
8 ounces drained pitted cherries in syrup, plus
1 tablespoon syrup from the jar or can
2 tablespoons granulated sugar
1 tablespoon cornstarch
2 tablespoons Kirsch
1 egg, separated
2 tablespoons water
2 tablespoons apricot jam

MAKES 12

1 Pour the egg and water into the pan. Reverse the order in which you add the liquid and dry ingredients if necessary.

2 Sprinkle the flour and cinnamon over, covering the liquid. Add the sugar, salt and 2 tablespoons of the butter, placing them in separate corners. Make a shallow indentation in the flour; add the yeast. Set the bread machine to the dough setting; use basic or pizza dough setting (if available). Press Start. When the cycle has finished, remove the dough and place on a lightly floured surface. Punch down gently, then roll out to a rectangle about ½ inch thick.

3 Divide the remaining butter into three and dot one portion over the top two-thirds of the dough, leaving the edges clear. Fold the unbuttered portion of dough over half the buttered area and fold the remaining portion on top. Seal the edges with a rolling pin. Give the dough a quarter turn and repeat the buttering and folding. Wrap the dough in plastic wrap and chill for 30 minutes. Repeat the folding and chilling with the remaining butter, then repeat again, this time without any butter. Wrap and chill the dough for 30 minutes.

4 Make the filling. Put the cherries, cherry syrup, granulated sugar, cornstarch and Kirsch in a pan and toss. Cook over a medium heat for 3–4 minutes, stirring until thickened. Let cool.

5 Roll out the dough to a rectangle measuring 16 × 12 inches. Cut into 4 inch squares. Place a tablespoon of filling in the middle of each square. Brush one corner of each pastry square with lightly beaten egg white, then bring the opposite corner over to meet it, setting it back slightly to leave some of the cherry filling exposed. Press down to seal.

6 Place the turnovers on lightly greased baking sheets. Cover with oiled plastic wrap and let rise for 30 minutes. Preheat the oven to 400°F.

7 Mix the egg yolk with half the water and brush over the dough. Bake for 15 minutes, or until golden. Mix the jam and remaining water in a pan; heat until warm. Brush over the pastries and turn out onto a wire rack to cool.

GINGER AND RAISIN WHIRLS

Tasty spirals of buttery pastry, studded with dried fruit and crystallized ginger.

1 quantity Danish pastry dough—
see Cherry Turnovers

FOR THE FILLING
3 tablespoons butter, softened
3 tablespoons granulated sugar
½ teaspoon grated nutmeg
2 tablespoons crystallized ginger
2 tablespoons candied orange peel
½ cup raisins

FOR THE GLAZE AND ICING
1 egg yolk, beaten with
1 tablespoon water
2 tablespoons confectioners' sugar, sifted
1 tablespoon orange juice

MAKES 12

1 Roll the pastry into a 12 × 9 inches rectangle. Cream the butter, sugar and nutmeg together and spread over the dough. Finely chop the ginger and peel. Sprinkle over the dough with the raisins. Lightly oil two baking sheets.

2 Tightly roll up the dough from one long side, as far as the center. Repeat with the remaining long side, so the two meet at the center. Brush the edges where the rolls meet with egg glaze.

3 Cut into 12 slices and place, spaced well apart, on the prepared baking sheets. Cover with oiled plastic wrap and let rise for 30 minutes.

4 Preheat the oven to 400°F. Brush the whirls with the egg glaze and bake for 12–15 minutes, or until golden. Turn out onto a wire rack to cool. Mix the confectioners' sugar and orange juice together and use to ice the pastries.

SWEET BREADS AND YEAST CAKES

Fresh fruit-colored loaves and rich yeast cakes filled with nuts, dried fruits or chocolate are all part of this diverse range of breads. A bread machine is the perfect tool for mixing and proving the rich doughs of Continental specialities, often prepared for special occasions.

BLUEBERRY AND OATMEAL BREAD

The blueberries add a subtle fruitiness to this loaf, while the oatmeal contributes texture and a nutty flavor. This is best eaten on the day it is baked, which shouldn't be a problem.

SMALL
½ cup water
½ cup milk
1 egg
scant 3 cups unbleached white bread flour, plus 2 tablespoons for coating the blueberries
¼ cup rolled oats
1 teaspoon ground apple pie spice
3 tablespoons granulated sugar
½ teaspoon salt
2 tablespoons butter
1 teaspoon rapid-rise active dry yeast
½ cup blueberries

MEDIUM
¾ cup water
¾ cup milk
1 egg
4 cups unbleached white bread flour, plus 2 tablespoons for coating the blueberries
½ cup rolled oats
1½ teaspoons ground apple pie spice
¼ cup granulated sugar
¾ teaspoon salt
3 tablespoons butter
1½ teaspoons rapid-rise active dry yeast
¾ cup blueberries

LARGE
⅞ cup water
⅞ cup milk
2 eggs
5½ cups unbleached white bread flour, plus 2 tablespoons for coating the blueberries
½ cup rolled oats
2 teaspoons ground apple pie spice
5 tablespoons granulated sugar
¾ teaspoon salt
¼ cup butter
2 teaspoons rapid-rise active dry yeast
scant 1 cup blueberries

MAKES 1 LOAF

COOK'S TIP
Use the light crust setting if your bread machine produces a rich, fairly dark crust for a sweet loaf.

1 Pour the water, milk and egg into the bread machine pan. If the instructions for your machine specify that the yeast is to be placed in the pan first, reverse the order in which you add the liquid and dry ingredients.

2 Sprinkle the flour over, ensuring it covers the liquid. Add the oatmeal and spice. Add the sugar, salt and butter in separate corners. Make an indentation in the center of the flour (but not down as far as the liquid) and add the yeast.

3 Set the bread machine to the basic/normal setting, with raisin setting (if available), medium crust. Press Start. Toss the berries with the extra flour to coat. Add to the dough when the machine beeps, or after the first kneading.

4 Remove the bread from the pan at the end of the baking cycle and turn out onto a wire rack to cool.

CRANBERRY AND ORANGE BREAD

The distinctive tart flavor of cranberries is intensified when these American fruits are dried. They combine well here with orange zest and pecans.

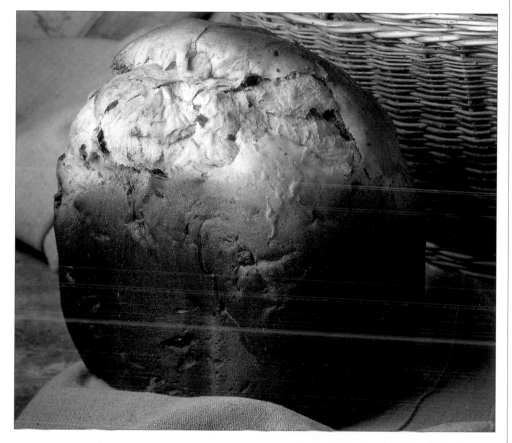

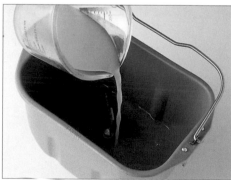

1 Pour the water, orange juice and egg into the bread machine pan. If the instructions for your machine specify that the yeast is to be placed in the pan first, reverse the order in which you add the liquid and dry ingredients.

2 Sprinkle the flour over, ensuring that it covers the water. Add the evaporated milk. Place the sugar, salt and butter in separate corners of the bread pan. Make a shallow indentation in the center of the flour (but not down as far as the liquid) and add the yeast.

3 Set the bread machine to the basic/normal setting, with raisin setting (if available), medium crust. Press Start. Add the orange zest, cranberries and pecans when the machine beeps, or after the first kneading.

4 Remove the bread from the pan at the end of the baking cycle and turn out onto a wire rack. Mix the orange juice and sugar in a small pan. Heat, stirring, until the sugar dissolves, then boil until syrupy. Brush the syrup over the loaf and let cool.

SMALL
½ cup water
½ cup orange juice
1 egg
3¼ cups unbleached
white bread flour
1 tablespoon nonfat dry milk
3 tablespoons sugar
½ teaspoon salt
2 tablespoons butter
1 teaspoon rapid-rise active dry yeast
2 teaspoons grated orange zest
⅓ cup dried cranberries
¼ cup pecans, chopped
2 tablespoons each fresh orange juice
and sugar, for glazing

MEDIUM
¾ cup water
¾ cup orange juice
1 egg
4½ cups unbleached
white bread flour
2 tablespoons nonfat dry milk
¼ cup sugar
¾ teaspoon salt
3 tablespoons butter
1½ teaspoons rapid-rise active dry
yeast
1 tablespoon grated orange zest
scant ½ cup dried cranberries
3 tablespoons pecans, chopped
2 tablespoons each fresh orange juice
and sugar, for glazing

LARGE
1 cup water
1 cup orange juice
2 eggs
6 cups unbleached white bread flour
3 tablespoons nonfat dry milk
5 tablespoons sugar
1 teaspoon salt
¼ cup butter
1½ teaspoons rapid-rise active dry yeast
4 teaspoons grated orange zest
⅔ cup dried cranberries
½ cup pecans, chopped
2 tablespoons each fresh orange juice
and sugar, for glazing

MAKES 1 LOAF

THREE CHOCOLATE BREAD

If you like chocolate, you'll adore this bread. The recipe suggests three specific types of chocolate, but you can combine your own favorites.

SMALL
1 egg
1 cup water
3¼ cups unbleached white
bread flour
1 tablespoon sugar
½ teaspoon salt
1½ tablespoons butter
1 teaspoon rapid-rise active dry yeast
1½ ounces milk chocolate with
raisins and almonds
1½ ounces semi-sweet chocolate
with ginger
2 ounces Belgian milk chocolate

MEDIUM
1 egg
1¼ cup water
4½ cups unbleached white
bread flour
2 tablespoons sugar
1 teaspoon salt
2 tablespoons butter
1½ teaspoons rapid-rise active dry yeast
2 ounces milk chocolate with raisins
and almonds
2 ounces semi-sweet chocolate
with ginger
3 ounces Belgian milk chocolate

LARGE
2 eggs
1½ cups water
6 cups unbleached white bread flour
3 tablespoons sugar
1½ teaspoons salt
3 tablespoons butter
1½ teaspoons rapid-rise active dry yeast
3 ounces milk chocolate with raisins
and almonds
3 ounces semi-sweet chocolate
with ginger
4 ounces Belgian milk chocolate

MAKES 1 LOAF

COOK'S TIP
Gradually add the chocolate to the bread machine pan, making sure that it is mixing into the dough before adding more.

1 Pour the water into the bread pan and add the eggs. If necessary, reverse the order in which you add the liquid and dry ingredients.

2 Sprinkle the flour over, ensuring that it covers the water. Add the sugar, salt and butter, placing them in separate corners of the bread pan. Make a shallow indentation in the center of the flour; add the yeast.

3 Set the bread machine to the basic/normal setting, with raisin setting (if available), medium crust. Press Start. Coarsely chop all the chocolate (it is not necessary to keep them separate). Add when the machine beeps, or after the first kneading (see Cook's Tip).

4 Remove the bread at the end of the baking cycle and turn out onto a wire rack to cool.

LEMON AND MACADAMIA BREAD

Originally from Australia, macadamia nuts were introduced into California and Hawaii about 50 years ago and are now very popular. Their buttery taste combines well with the tangy flavor of the lemon zest and yogurt in this delicious bread.

1 Pour the egg(s), yogurt and milk into the pan. If necessary, reverse the order of adding the wet and dry ingredients.

2 Sprinkle the flour over, ensuring that it covers the water. Add the sugar, salt and butter, placing them in separate corners of the bread pan. Make a shallow indentation in the flour (but not down as far as the liquid) and add the yeast.

3 Set the bread machine to the basic/normal setting, with raisin setting (if available), medium crust. Press Start. Add the nuts and lemon zest when the machine beeps, or after the first kneading finishes.

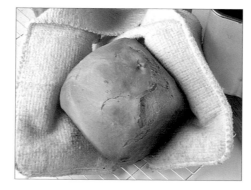

4 Remove the lemon and macadamia bread from the bread pan at the end of the baking cycle and turn out onto a wire rack to cool.

SMALL
1 egg
generous ½ cup lemon yogurt
⅔ *cup milk*
3¼ *cups unbleached white
bread flour*
3 *tablespoons sugar*
½ *teaspoon salt*
2 *tablespoons butter*
1 *teaspoon rapid-rise active dry yeast*
¼ *cup macadamia
nuts, chopped*
2 *teaspoons grated lemon zest*

MEDIUM
1 egg
¾ *cup lemon yogurt*
⅔ *cup milk*
4½ *cups unbleached white
bread flour*
¼ *cup sugar*
¾ *teaspoon salt*
3 *tablespoons butter*
1½ *teaspoons rapid-rise active dry
yeast*
⅓ *cup macadamia
nuts, chopped*
1 *tablespoon grated lemon zest*

LARGE
2 eggs
⅞ *cup lemon yogurt*
¾ *cup milk*
6 *cups unbleached white bread flour*
5 *tablespoons sugar*
1 *teaspoon salt*
¼ *cup butter*
1½ *teaspoons rapid-rise active
dry yeast*
½ *cup macadamia
nuts, chopped*
4 *teaspoons grated lemon zest*

MAKES 1 LOAF

COOK'S TIP
Select light crust setting if your bread machine tends to produce a dark crust when you make a sweet bread.

RUM RAISIN LOAF

*Juicy raisins, plumped up with dark rum, flavor this loaf.
It's more than good enough to serve just as it is, but slices can also be
lightly toasted and buttered.*

SMALL
generous ½ cup raisins
1½ tablespoons dark rum
1 egg
1 cup milk
3 cups unbleached white bread flour
¼ teaspoon ground ginger
2 tablespoons sugar
½ teaspoon salt
3 tablespoons butter
1 teaspoon rapid-rise active dry yeast
2 teaspoons honey, warmed

MEDIUM
⅔ cups raisins
2 tablespoons dark rum
1 egg
1¼ cups milk
4½ cups unbleached white
bread flour
½ teaspoon ground ginger
3 tablespoons sugar
¾ teaspoon salt
¼ cup butter
1½ teaspoons rapid-rise active
dry yeast
1 tablespoon honey, warmed

LARGE
⅘ cup raisins
3 tablespoons dark rum
2 eggs, lightly beaten
1½ cups milk
6 cups unbleached white bread flour
1 teaspoon ground ginger
¼ cup sugar
1 teaspoon salt
5 tablespoons butter
1½ teaspoons rapid-rise active
dry yeast
1 tablespoon honey, warmed

MAKES 1 LOAF

1 Place the raisins and rum in a small bowl and let soak for 2 hours, or longer if you can. Add the egg and milk to the bread machine pan. If the instructions for your machine specify that the yeast is to be placed in the pan first, reverse the order in which you add the liquid and dry ingredients.

2 Sprinkle the flour over, ensuring that it covers the liquid completely. Add the ground ginger. Add the sugar, salt and butter, placing them in separate corners of the bread machine pan. Make a shallow indentation in the center of the flour (but not down as far as the liquid) and pour in the yeast.

3 Set the bread machine to the basic/normal setting, with raisin setting (if available), medium crust. Press Start. Add the raisins when the machine beeps to add extra ingredients, or after the first kneading.

4 Remove the bread at the end of the baking cycle and turn out onto a wire rack. Brush the top with honey and let the loaf cool.

MANGO AND BANANA BREAD

Tropical fruit juice, fresh banana and dried mango give this light-textured loaf its Caribbean flavor.

1 Pour the fruit juice and buttermilk into the bread machine pan. Add the mashed banana(s) to the bread pan, with the honey. If necessary for your machine, reverse the order in which you add the liquid and dry ingredients.

2 Sprinkle the flour over, ensuring that it covers the liquid. Place the salt and butter in separate corners of the bread pan. Make a shallow indentation in the center of the flour and add the yeast.

3 Set the bread machine to the basic/normal setting, with raisin setting (if available), medium crust. Press Start.

4 Add the chopped mango pieces when the machine beeps to add extra ingredients, or 5 minutes before the end of the kneading cycle.

5 Remove the bread from the pan at the end of the baking cycle and turn out onto a wire rack to cool.

SMALL
2 tablespoons orange and
mango juice
⅔ cup buttermilk
1 medium banana, peeled
and mashed
2 tablespoons honey
3 cups unbleached white bread flour
1 teaspoon salt
2 tablespoons butter
1 teaspoon rapid-rise active dry yeast
¼ cup dried mango, chopped

MEDIUM
¼ cup orange and
mango juice
⅞ cup buttermilk
1 large banana, peeled
and mashed
3 tablespoons honey
4½ cups unbleached white
bread flour
1 teaspoon salt
3 tablespoons butter
1 teaspoon rapid-rise active dry yeast
⅓ cup dried mango, chopped

LARGE
¼ cup orange and mango juice
1⅛ cups buttermilk
2 medium bananas, peeled and
mashed
¼ cup honey
6 cups unbleached white bread flour
1½ teaspoons salt
¼ cup butter
1½ teaspoons rapid-rise active
dry yeast
½ cup dried mango, chopped

MAKES 1 LOAF

COOK'S TIP
Select ripe bananas if you can for
this recipe, as they are softer
and easier to mash.

AUSTRIAN COFFEE CAKE

This attractive cake is layered with marzipan and fresh cherries and has just a hint of cinnamon and apple. It is a rich cake, perfect with freshly made coffee, or try it warm as a tasty dessert, served with whipped cream, crème fraîche or yogurt.

⅔ cup water
1 egg
¾ cup grated tart green apple
4 cups unbleached white bread flour
2 tablespoons nonfat dry milk
¼ cup sugar
3 tablespoons butter, melted
1½ teaspoons rapid-rise active
dry yeast

FOR THE FILLING
8 ounces cherries, pitted
8 ounces white almond paste, grated
1 teaspoon ground cinnamon

FOR THE TOPPING
beaten egg white
1 tablespoon demerara sugar
2 tablespoons flaked almonds

MAKES 1 CAKE

1 Pour the water and egg into the bread machine pan. Sprinkle the grated apple over. If the instructions for your machine specify that the yeast is to be placed in the pan first, simply reverse the order in which you add the liquid and dry ingredients.

2 Sprinkle the flour over, ensuring that it covers the water, egg and apple completely. Add the milk then add the sugar and butter, placing them in separate corners of the bread pan.

3 Make a shallow indentation in the center of the flour (but not down as far as the liquid underneath) and pour the yeast into the hollow.

4 Set the bread machine to the dough setting; use basic dough setting (if available). Press Start.

5 When the dough cycle has finished, remove the dough from the machine and place it on a lightly floured surface. Punch it down gently, then roll it out to form a 16-inch square.

6 Arrange the cherries on top and then scatter the grated almond paste and ground cinnamon over the fruit.

7 Carefully roll the dough up, as you would when making a jelly roll, then gently roll and stretch the sausage shape until it is 22 inches long. Twist the roll into a loose coil and place in a 9-inch nonstick springform cake pan.

COOK'S TIP
Try this cake layered with thick slices of fresh apricots or plums when cherries are out of season.

8 Cover the pan with lightly oiled plastic wrap and leave in a warm place for about 30–45 minutes, to allow the dough to rise. Meanwhile, preheat the oven to 375°F.

9 Brush the top of the risen dough with egg white and sprinkle with demerara sugar and flaked almonds.

10 Bake for 30–35 minutes, or until the cake is golden and well risen. Let it cool for a few minutes in the pan, then transfer the cake to a wire rack to cool. Serve warm or cold, cut into wedges.

SWISS PEAR AND RED CURRANT TART

Juicy pears and red currants in a nutmeg cream custard provide an unforgettable filling for this Swiss tart.

⅜ cup milk
1 egg
2 cups unbleached white bread flour
½ teaspoon salt
2 tablespoons sugar
2 tablespoons butter, melted
1 teaspoon rapid-rise active dry yeast
confectioners' sugar, for dusting

FOR THE FILLING
½ cup light cream
2 eggs
2 tablespoons sugar
½ teaspoon freshly grated nutmeg
3 pears, peeled, halved and cored
⅓ cup red currants

SERVES 6–8

1 Pour the milk and egg into the bread machine pan. If the instructions for your bread machine specify it, reverse the order in which you add the liquid and dry ingredients.

2 Sprinkle the flour over, ensuring that it covers the liquid completely. Add the salt, sugar and butter, placing them in separate corners of the bread pan. Make a shallow indentation in the center of the flour (but not down as far as the liquid) and add the yeast.

3 Set the bread machine to the dough setting; use basic dough setting (if available). Press Start. Lightly oil a 10-inch pizza pan, shallow pie pan or flan tin.

4 When the dough cycle has finished, remove the dough from the machine and place it on a lightly floured surface. Punch it down gently.

5 Roll out the dough to a 11-inch round. Place it in the oiled pizza pan or pie or flan pan. With your fingers, press the dough outward and upward so that it covers the bottom and sides of the pan evenly. Then preheat the oven to 375°F.

6 Make the filling by beating the cream with the eggs, sugar and nutmeg in a bowl. Pour it into the dough-lined pan, then arrange the pears on top, placing them cut side down. Sprinkle the red currants in the center.

7 Bake the tart for 35–40 minutes, or until the filling has set and the crust is golden. Let it cool for a few minutes in the pan, then sprinkle it with sugar. Cut it into wedges and serve immediately.

APRICOT AND VANILLA SLICES

Fresh apricots are perfect for these fruit slices, but there's no need to deny yourself when they are out of season. Just use well-drained canned ones.

½ cup water
2 cups unbleached white bread flour
½ teaspoon salt
2 tablespoons sugar
2 tablespoons butter, melted
1 teaspoon rapid-rise active dry yeast

FOR THE FILLING
3 tablespoons sugar
1 tablespoon cornstarch
⅔ cup mascarpone cheese
¾ cup cottage cheese
2 eggs, lightly beaten
½ teaspoon pure vanilla extract
2 tablespoons apricot preserves
9 apricots, halved and pitted

MAKES ABOUT 14

VARIATION
This tastes just as good when made with fresh nectarines. Use raspberry jam instead of the apricot preserves.

1 Pour the water into the bread machine pan. If the instructions for your bread machine specify that the yeast is to be placed in the pan first, simply reverse the order in which you add the liquid and dry ingredients.

2 Sprinkle the flour over, ensuring that it covers the water. Add the salt, sugar and butter, placing them in separate corners of the bread pan.

3 Make a shallow indentation in the center of the flour (but not down as far as the liquid underneath) and add the yeast.

4 Set the bread machine to the dough setting; use basic dough setting (if available). Press Start. Then lightly oil a 13 × 8-inch jelly roll pan.

5 When the dough cycle has finished, remove the dough from the machine and place it on a lightly floured surface.

6 Punch the dough down gently, then roll out to a rectangle, measuring 14 × 9 inches. Lift it on to the jelly roll pan. Using your fingers, press the dough outward and upward so that it covers the bottom and sides of the pan evenly. Cover with oiled plastic wrap. Set aside.

7 Preheat the oven to 400°F. Make the filling. Mix the sugar and cornstarch in a cup or small bowl. Place the mascarpone and cottage cheese in a large mixing bowl and beat in the sugar mixture, followed by the eggs and vanilla extract.

8 Spread the apricot preserves evenly over the dough, then spread the vanilla mixture on top. Arrange the apricots over the filling, placing them cut-side down.

9 Bake for 25–30 minutes, or until the filling is set and the dough has risen and is golden. Let cool slightly before cutting into slices. Serve warm.

PEACH STREUSELKUCHEN

This peach-filled German yeast cake is finished with a crunchy almond and cinnamon topping which is quite irresistible.

7 tablespoons milk
1 egg
2¼ cups unbleached white bread flour
½ teaspoon salt
3 tablespoons sugar
3 tablespoons butter, melted
1 teaspoon rapid-rise active dry yeast
4 fresh peaches, halved and pitted

FOR THE TOPPING
¾ cup all-purpose flour
⅓ cup ground almonds
¼ cup butter, diced and softened
4 tablespoons sugar
1 teaspoon ground cinnamon

SERVES 8

1 Pour the milk and egg into the bread pan. If the instructions for your bread machine specify that the yeast should go in first, reverse the order of wet and dry ingredients.

2 Sprinkle the flour over, ensuring that it covers the milk and egg completely. Then add the salt, sugar and butter, placing them in three separate corners of the bread pan. Make a shallow indentation in the center of the flour (but not down as far as the liquid) and add the yeast.

3 Set the bread machine to the dough setting; use basic dough setting (if available). Press Start. Lightly oil a 10-inch springform cake pan.

4 When the dough cycle has finished, remove the dough from the pan and place it on a lightly floured surface. Punch it down gently, then roll it out to fit the pan. Ease it into position.

5 Slice the peaches thickly and arrange them on top of the dough. Next, make the topping. Rub the flour, ground almonds and butter together until the mixture resembles coarse bread crumbs. Stir in the sugar and cinnamon. Sprinkle the topping over the peaches.

6 Cover the dough with lightly oiled plastic wrap and set aside in a warm place for about 20–25 minutes, to rise slightly. Meanwhile, preheat the oven to 375°F.

7 Bake the cake for 25–30 minutes, or until evenly golden. Let it cool in the pan for a few minutes and serve warm, or turn out onto a wire rack to allow to cool completely.

BAVARIAN PLUM CAKE

As this bakes, the juices from the plums trickle through to the crust, making a deliciously succulent, fruity cake. Serve it with coffee or as a dessert with crème fraîche or ice cream.

6 tablespoons milk
1 egg
2 cups unbleached white bread flour
1 teaspoon ground cinnamon
½ teaspoon salt
3 tablespoons sugar
2 tablespoons butter, melted
1 teaspoon rapid-rise active dry yeast
1½ pounds plums
confectioners' sugar, for dusting

SERVES 8

3 Make a shallow indentation in the center of the flour (but not down as far as the liquid) and add the yeast.

4 Set the bread machine to the dough setting; use basic dough setting (if available). Press Start. Lightly oil a 10½ × 7-inch rectangular baking pan that is about 1½ inches deep.

5 When the dough cycle has finished, remove the dough from the machine and place it on a lightly floured surface. Punch it down gently, then roll it out to fit the pan. Using your fingertips, ease it into position.

6 Cut the plums into quarters and remove the stones. Arrange them on the dough, so that they overlap slightly. Cover with lightly oiled plastic wrap and leave the cake in a warm place for 30–45 minutes, to rise. Meanwhile, preheat the oven to 375°F.

1 Pour the milk into the bread machine pan and add the egg. If the instructions for your machine specify that the yeast is to be placed in the pan first, simply reverse the order in which you add the liquid and dry ingredients.

VARIATION
Replace the plums with apple wedges or nectarine slices. Use dessert apples as cooking apples will be too tart. Allow four to five depending on their size. Sprinkle the top with demerara sugar 5 minutes before the end of baking, and return to the oven.

2 Sprinkle the flour over, ensuring that it covers the milk and egg completely. Add the ground cinnamon. Place the salt, sugar and butter in separate corners of the bread pan.

7 Bake the cake for 30–35 minutes, or until golden and well risen. Dust with confectioners' sugar and serve warm.

1 teaspoon saffron threads
⅞ cup milk
2 eggs
4½ cups unbleached white
bread flour
1 teaspoon ground cardamom seeds
½ teaspoon salt
¼ cup sugar
¼ cup butter, melted
1 teaspoon rapid-rise active dry yeast

FOR THE GLAZE
1 egg yolk
1 tablespoon water

FOR THE TOPPING
3 tablespoons flaked almonds
3 tablespoons granulated sugar
1 tablespoon rum
1 tablespoon candied lime peel,
chopped (optional)

SERVES 8–10

VARIATION
Instead of candied lime peel, other ingredients can be used for the topping, if preferred. Try angelica or candied orange peel instead. Glacé fruits such as cherries or peaches are also good, or you could use dried mango or dried pear.

1 Place the saffron strands in a small mixing bowl. Heat half of the milk in a small saucepan, pour it over the saffron and set aside to infuse until the milk is at room temperature.

FINNISH FESTIVE WREATH

This traditional sweet bread, enriched with egg and delicately scented with saffron and cardamom, is called pulla in its native Finland. For festive occasions, elaborately shaped versions of the bread, like this pretty wreath, are prepared.

2 Pour the saffron milk into the bread machine pan, then add the remaining milk and the eggs. However, if the instructions for your bread machine specify that the yeast is to be placed in the bread pan first, simply reverse the order in which you add the liquid and dry ingredients.

3 Sprinkle the flour over, ensuring that it covers the liquid completely, then add the cardamom seeds.

4 Add the salt, sugar and butter, placing them in separate corners of the bread pan. Make a shallow indentation in the center of the flour (but not down as far as the milk and eggs) and add the yeast.

5 Set the bread machine to the dough setting; use basic dough setting (if available). Press Start. Lightly oil a baking sheet.

6 When the dough cycle has finished, remove the dough from the bread machine pan and place it on a surface that has been lightly floured. Punch the dough down gently, then divide it into three equal pieces.

7 Roll each piece of dough into a rope, about 26 inches long. Place the ropes lengthwise, next to each other, to begin the braid.

8 Starting from the center, braid the pieces together, working toward yourself and from left to right. Turn the dough around and repeat the braiding process. Bring the ends of the braid together to form a circular wreath and pinch to seal.

9 Place the wreath on the prepared baking sheet. Cover with oiled plastic wrap and leave for 45–60 minutes, or until it has almost doubled in size.

10 Meanwhile, preheat the oven to 375°F. Make the glaze by mixing the egg yolk and water in a bowl. In a separate bowl, mix the almonds, sugar, rum and peel for the topping. Brush the glaze over the loaf and sprinkle the almond mixture on top.

11 Bake for 20 minutes, then reduce the oven temperature to 350°F and bake for 10–15 minutes more, or until the wreath is golden and well risen. Turn out onto wire rack to cool.

2 tablespoons instant coffee granules
2 tablespoons hot water
scant ⅔ cup milk
1 egg, plus 2 egg yolks
3½ cups unbleached white
bread flour
1 tablespoon cocoa powder
1 teaspoon ground cinnamon
½ teaspoon salt
6 tablespoons sugar
6 tablespoons butter, softened
1½ teaspoons rapid-rise active dry yeast
4 ounces semisweet chocolate,
coarsely chopped
3 tablespoons pine nuts, lightly toasted
melted butter, for glazing

SERVES 8–10

COOK'S TIP
The dough for this bread is quite rich and may require a longer rising time than that provided for by your bread machine. Check the dough at the end of the dough cycle. If it does not appear to have risen very much in the bread pan, leave the dough in the machine, with the machine switched off and the lid closed, for a further 30 minutes to allow it to rise to the required degree.

1 In a small bowl, dissolve the coffee granules in the hot water. Pour the mixture into the bread machine pan and then add the milk, egg and egg yolks. If the instructions for your bread machine specify that the yeast is to be placed in the pan first, simply reverse the order in which you add the liquid and dry ingredients.

MOCHA PANETTONE

Panettone is the traditional Italian Christmas bread from Milan. This tall domed loaf is usually filled with dried fruits; for a change try this coffee-flavored bread studded with chocolate and pine nuts.

2 Sift the flour and cocoa powder together. Sprinkle the mixture over the liquid, ensuring that it is completely covered. Add the ground cinnamon. Place the salt, sugar and butter in separate corners of the bread pan. Make a shallow indentation in the center of the flour (but not down as far as the liquid) and add the yeast.

3 Set the bread machine to the dough setting; use basic dough setting (if available). Press Start. Lightly oil a 6-inch deep cake pan or soufflé dish. Using a double sheet of waxed paper that is 3 inches wider than the depth of the pan or dish, line the container so that the excess paper creates a collar.

4 When the dough cycle has finished, remove the dough from the machine and place it on a lightly floured surface. Punch it down gently. Gently knead in the chocolate and toasted pine nuts and shape the dough into a ball. Cover it with lightly oiled plastic wrap and let rest for 5 minutes.

5 Shape the dough into a plump round loaf that has the same diameter as the cake pan or soufflé dish, and place in the bottom of the container. Cover with oiled plastic wrap and let the dough rise in a slightly warm place for 45–60 minutes, or until the dough has almost reached the top of the waxed paper collar.

6 Meanwhile, preheat the oven to 400°F. Brush the top of the loaf with the melted butter and cut a deep cross in the top of the bread. Bake the bread for 10 minutes.

7 Reduce the oven temperature to 350°F and continue to bake the panettone for 30–35 minutes more, or until it is evenly golden all over and a metal skewer inserted in the center comes out clean, without any crumb sticking to it.

8 Leave the panettone in the pan or dish for 5–10 minutes, then turn out onto a wire rack and set aside until it is quite cold before slicing.

STRAWBERRY CHOCOLATE SAVARIN

This light spongy cake is soaked in a wine and brandy syrup before being filled with succulent fresh strawberries to make an exquisite dessert.

7 tablespoons milk
4 eggs
2 cups unbleached white bread flour
3 tablespoons cocoa powder
½ teaspoon salt
2 tablespoons sugar
7 tablespoons butter, melted
1 teaspoon rapid-rise active dry yeast
*cape gooseberry and strawberry
leaves to decorate*

FOR THE SYRUP
½ cup granulated sugar
scant ⅓ cup water
scant ⅓ cup white wine
3 tablespoons brandy

FOR THE FILLING
*⅔ cup heavy cream, whipped, or
crème fraîche*
2 cups strawberries, halved
1 cup raspberries

SERVES 6–8

VARIATION
The savarin can be filled with other fruits, such as grapes, raspberries, currants, peaches or blackberries. Alternatively, fill with whipped cream, and sprinkle chopped nuts over the top.

1 Pour the milk and eggs into the bread pan. If your machine specifies that the yeast is to be placed in the pan first, reverse the order in which you add the liquid and dry ingredients.

2 Sift the flour and cocoa powder together. Sprinkle the mixture over the liquid in the pan, covering it completely. Place the salt, sugar and butter in separate corners. Make an indentation in the center of the flour; add the yeast.

3 Set the machine to the dough setting; use basic dough setting (if available). Press Start. Lightly oil a 6¼ cup savarin or ring mold.

4 When the machine has finished mixing the ingredients, leave it on the dough setting for 20 minutes then stop the machine. Pour the dough mixture into the prepared mold, cover with oiled plastic wrap and set aside in a warm place for 45–60 minutes, or until the dough almost reaches the top of the pan.

5 Meanwhile, preheat the oven to 400°F. Bake the savarin for 25–30 minutes, or until it is golden and risen. Turn out onto a wire rack to cool, with a plate beneath the rack.

6 Make the syrup. Put the sugar, water and wine in a small pan. Heat gently, stirring until the sugar dissolves, then bring to a boil. Lower the heat and simmer for 2 minutes, then remove from the heat and stir in the brandy.

7 Spoon the syrup over the savarin. Repeat with any syrup that has collected on the plate. Transfer to a serving plate; let cool. To serve, fill the center with the cream or crème fraîche and top with the strawberries and raspberries. Decorate with cape gooseberry and strawberry leaves.

PEACH BRANDY BABAS

These light, delicate sponges are moistened with a syrup flavored with peach brandy before being filled with whipped cream and fruit. You can vary the flavor of the syrup by using orange or coconut liqueur or dark rum.

1 Pour the milk and eggs into the bread pan. If the instructions for your machine specify that the yeast is to be placed in the pan first, reverse the order in which you add the liquid and dry ingredients to the pan.

2 Sprinkle the flour over, ensuring that it covers the liquid. Add the cinnamon, then place the salt and sugar in separate corners. Make a shallow indentation in the center of the flour (but not down as far as the liquid) and add the yeast.

3 Set the bread machine to the dough setting; use basic dough setting (if available). Press Start. Lightly oil eight small savarin tins, each with a diameter of 10cm/4in.

4 When the machine has finished mixing the dough, let the dough cycle continue for a further 15 minutes, then stop the machine and scrape the dough into a bowl. Gradually beat in the melted butter.

5 Pour the batter into the prepared tins, half filling them. Cover with lightly oiled plastic wrap and leave in a warm place until the batter reaches the tin tops.

6 Meanwhile, preheat the oven to 375°F. Bake the babas for 20 minutes, or until they are golden and have risen well. Turn the babas out onto a wire rack to cool. Slide a large tray under the rack.

7 To make the syrup for the babas, place the granulated sugar and water in a small saucepan and heat gently, stirring occasionally, until the sugar has dissolved. Bring to the boil and boil hard for 2 minutes without stirring. Remove the syrup from the heat and stir in the peach brandy. Spoon the syrup over the babas. Then scrape up any syrup which has dripped on to the tray with a spatula and repeat the process until all the syrup is absorbed.

8 When the babas are cold, whip the cream, sugar and vanilla extract in a bowl until the cream just forms soft peaks. Fill the babas with the flavored cream and decorate them with the fresh fruits of your choice.

7 tablespoons milk
4 eggs
2 cups unbleached white bread flour
1 teaspoon ground cinnamon
½ teaspoon salt
2 tablespoons sugar
1 teaspoon rapid-rise active dry yeast
7 tablespoons butter, melted

FOR THE SYRUP
½ cup granulated sugar
⅔ cup water
6 tablespoons peach brandy

FOR THE DECORATION
⅔ cup heavy cream
1 tablespoon sugar
3–4 drops pure vanilla extract
fresh fruits, such as grapes, star fruit and red currants, to decorate

MAKES 8

MIXED PEEL BRAID

6 tablespoons milk
1 egg
2½ cups unbleached white
bread flour
1 teaspoon ground apple pie spice
½ teaspoon salt
2 tablespoons sugar
¼ cup butter, melted
1 teaspoon rapid-rise active dry yeast

FOR THE FILLING
⅔ cup mixed peel
⅓ cup golden raisins
¼ cup walnut pieces, chopped
2 tablespoons chopped candied ginger
3 tablespoons three citrus
fruit marmalade

FOR THE GLAZE
1 egg yolk
1 tablespoon sugar
1 tablespoon milk

SERVES 8

A succulent citrus filling with a hint of ginger provides the pleasant surprise in this attractively braided coffee-time cake.

1 Pour the milk and egg into the bread machine pan. If necessary for your bread machine, reverse the order of adding the wet and dry ingredients.

2 Sprinkle the flour over the liquid. Add the apple pie spice. Put the salt, sugar and butter in separate corners. Make a shallow indentation in the center of the flour and add the yeast.

3 Set the bread machine to the dough setting; use basic dough setting (if available). Press Start. Lightly oil a baking sheet.

4 When the dough cycle has finished, remove the dough from the machine and place it on a lightly floured surface. Punch it down gently, then roll it out to a 11 × 16-inch rectangle.

5 Make the filling by combining the mixed peel, golden raisins, walnuts, ginger and marmalade in a bowl. Spread the mixture lengthwise over the middle third of the rolled-out dough, leaving a 1-inch border at either end. Using a sharp knife, cut the two strips of dough either side of the filling into diagonal strips angled toward you, ¾ inch wide.

6 Working from the far end, fold in the end piece of dough, then braid the dough strips over the filling. Tuck in the end to seal. Place the braid on the prepared baking sheet. Cover it with lightly oiled plastic wrap and leave in a warm place for 30–45 minutes to rise.

7 Meanwhile, preheat the oven to 400°F. Make the glaze by mixing the egg yolk, sugar and milk in a bowl. Brush the mixture over the braid. Bake for 10 minutes, then reduce the oven temperature to 375°F and bake for 10–15 minutes more, or until the braid is golden and well risen. Turn out onto a wire rack to cool.

HAZELNUT TWIST CAKE

Easy to make yet impressive, this sweet bread consists of layers of ground nuts, twisted through a rich dough, topped with a maple-flavored icing.

1 cup water
1 egg
4 cups unbleached white bread flour
3 tablespoons nonfat dry milk
grated zest of 1 orange
½ teaspoon salt
¼ cup sugar
6 tablespoons butter, melted
1½ teaspoons rapid-rise active dry yeast
flaked almonds or slivered hazelnuts, to decorate

FOR THE FILLING
1 cup ground hazelnuts
scant 1 cup ground almonds
scant ½ cup light brown sugar
½ teaspoon freshly grated nutmeg
2 egg whites
1 tablespoon brandy

FOR THE TOPPING
4 tablespoons confectioners' sugar
1 tablespoon hot water
2 tablespoons natural maple syrup

SERVES 6–8

1 Pour the water and egg into the bread pan. Reverse the order in which you add the wet and dry ingredients if necessary.

2 Sprinkle the flour over, covering the liquid. Add the milk and orange zest. Place the salt, sugar and butter in separate corners. Make an indentation in the center of the flour; add the yeast.

3 Set the bread machine to the dough setting; use basic dough setting (if available). Press Start. Lightly oil a 9-inch springform ring cake pan.

4 When the dough cycle has finished, place the dough on a lightly floured surface. Punch it down gently, then roll it out to a 26 × 18 inch rectangle. Cut the dough in half lengthwise.

5 Make the filling by mixing all of the ingredients in a bowl. Divide the filling in half. Spread one portion over each piece of dough, leaving a ½ inch border along one long edge of each piece.

6 Starting from the other long edge, roll up each piece of dough, jelly roll fashion. Place the two pieces next to each other and twist them together.

7 Brush the ends of the dough rope with a little water. Loop the rope in the prepared springform pan and gently press the ends together to seal.

8 Cover the pan with lightly oiled plastic wrap and then leave in a warm place for 30–45 minutes, or until the dough has risen and is puffy. Preheat the oven to 400°F.

9 Bake the cake for 30–35 minutes, or until it is golden and well risen. Let cool slightly, then turn the cake out onto a wire rack.

10 Make the icing by mixing the confectioners' sugar, hot water and maple syrup in a bowl. Drizzle over the warm cake. Sprinkle with a few flaked almonds or slivered hazelnuts and let cool completely before serving.

2 tablespoons milk
2 eggs
2 cups unbleached white bread flour
½ teaspoon salt
1 tablespoon sugar
2 ounces butter, melted
1½ teaspoons rapid-rise active
dry yeast

FOR THE GLAZE
1 egg yolk
1 tablespoon milk

MAKES 12

COOK'S TIP
This is a rich dough and may need
more than the standard rising time. If
it has not risen very much by the time
the dough program ends, leave the
dough in the machine for
another 30 minutes, turning off the
machine and leaving the lid shut.

1 Pour the milk and eggs into the bread
machine pan. If the instructions for your
bread machine specify that the yeast is
to be placed in the pan first, simply
reverse the order in which you add the
liquid and dry ingredients.

2 Sprinkle over the flour, ensuring that
it covers the liquid. Add the salt, sugar
and butter, placing them in separate
corners of the bread pan. Make a
shallow indentation in the center of the
flour (but not down as far as the liquid)
and add the yeast.

3 Set the bread machine to the dough
setting; use basic dough setting (if
available). Press Start. Lightly oil
12 small brioche molds.

4 When the dough cycle has finished,
remove the dough from the machine and
place it on a lightly floured surface.
Knock it back gently. Slice off a quarter
of the dough, cover with oiled plastic
wrap and set aside. Divide the remaining
dough into 12 pieces.

MINI BRIOCHE

Rich yet light, these buttery breads, with their characteristic fluted shape,
can be eaten with both sweet and savoury foods.

5 Knead each piece of dough into a
small round. Place each round in an
oiled mold. Divide the reserved piece
of dough into 12 and shape into small
pear shapes.

6 To shape each mini brioche, make a
small hole or cut a cross in the top of
each large piece of dough. Place the
pear-shaped pieces of dough on top,
narrow end down. Cover with lightly
oiled plastic wrap and set aside in a
warm place for 30–45 minutes, or until
well risen. Meanwhile preheat the oven
to 425°F.

7 Make the glaze by mixing the egg yolk
and milk together. Brush the mixture
over each brioche. Bake for 15 minutes,
or until the brioche are golden and have
risen well. Transfer them to a wire rack
to cool. Serve warm or cold.

LEMON AND PISTACHIO STRUDEL

*For a special occasion serve this superb strudel, which is made up of
thin layers of dough interleaved with a tasty fruit and goat cheese filling.*

1 Pour the milk and egg into the bread
machine pan. If the instructions for your
bread machine specify that the yeast is
to be placed in the pan first, simply
reverse the order in which you add the
liquid and dry ingredients.

2 Sprinkle the flour over, ensuring that
it covers the liquid. Add the salt, sugar
and butter, placing them in separate
corners of the bread pan. Make a
shallow indentation in the center of the
flour (but not down as far as the liquid)
and add the yeast.

3 Set the bread machine to the dough
setting; use basic dough setting (if
available). Press Start. Then lightly oil
a baking sheet.

4 Make the filling. Put both types of
cheese, the egg yolks, sugar, lemon zest
and vanilla in a bowl. Mix well. Stir in
the raisins, pistachios and apricots.

5 When the dough cycle has finished,
place the dough on a lightly floured
surface. Punch down gently. Roll out to
a rectangle 14 × 10 inches.

6 tablespoons milk
1 egg
2 cups unbleached white bread flour
½ teaspoon salt
1 tablespoon sugar
¼ cup butter
1 teaspoon rapid-rise active dry yeast
confectioners' sugar, for dusting

FOR THE FILLING
4 ounces montrachet or soft
goat cheese
½ cup cottage cheese, sieved
2 egg yolks
¼ cup sugar
grated zest of 1 lemon
½ teaspoon pure vanilla extract
⅓ cup raisins
⅓ cup pistachios, peeled
¼ cup dried apricots, chopped
¼ cup butter, melted
½ cup ground almonds

SERVES 6–8

6 Brush the dough with melted butter
and sprinkle with the ground almonds.
Spread the cheese filling over, leaving a
narrow border around the edges. Fold in
the edges along both long sides.

7 Starting from a short side, roll up like
a jelly roll. Place on the baking sheet,
seam side down. Cover with lightly oiled
plastic wrap. Let rise for 30 minutes.
Preheat the oven to 375°F.

8 Bake for 25–30 minutes. Turn out
onto a wire rack to cool. Dust with
confectioners' sugar and serve warm.

EASTER TEA RING

This Easter tea ring is too good to serve just once a year. Bake it as a family weekend treat whenever you feel self-indulgent. Perfect for a mid-morning coffee break or for tea time.

6 tablespoons milk
1 egg
2 cups unbleached white bread flour
½ teaspoon salt
2 tablespoons sugar
2 tablespoons butter
1 teaspoon rapid-rise active dry yeast

FOR THE FILLING
½ cup dried apricots
1 tablespoon butter
¼ cup light brown sugar
1½ teaspoons ground cinnamon
½ teaspoon allspice
⅓ cup golden raisins
milk, for brushing

FOR THE DECORATION
3 tablespoons confectioners' sugar
1–2 tablespoons orange liqueur or orange juice
pecans
candied fruits

SERVES 8–10

1 Pour the milk and egg into the bread machine pan. If the instructions for your bread machine specify that the yeast is to be placed in the pan first, simply reverse the order in which you add the liquid and dry ingredients.

2 Sprinkle over the flour, ensuring that it covers the liquid. Add the salt, sugar and butter, placing them in separate corners of the bread pan. Make a shallow indentation in the center of the flour (but not down as far as the liquid) and add the yeast.

3 Set the bread machine to the dough setting; use basic dough setting (if available). Press Start. Then lightly oil a baking sheet.

4 When the dough cycle has finished, remove the dough from the bread pan. Place it on a surface that has been lightly floured. Punch the dough down gently, then roll it out into a 12 × 18 inch rectangle.

5 Chop the dried apricots into small pieces. Melt the butter for the filling and brush it over the dough. Then sprinkle the dough with the muscovado sugar, ground cinnamon, allspice, golden raisins and chopped apricots.

6 Starting from one long edge, roll up the rectangle of dough, as when making a jelly roll. Turn the dough so that the seam is underneath.

7 Curl the dough into a circle, brush the ends with a little milk and seal. Place on the prepared baking sheet.

8 Using a pair of scissors, snip through the circle at 1½-inch intervals, each time cutting two-thirds of the way through the dough. Twist the sections so they start to fall sideways.

9 Cover the ring with lightly oiled plastic wrap and leave in a warm place for about 30 minutes, or until the dough is well risen and puffy. Preheat oven to 400°F.

10 Bake the ring for 20–25 minutes, or until golden. Turn out onto a wire rack to cool.

11 While the tea ring is still warm, make the decoration by mixing together the confectioners' sugar and liqueur or orange juice. Drizzle the mixture over the ring, then arrange pecans and candied fruit on top. Cool completely before serving.

VARIATION
There is a vast range of dried fruits available in the supermarkets. Vary the golden raisins and apricots; try dried peaches, mango, melon, cherries and raisins, to name a few. Just make sure that the total quantity stays the same as in the recipe.

POLISH BABKA

Vodka is the surprise ingredient in this classic Polish cake, made at Eastertime. The dough is enriched with eggs and flavored with citrus zest and raisins.

¼ cup vodka
½ teaspoon saffron threads
1 tablespoon grated orange zest
1 tablespoon grated lemon zest
½ cup butter, softened
6 tablespoons sugar
3 eggs
2 tablespoons water
3½ cups unbleached white bread flour
½ teaspoon salt
2 teaspoons rapid-rise active dry yeast
½ cup raisins
½ cup dried sour cherries

FOR THE ICING
1 cup confectioners' sugar
1 tablespoon lemon juice

FOR THE DECORATION
toasted flaked almonds
pared orange rind or candied orange peel

SERVES 8–10

1 Seep the vodka, saffron and citrus zest together for 30 minutes. Beat the butter and sugar in a bowl until pale and creamy. Tip the saffron mixture into the bread pan, then add the eggs and water. If necessary, reverse the order in which you add the liquid and dry ingredients.

2 Add the flour, covering the liquid. Add the salt in a corner. Make an indentation in the flour; add the yeast. Set to the dough setting; use basic raisin dough setting (if available). Press Start.

3 Mix for 5 minutes, then add the creamed butter and sugar mixture.

4 Add the raisins and dried sour cherries when the machine beeps, or 5 minutes before the end of the kneading cycle. Lightly oil a brioche pan. When the cycle has finished, remove the dough from the pan and place on a floured surface.

5 Punch the dough down gently, and shape it into a plump ball. Place the dough in the prepared pan, cover with lightly oiled plastic wrap and set aside in a warm place for about 2 hours, or until it has risen almost to the top of the pan.

6 Preheat the oven to 400°F. Bake the babka for 20 minutes. Reduce the oven temperature to 375°F and continue to bake for 15–20 minutes more, until golden.

7 Turn the babka out onto a wire rack to cool. Meanwhile, make the icing. Place the confectioners' sugar in a small bowl and add the lemon juice and 1 tablespoon hot water. Mix well, then drizzle the icing over the cake. Sprinkle over the almonds and pared orange zest or candied orange peel to decorate.

SPICED FRUIT KUGELHOPF

Golden raisins steeped in spiced rum flavor this brioche-style bread, which is baked in a special fluted mold with a central funnel.

1 Mix the rum, ginger, cloves, cinnamon stick and nutmeg in a small saucepan and place over a medium heat until hot, but not bubbling. Remove from the heat, add the golden raisins and set aside in the pan for 30 minutes.

2 Pour the milk into the machine pan. Add three of the eggs, then separate the remaining eggs, setting the whites aside, and add the egg yolks to the pan.

3 Remove the cloves and cinnamon from the saucepan and discard (although the cinnamon stick can be dried for re-use later). Place a sieve over the bread pan and drain the golden raisins in it so that the juices fall through into the pan. Set the raisins aside. If the instructions for your bread machine specify that the yeast is to be placed in the machine pan first, then simply reverse the order in which you add the liquid and dry ingredients to the pan.

4 Sprinkle the flour over, ensuring that it covers the liquid mixture completely. Add the salt and sugar in separate corners of the bread pan. Make a shallow indentation in the center of the flour (but not down as far as the liquid) and add the yeast.

5 Set the bread machine to the dough setting; use basic dough setting (if available). Press Start. Mix for 5 minutes, then gradually add the melted butter. Lightly oil a nonstick kugelhopf pan.

6 When the dough cycle has finished, put the dough in a large mixing bowl. In a separate, grease-free bowl, whisk the egg whites to soft peaks. Add the reserved golden raisins and cut mixed peel to the dough and fold in, using your hands. Gradually fold in the egg whites to form a soft dough.

7 Spoon the dough into the kugelhopf pan in three or four batches, making sure it is evenly distributed. Cover with lightly oiled plastic wrap and leave in a slightly warm place for 1–1½ hours, or until the dough has risen and is almost at the top of the pan.

8 Preheat the oven to 375°F. Bake the kugelhopf for 50–60 minutes or until it has browned and is firm to the touch. You can cover the surface with waxed paper if it starts to brown too quickly. Turn out onto a wire rack to cool. Dust with confectioners' sugar.

7 tablespoons dark rum
1 teaspoon ground ginger
3 whole cloves
1 cinnamon stick
1 teaspoon freshly grated nutmeg
⅔ cup golden raisins
2 tablespoons milk
5 eggs
4½ cups unbleached white bread flour
½ teaspoon salt
6 tablespoons sugar
2 teaspoons rapid-rise active dry yeast
6 tablespoons butter, melted
½ cup cut mixed peel
confectioners' sugar, for dusting

MAKES 1 LOAF

COOK'S TIP
This bread is best made in a medium or large bread machine as these have longer rising times. If you have a small machine you may need to increase the rising time in the kugelhopf pan.

TEABREADS AND CAKES

Traditional teabreads and cakes use baking powder or baking soda rather than yeast as a rising agent, giving them a light texture and a good flavor. Classic cakes, such as Madeira Cake, Marble Cake and sticky Gingerbread, can easily be baked in a bread machine. For more exotic combinations, there are recipes for Tropical Fruit Loaf, flavored with pinapple, mango, papaya and melon; Raspberry and Almond Teabread or sugar-topped Pear and Cherry Cake.

MADEIRA CAKE

Delicately flavored with vanilla, this classic plain cake has a firm yet light texture. Serve the traditional way with a glass of its namesake.

SMALL
½ cup butter, cut into pieces
generous ½ cup sugar
a few drops of pure vanilla extract
generous 1 cup self-rising flour
6 tablespoons all-purpose flour
2 eggs, lightly beaten
¼ cup milk

MEDIUM
⅔ cup butter, cut into pieces
¾ cup sugar
¼ teaspoon pure vanilla extract
generous 1¼ cups self-rising flour
6 tablespoons all-purpose flour
3 eggs, lightly beaten
¼ cup milk

LARGE
¾ cup butter, cut into pieces
⅞ cup sugar
¼ teaspoon pure vanilla extract
1½ cups self-rising flour
½ cup all-purpose flour
3 eggs, lightly beaten
¼ cup milk

MAKES 1 CAKE

1 To prepare the bread machine, remove the kneading blade from the bread pan and then line the pan with nonstick baking parchment or alternatively with greased waxed paper.

2 Cream the butter and sugar together until the mixture is very light and fluffy, then beat in the pure vanilla extract.

3 Sift the flours together. Gradually beat the eggs into the creamed mixture, beating well after each addition, and adding a little flour if the mixture starts to curdle.

COOK'S TIP
Cakes cooked in a bread pan tend to have browner sides than when cooked conventionally, in an oven, as the cooking element is around the sides of the bread pan. Cakes such as this, which have a high proportion of fat and sugar, need to be watched closely, as the edges will easily overcook.

4 Fold in the remaining flour mixture, using a metal spoon, then add enough of the milk to give a dropping consistency.

5 Spoon the mixture into the prepared bread pan and set the bread machine on the bake only setting. Set the timer, if possible, for the recommended time. If, on your bread machine, the minimum time on the bake only setting is for longer than the time suggested here, set the timer and check the cake after the shortest recommended time. Bake the small madeira cake for 40–45 minutes, the medium for 45–50 minutes and the large cake for 55–60 minutes.

6 The cake should be well risen and firm to the touch. Test by inserting a skewer into the center of the cake. It should come out clean. If necessary, bake for a few minutes more.

7 Remove the bread pan from the machine. Let stand for about 2–3 minutes, then turn the madeira cake out onto a wire rack to cool.

CRUNCHY PEAR AND CHERRY CAKE

Made from quick all-in-one cake mixture and filled with juicy pears and cherries, this cake has a crunchy demerara sugar topping that contrasts beautifully with the soft crumb.

1 Remove the kneading blade from the bread pan and line the pan with nonstick baking parchment or greased waxed paper.

2 Mix the margarine and sugar in a large bowl. Add the eggs, milk, flour and baking powder. Beat together for 1–2 minutes. Fold in the pears, cherries and ginger, using a metal spoon.

3 Spoon the mixture into the prepared pan and sprinkle half the demerara sugar over the top. Set the machine to the bake only setting. Set the timer, if possible, for the recommended time. If not, set the timer and check the cake after the shortest recommended time. Bake the small cake for 45–50 minutes, the medium cake for 50–55 minutes and the large cake for 65–70 minutes.

4 Sprinkle the remaining sugar over after 25 minutes if baking the small cake, after 30 minutes if baking the medium cake, and after 35 minutes if baking the large cake.

5 Remove the bread pan from the machine. Let the cake stand for 2–3 minutes, then turn out onto a wire rack to cool.

SMALL

6 tablespoons soft margarine
scant ½ cup sugar
2 eggs
2 tablespoons milk
1½ cups all-purpose flour
1½ teaspoon baking powder
½ cup dried pears, chopped
2 tablespoons candied cherries, quartered
2 tablespoons crystallized ginger, chopped
1½ tablespoons demerara sugar

MEDIUM

7 tablespoons soft margarine
½ cup sugar
2 eggs
4 tablespoons milk
2 cups all-purpose flour
2 teaspoons baking powder
generous ½ cup dried pears, chopped
generous ¼ cup glacé cherries, quartered
3 tablespoons crystallized ginger, chopped
2 tablespoons demerara sugar

LARGE

⅔ cup soft margarine
¾ cup sugar
3 eggs
4 tablespoons milk
2½ cups all-purpose flour
2½ teaspoon baking powder
¾ cup dried pears, chopped
scant ½ cup glacé cherries, quartered
4 tablespoons crystallized ginger, chopped
2 tablespoons demerara sugar

MAKES 1 CAKE

COOK'S TIP
Rinse and dry the candied cherries thoroughly before adding them to the cake.

HONEY CAKE

If you like the taste of honey, you are sure to love this cake. Serve it with tea or coffee or as a dessert with fresh fruit and crème fraîche.

SMALL
3 tablespoons butter
7 tablespoons honey
¾ cup all-purpose flour
pinch of salt
1 teaspoon baking powder
½ teaspoon baking soda
½ teaspoon ground apple pie spice
3¾ cups whole-wheat flour
2 tablespoons milk
1 egg, lightly beaten
2 tablespoons thick-cut orange
marmalade, to glaze

MEDIUM
¼ cup butter
⅔ cup honey
1 cup all-purpose flour
pinch of salt
1½ teaspoons baking powder
½ teaspoon baking soda
1 teaspoon ground mixed spice
1 cup whole-wheat flour
2 eggs, lightly beaten
3 tablespoons thick-cut orange
marmalade, to glaze

LARGE
5 tablespoons butter
generous ¾ cup honey
1¼ cups all-purpose flour
pinch of salt
2 teaspoons baking powder
¾ teaspoon baking soda
1 teaspoon ground mixed spice
1¼ cups whole-wheat flour
3 tablespoons milk
2 eggs, lightly beaten
4 tablespoons thick-cut orange
marmalade, to glaze

MAKES 1 CAKE

1 Remove the kneading blade from the bread pan and line the pan with nonstick baking parchment or greased waxed paper.

2 Place the butter and honey in a small saucepan and heat gently, stirring all the time, until the butter has melted.

3 Sift the all-purpose flour, salt, baking powder, baking soda and mixed spice into a mixing bowl. Stir in the whole-wheat flour.

4 Stir the milk, if using, into the beaten egg, if making the small or large cake. Gradually pour onto the flour mixture, alternately with the honey and butter mixture, beating well after each addition of liquid.

5 Spoon the mixture into the prepared bread pan. Set the bread machine to the bake only setting. Set the timer, if possible, for the recommended time. If not, set the timer and check the cake after the shortest recommended time. Bake the small cake for 35–40 minutes, the medium cake for 40–45 minutes and the large cake for 50–55 minutes, or until well risen and firm to the touch.

6 Test by inserting a skewer into the center of the cake. It should come out clean. If necessary, bake the cake for a few minutes more.

7 Remove the pan from the machine. Let stand for 2–3 minutes, then turn the cake out onto a wire rack.

8 Melt the marmalade in a small pan and brush it over the warm cake, to glaze.

GINGERBREAD

This tea-time favorite can be baked easily in your bread machine. Store it in an airtight container for a couple of days to allow the characteristic moist, sticky texture to develop fully.

1 Remove the blade from the bread pan and line with nonstick baking parch- ment or greased waxed paper. Sift the flour, ginger, baking powder, baking soda and apple pie spice together into a large bowl.

2 Melt the sugar, butter, syrup and molasses in a saucepan over a low heat.

3 Make a well in the center of the dry ingredients and pour in the melted mixture. Add the milk, egg and preserved ginger and mix thoroughly.

4 Pour the mixture into the bread pan and set the machine to the bake only setting. Set the timer, if possible, for the recommended time. If not, set the timer and check the gingerbread after the shortest recommended time. Bake the small gingerbread for 45–50 minutes, the medium for 50–55 minutes and the large for 65–70 minutes, or until well risen.

5 Remove the bread pan from the machine. Let stand for 2–3 minutes, then turn the gingerbread out onto a wire rack to cool.

SMALL

1½ cups all-purpose flour
¾ teaspoon ground ginger
1 teaspoon baking powder
¼ teaspoon baking soda
½ teaspoon ground apple pie spice
6 tablespoons light muscovado sugar
¼ cup butter, cut into pieces
scant ⅓ cup golden syrup or
corn syrup
3 tablespoons molasses
7 tablespoons milk
1 egg, lightly beaten
¼ cup drained bottled preserved
ginger, thinly sliced

MEDIUM

2 cups all-purpose flour
1 teaspoon ground ginger
1½ teaspoons baking powder
⅓ teaspoon baking soda
½ teaspoon ground apple pie spice
½ cup light brown sugar
6 tablespoons butter, cut into pieces
generous ⅓ cup golden syrup or
corn syrup
4 tablespoons molasses
⅔ cup milk
1 egg, lightly beaten
⅓ cup drained bottled preserved
ginger, thinly sliced

LARGE

2½ cups all-purpose flour
1½ teaspoons ground ginger
2 teaspoons baking powder
¾ teaspoon baking soda
¾ teaspoon ground apple pie spice
generous ½ cup light brown sugar
½ cup butter, cut into pieces
scant ½ cup golden syrup or
corn syrup
4 tablespoons molasses
⅞ cup milk
1 egg, lightly beaten
⅓ cup drained bottled preserved
ginger, thinly sliced

MAKES 1 LOAF

COCONUT CAKE

Dried shredded coconut gives this simple, speedy cake a wonderful moist texture and delectable aroma.

SMALL
6 tablespoons butter or
margarine, softened
generous ½ cup sugar
2 eggs, lightly beaten
1⅓ cups dry shredded coconut
¾ cup self-rising flour
¼ cup sour cream
1 teaspoon grated lemon zest

MEDIUM
7 tablespoons butter or margarine,
softened
¾ cup sugar
2 large eggs, lightly beaten
1⅔ cups dry shredded coconut
scant 1 cup self-rising flour
scant ⅓ cup sour cream
1½ teaspoons grated lemon zest

LARGE
½ cup butter or
margarine, softened
scant 1 cup sugar
3 eggs, lightly beaten
2 cups dry shredded coconut
1 cup self-rising flour
⅜ cup soured cream
2 teaspoons grated lemon zest

MAKES 1 CAKE

1 Remove the kneading blade from the bread pan and line the pan with nonstick parchment paper or greased waxed paper.

2 Cream the butter or margarine and sugar together until pale and fluffy, then add the eggs a little at a time, beating well after each addition.

3 Add the dry shredded coconut, flour, sour cream and lemon zest. Gradually mix together, using a non-metallic spoon.

4 Spoon into the pan. Set the machine to the bake only setting. Set the timer, if possible, for the recommended time. If not, set the timer and check after the shortest recommended time. Bake the small or medium cake for 45–50 minutes and the large cake for 65–70 minutes.

5 Test by inserting a skewer into the center of the cake. It should come out clean. If necessary, bake for a few minutes more.

6 Remove the bread pan from the machine. Let stand for 2–3 minutes, then turn the cake out onto a wire rack to cool.

COOK'S TIP
This is delicious with a lemon syrup drizzled over the cooked cake. Heat 2 tablespoons lemon juice with scant ½ cup granulated sugar and 6 tablespoons water in a saucepan, stirring until the sugar has dissolved. Bring to a boil, then simmer for 2–3 minutes before drizzling the syrup over the warm coconut cake.

RASPBERRY AND ALMOND TEABREAD

Fresh raspberries and almonds combine perfectly to flavor this mouthwatering cake. Toasted flaked almonds make a crunchy topping.

1 Remove the kneading blade from the bread pan and line the pan with nonstick parchment paper or greased waxed paper.

2 Sift the flour into a large bowl. Add the butter and rub in with your fingertips until the mixture resembles fine bread crumbs.

3 Stir in the sugar and ground almonds. Gradually beat in the egg(s). If making the small or large teabread, beat in the milk.

4 Fold in the raspberries, then spoon the mixture into the prepared pan. Sprinkle the flaked almonds over.

SMALL
1¼ cups self-rising flour
5 tablespoons butter, cut into pieces
generous ⅓ *cup sugar*
¼ cup ground almonds
1 egg, lightly beaten
2 tablespoons milk
1 cup raspberries
1½ tablespoons toasted flaked almonds

MEDIUM
1½ cups self-rising flour
7 tablespoons butter, cut into pieces
½ cup sugar
⅓ cup ground almonds
2 eggs, lightly beaten
1¼ cups raspberries
2 tablespoons toasted flaked almonds

LARGE
2 cups self-rising flour
½ cup butter, cut into pieces
generous ½ *cup sugar*
½ cup ground almonds
2 eggs, lightly beaten
3 tablespoons milk
1½ cups raspberries
2 tablespoons toasted flaked almonds
MAKES 1 TEABREAD

COOK'S TIP
This cake is best eaten on the day it is made, when the fresh raspberries will be at their best.

5 Set the bread machine to the bake only setting. Set the timer, if possible, for the recommended time. If not, set the timer and check after the shortest recommended time. Bake the small teabread for 35–40 minutes, the medium for 45–50 minutes and the large cake for 65–70 minutes or until well risen.

6 Test by inserting a skewer into the center of the teabread. It should come out clean. If necessary, bake for a few minutes more. Then remove the pan from the machine. Turn out onto a wire rack to cool after 2–3 minutes.

PASSION CAKE

Don't be misled into assuming this cake contains passion fruit. It is actually a carrot and walnut cake and a very good one, too. Topped with a tangy lemon cheese icing, it makes the perfect tea-time treat.

SMALL
½ cup butter
½ cup soft light brown sugar
2 eggs, separated
1 teaspoon lemon juice, plus
1 teaspoon for the topping
1 cup self-rising flour
½ teaspoon baking powder
¼ cup ground almonds
generous ½ cup walnut pieces,
chopped
scant 1¼ cups grated carrot
½ cup mascarpone cheese
2 tablespoons confectioners' sugar
1½ tablespoons walnut pieces,
to decorate

MEDIUM
scant ⅔ cup butter
scant ⅔ cup light brown sugar
2 eggs, separated
2 teaspoons lemon juice, plus
1 teaspoon for the topping
1 tablespoon milk
1¼ cups self-rising flour
¾ teaspoon baking powder
⅓ cup ground almonds
¾ cup walnut pieces, chopped
scant 1½ cups grated carrot
⅔ cup mascarpone cheese
3 tablespoons confectioners' sugar
2 tablespoons walnut pieces,
to decorate

LARGE
¾ cup butter
¾ cup light brown sugar
3 eggs, separated
1 tablespoon lemon juice, plus
1½ teaspoons for the topping
1½ cups self-rising flour
1 teaspoon baking powder
½ cup ground almonds
1 cup walnut pieces, chopped
generous 1½ cups grated carrot
¾ cup mascarpone cheese
3 tablespoons confectioners' sugar
3 tablespoons walnut pieces,
to decorate

MAKES 1 CAKE

1 Remove the kneading blade from the bread pan and line the pan with nonstick baking parchment or greased waxed paper.

2 Place the butter and sugar together in a large mixing bowl and cream until light and fluffy. Beat in the egg yolks, one at a time, then beat in the lemon juice. If making the medium cake, beat in the milk.

3 Fold in the flour and the baking powder, then add the ground almonds and chopped walnut pieces.

4 Meanwhile, beat the egg whites in a grease-free bowl until stiff.

5 Fold the egg whites into the creamed cake mixture, together with the grated carrot and mix.

6 Spoon the mixture into the prepared bread pan and set the machine to the bake only setting. Set the timer, if possible, for the recommended time. If, on your bread machine, the minimum time on the "bake only" setting is for longer than the time suggested here, set the timer and check after the shortest recommended time. Bake the small and the medium cake for 45–50 minutes and the large cake for 65–70 minutes.

7 The passion cake should be well risen and firm to the touch. Test by inserting a skewer into the center of the cake. It should come out clean. If necessary, bake for a few minutes more.

8 Remove the pan from the machine. Let the cake stand for 2–3 minutes, then turn out onto a wire rack to cool.

9 To finish the cake, beat the mascarpone cheese with the confectioners' sugar and lemon juice. Spread the topping mixture over the top of the cake and sprinkle with the walnut pieces.

COOK'S TIP
If you can't locate mascarpone cheese, use cream cheese instead. It doesn't matter whether it is plain or reduced fat cheese.

MIXED FRUIT TEABREAD

When mixed dried fruits are plumped up by being soaked in orange juice before baking, the result is a succulent teabread that keeps well.

SMALL
½ cup golden raisins
⅓ cup raisins
2 tablespoons currants
1 tablespoon cut mixed peel
6 tablespoons light brown sugar
⅔ cup orange juice
1 egg, lightly beaten
generous ½ cup all-purpose flour
generous ½ cup
whole-wheat flour
1 teaspoon baking powder
¼ teaspoon ground cinnamon
¼ teaspoon freshly grated nutmeg

MEDIUM
⅔ cup golden raisins
½ cup raisins
3 tablespoons currants
2 tablespoons cut mixed peel
½ cup light brown sugar
⅞ cup orange juice
1 egg, lightly beaten
generous ¾ cup all-purpose flour
generous ¾ cup
whole-wheat flour
1½ teaspoons baking powder
½ teaspoon ground cinnamon
½ teaspoon freshly grated nutmeg

LARGE
1 cup golden raisins
¾ cup raisins
¼ cup currants
2 tablespoons cut mixed peel
¾ cup light brown sugar
generous 1¼ cups orange juice
1 egg, lightly beaten
1 cup all-purpose flour
1 cup whole-wheat flour
1½ teaspoons baking powder
½ teaspoon ground cinnamon
½ teaspoon freshly grated nutmeg

MAKES 1 TEABREAD

1 Place the dried fruit, peel and sugar in a bowl. Pour over the orange juice and let soak for 8 hours or overnight.

2 Remove the kneading blade from the bread pan and line the pan with nonstick baking parchment or greased waxed paper.

3 Add the egg, both types of flour, the baking powder, and spices to the fruit mixture and beat thoroughly to combine. Spoon the mixture into the prepared bread pan.

4 Set the machine to the bake only setting. Set the timer, if possible, for the recommended time. If not, set the timer and check the cake after the recommended time. Bake the small cake for 40–45 minutes, the medium for 55–60 minutes and the large cake for 75–80 minutes. Check after the shortest recommended time. It should be well risen and firm to the touch.

5 Remove the bread pan from the machine. Turn the cake out onto a wire rack after 2–3 minutes.

VANILLA-CHOCOLATE MARBLE CAKE

White and dark chocolate, marbled together, make a cake that tastes as good as it looks. Serve it for tea, or cut it into chunks, mix it with fresh peach slices and add a sprinkling of orange or peach liqueur for an impressive dessert.

1 Remove the blade from the bread pan and line with nonstick baking parchment or greased waxed paper. Cream the margarine or butter and sugar together until light and fluffy. Slowly add the eggs, beating thoroughly. Place half the mixture in another bowl.

2 Place the white chocolate in a heatproof bowl over a pan of simmering water. Stir until melted.

3 Melt the plain chocolate in a separate bowl, in the same way. Stir the white chocolate and the vanilla extract into one bowl of creamed mixture and the plain chocolate into the other. Divide the flour equally between the two bowls and lightly fold it in with a metal spoon.

4 Put alternate spoonfuls of the two mixtures into the prepared bread pan. Use a round-bladed knife to swirl the mixtures together to marble them.

5 Set the bread machine to the bake only setting. Set the timer, if possible, for the recommended time. If not, set the timer and check the cake after the shortest recommended time. Bake the small cake for 45–50 minutes, the medium for 50–55 minutes and the large for 65–70 minutes, until well risen.

SMALL
½ cup margarine or butter
generous ½ cup sugar
2 eggs, lightly beaten
1½ ounces white chocolate, broken into pieces
1½ ounces semi-sweet chocolate, broken into pieces
¼ teaspoon pure vanilla extract
1½ cups self-rising flour
confectioners' sugar and cocoa powder, for dusting

MEDIUM
generous ½ cup margarine or butter
scant ¾ cup sugar
2 eggs, lightly beaten
2 ounces white chocolate, broken into pieces
2 ounces semi-sweet chocolate, broken into pieces
½ teaspoon pure vanilla extract
1¾ cups self-rising flour
confectioners' sugar and cocoa powder, for dusting

LARGE
scant 1 cup margarine or butter
1 cup sugar
3 eggs, lightly beaten
3 ounces white chocolate, broken into pieces
3 ounces semi-sweet chocolate, broken into pieces
½ teaspoon pure vanilla extract
2½ cups self-rising flour
confectioners' sugar and cocoa powder, for dusting

MAKES 1 CAKE

6 The cake should be just firm to the touch. Test by inserting a skewer into the center of the cake. It should come out clean. If necessary, bake for a few minutes more. Remove the pan from the machine. Stand for 2–3 minutes, then turn the cake out onto a wire rack. Dust with confectioners' sugar and cocoa powder and serve in slices or chunks.

BANANA AND PECAN TEABREAD

This moist, light teabread is flavored with banana, lightly spiced with nutmeg and studded with golden raisins and pecans. Weigh the bananas after peeling them—it is important to use the precise quantities given.

SMALL

6 tablespoons butter, softened
generous ¾ cup sugar
2 eggs, lightly beaten
1½ cups self-rising
flour, sifted
5½ ounces peeled ripe bananas
5 tablespoons buttermilk
¼ teaspoon baking powder
½ teaspoon freshly grated nutmeg
generous ½ cup golden raisins
generous ½ cup pecans,
chopped
1 tablespoon apricot
jam, melted
1 tablespoon banana chips

MEDIUM

7 tablespoons butter, softened
⅞ cup sugar
2 large eggs, lightly beaten
1¾ cups self-rising
flour, sifted
7 ounces peeled ripe bananas
6 tablespoons buttermilk
½ teaspoon baking powder
1 teaspoon freshly grated nutmeg
⅔ cup golden raisins
¾ cup pecans, chopped
2 tablespoons apricot
jam, melted
2 tablespoons banana chips

LARGE

½ cup butter, softened
1 cup sugar
3 eggs, lightly beaten
2 cups self-rising
flour, sifted
8 ounces peeled ripe bananas
7 tablespoons buttermilk
½ teaspoon baking powder
1 teaspoon freshly grated nutmeg
scant 1 cup golden raisins
scant 1 cup pecans, chopped
2 tablespoons apricot
jam, melted
2 tablespoons banana chips

MAKES 1 TEABREAD

1 Remove the kneading blade from the bread pan and line the pan with nonstick baking parchment or greased waxed paper.

2 Cream the butter and sugar in a mixing bowl until pale and fluffy. Gradually beat in the eggs, beating well after each addition, and adding a little of the flour if the mixture starts to curdle.

3 Mash the bananas until completely smooth. Beat into the creamed mixture with the buttermilk.

4 Sift the remaining flour and the baking powder into the bowl. Add the nutmeg, raisins and pecans; beat until smooth.

5 Spoon into the prepared bread pan. Set the machine to the bake only setting. Set the timer, if possible, for the recommended time. If not, set the timer and check the cake after the shortest recommended time. Bake the small or medium cake for 55–60 minutes and the large cake for 65–70 minutes. Test by inserting a skewer in the center of the teabread. It should come out clean. If necessary, bake for a few minutes more.

6 Remove the pan from the machine. Let stand for about 5 minutes, then turn the cake out onto a wire rack.

7 While the cake is still warm, brush the top with the melted jam and sprinkle over the banana chips. Let cool completely before serving.

APRICOT, PRUNE AND PEACH TEABREAD

The succulent dried fruits complement the crunchy texture of the hazelnuts and multi-grain flour. Serve this unusual fruit bread in slices, either plain or spread thinly with butter.

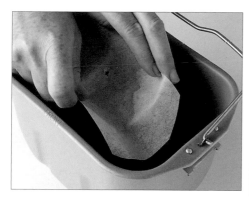

1 Remove the kneading blade from the bread pan and line the pan with nonstick baking parchment or greased waxed paper.

2 Chop the apricots, prunes and the peaches. Sift the flour, apple pie spice and baking powder together into a large bowl. Add the butter and rub in with your fingers until the mixture resembles fine bread crumbs.

3 Stir in the sugar, apricots, prunes, peaches and hazelnuts. Gradually beat in the milk and egg.

4 Spoon the mixture into the prepared bread pan. Set the machine to the bake only setting. Set the timer, if possible, for the recommended time. If not, set the timer and check the cake after the shortest recommended time. Bake the small cake for 40–45 minutes, the medium cake for 45–50 minutes and the large cake for 60–65 minutes, or until well risen and firm to the touch.

5 Test by inserting a skewer in the center of the teabread. It should come out clean. If necessary, bake for a few minutes more. Then remove the bread pan from the machine. Let stand for 2–3 minutes, then turn the teabread out onto a wire rack to cool.

SMALL
generous ¼ cup dried apricots
generous ¼ cup prunes, pitted
¼ cup dried peaches
1½ cups multi-grain flour
1 teaspoon ground apple pie spice
1½ teaspoons baking powder
¼ cup butter, diced
¼ cup light brown sugar
⅓ cup hazelnuts, halved
7 tablespoons milk
1 egg, lightly beaten

MEDIUM
generous ⅓ cup dried apricots
generous ⅓ cup prunes, pitted
generous ¼ cup dried peaches
2 cups multi-grain flour
1½ teaspoons ground apple pie spice
2 teaspoons baking powder
5 tablespoons butter, diced
5 tablespoons light brown sugar
½ cup hazelnuts, halved
⅔ cup milk
1 egg, lightly beaten

LARGE
scant ½ cup dried apricots
scant ½ cup prunes, pitted
scant ⅓ cup dried peaches
2½ cups multi-grain flour
1½ teaspoons ground apple pie spice
2½ teaspoons baking powder
6 tablespoons butter, diced
6 tablespoons light brown sugar
½ cup hazelnuts, halved
⅞ cup milk
1 egg, lightly beaten

MAKES 1 TEABREAD

TROPICAL FRUIT LOAF

There's a tempting tropical taste in every slice of this wonderfully moist loaf. Speckled with delicious little chunks of papaya, mango, melon and pineapple, it is topped with a tangy lime—soft cheese icing and finished with fresh toasted coconut.

SMALL
generous 1 cup all-purpose flour
1 teaspoon baking powder
½ cup dry shredded coconut
5 tablespoons butter, cut into pieces
5 tablespoons sugar
generous ½ cup dried tropical fruits, coarsely chopped
7 tablespoons milk
1 egg, lightly beaten
grated zest and juice of ½ lime

FOR THE ICING AND THE DECORATION
scant ½ cup full-fat soft cheese
3 tablespoons confectioners' sugar
juice of ½ lime
pared lime zest and fresh coconut shavings or coconut shreds, to decorate

MEDIUM
1½ cups all-purpose flour
1 teaspoon baking powder
⅔ cup dry shredded coconut
7 tablespoons butter, cut into pieces
7 tablespoons sugar
scant 1 cup dried tropical fruits, coarsely chopped
½ cup + 1 tablespoon milk
1 egg, lightly beaten
grated zest and juice of ½ lime

ICING AND DECORATION FOR THE MEDIUM AND LARGE LOAVES
½ cup full-fat soft cheese
4 tablespoons confectioners' sugar
juice of ½ lime
pared lime zest and fresh coconut shavings or coconut shreds, to decorate

LARGE
2 cups all-purpose flour
1½ teaspoons baking powder
1 cup dry shredded coconut
½ cup butter, cut into pieces
⅔ cup sugar
1 cup dried tropical fruits, coarsely chopped
⅞ cup milk
1 large egg, lightly beaten
grated zest and juice of ½ lime

MAKES 1 LOAF

1 Remove the kneading blade from the bread pan and line the pan with nonstick baking parchment or greased waxed paper.

2 Sift the flour and baking powder into a large bowl. Then mix in the coconut. Add the butter and rub in with your fingers until the mixture resembles fine bread crumbs.

3 Stir in the sugar and dried tropical fruits. Gradually add the milk, egg, grated lime zest and juice, beating well after each addition.

4 Spoon the mixture into the prepared bread pan and set the bread machine on the bake only setting. Set the timer, if possible, for the recommended time. If, on your bread machine, the minimum time on the bake only setting is for longer than the time suggested here, set the timer and check the cake after the recommended time. Bake the small cake or medium cake for 45–50 minutes and the large cake for 65–70 minutes.

5 The fruit loaf should be well risen and firm to the touch. Test by inserting a skewer into the center of the loaf. It should come out perfectly clean.

6 Remove the bread pan from the bread machine. Let the loaf stand for about 5 minutes, then turn it out onto a wire rack to cool.

7 Meanwhile, make the icing. Cream the soft cheese, confectioners' sugar and lime juice together in a bowl. Spread the mixture over the top of the loaf.

8 Lightly toast the coconut shavings or shreds. Let cool for 2–3 minutes, then use them to decorate the top of the loaf, with the pared lime zest.

COOK'S TIP
When testing the cake with a skewer, try to avoid piercing a piece of dried fruit, or the skewer will come out sticky and might therefore give you a misleading result.

COFFEE BREAD

This quick and easy sweet bread keeps well and so makes a useful standby.

SMALL

1½ cups all-purpose flour
1½ teaspoons baking powder
pinch of salt
6 tablespoons light brown sugar
½ cup pecans, chopped
1½ teaspoons coffee granules
1½ tablespoons butter, melted
5 tablespoons milk
1 egg, lightly beaten

MEDIUM

1¾ cups all-purpose flour
2 teaspoons baking powder
pinch of salt
scant ½ cup light brown sugar
¾ cup pecans, chopped
2 teaspoons coffee granules
2 tablespoons butter, melted
7 tablespoons milk
2 eggs, lightly beaten

LARGE

2½ cups all-purpose flour
1 tablespoon baking powder
pinch of salt
⅔ cup light brown sugar
1 cup pecans, chopped
1 tablespoon coffee granules
3 tablespoons butter, melted
⅔ cup milk
2 eggs, lightly beaten

MAKES 1 LOAF

COOK'S TIP

For a special treat, drizzle the loaf with coffee glacé icing and decorate with pecan halves.

1 Remove the kneading blade from the bread pan and line the pan with nonstick baking parchment or greased waxed paper.

2 Sift the flour, baking powder and salt into a large bowl. Stir in the sugar and pecans. Dissolve the coffee granules with 1 tablespoon hot water in a cup.

3 Add the coffee, the melted butter, milk and egg(s), to the dry ingredients. Beat thoroughly to mix. Spoon the mixture into the prepared bread pan and set the bread machine to the bake only setting.

4 Set the timer, if possible, for the recommended time. If not, set the timer and check after the shortest recommended time. Bake the small cake for 40–45 minutes, the medium for 45–50 minutes and the large for 55–60 minutes.

5 Test by inserting a skewer into the center of the loaf. It should come out clean. If necessary, bake for a few minutes more.

6 Remove the bread pan from the machine. Let stand for 2–3 minutes, then turn the bread out onto a wire rack to cool.

PEANUT BUTTER TEABREAD

Peanut butter is used instead of butter or margarine in this tasty teabread, giving it a distinctive flavor and an interesting texture, thanks to the peanut pieces.

SMALL
¼ cup crunchy peanut butter
⅓ cup sugar
1 egg, lightly beaten
7 tablespoons milk
1¾ cups self-rising flour

MEDIUM
⅓ cup crunchy peanut butter
scant ½ cup sugar
1 egg, lightly beaten
¾ cup milk
generous 2½ cups self-rising flour

LARGE
scant ½ cup crunchy peanut butter
scant ¾ cup sugar
2 eggs, lightly beaten
⅞ cup milk
3½ cups self-rising flour

MAKES 1 TEABREAD

1 Remove the kneading blade from the bread pan and line the pan with nonstick baking parchment or greased waxed paper.

2 Cream the peanut butter and sugar in a bowl together until light and fluffy, then gradually beat in the egg(s).

3 Add the milk and flour and mix with a wooden spoon.

COOK'S TIP
Leave a rough finish on the top of the cake before baking to add character.

4 Spoon the mixture into the prepared bread pan and set the machine to the bake only setting.

5 Set the timer, if possible, for the recommended time. If, on your bread machine, the minimum time on the bake only setting is for longer than the time suggested here, then set the timer and check the teabread after the shortest recommended time. Bake the small or medium teabread for 45–50 minutes, and the large teabread for 60–65 minutes.

6 The teabread should be well risen and just firm to the touch. Test by inserting a skewer in the center of the teabread. It should come out clean. If necessary, bake for a few minutes more.

7 Remove the bread pan from the bread machine. Let stand in the pan for 2–3 minutes, then transfer the peanut butter teabread onto a wire rack to cool.

MOLASSES, DATE AND WALNUT CAKE

Layered with date purée and finished with a crunchy sugar and walnut topping, this cake is absolutely irresistible.

1 Remove the kneading blade from the bread pan and line the pan with nonstick baking parchment or greased waxed paper. Mix the dates, lemon zest and lemon juice in a saucepan. Add ¼ cup of water and bring to a boil, then simmer until soft. Purée in a blender or food processor until smooth.

2 Sift the flour and spices together. Cream the butter and sugar until pale and fluffy. Warm the molasses, golden syrup and milk in a saucepan, until just melted, then beat into the creamed butter mixture. Add the egg and beat in the flour mixture. Stir in the walnuts.

COOK'S TIP
Try increasing the quantities of the toppings by 25 percent if you are making a large cake, or decrease by 25 percent if you are making a small cake.

3 Place half the mixture in the bread pan. Spread the date purée over, leaving a narrow border of cake mix all round. Top with the remaining cake mixture, spreading it evenly over the date purée.

4 Set the machine to the bake only setting. Set the timer, if possible, for the recommended time. If not, set the timer and check after the recommended time. Bake the small cake for 35 minutes, the medium cake for 40 minutes and the large cake for 45 minutes.

5 Mix all of the topping ingredients together. When the cake has baked for the recommended time, sprinkle the topping over it and cook for 10–15 minutes more, until the topping starts to bubble and the cake is cooked. Remove the bread pan from the machine. Let stand for 10 minutes, then turn out onto a wire rack to cool.

STRAWBERRY TEABREAD

Perfect for a summertime treat, this hazelnut-flavored teabread is laced with luscious fresh strawberries.

SMALL
1 cup strawberries
½ cup butter, softened
generous ½ cup sugar
2 eggs, beaten
1¼ cups self-rising
flour, sifted
¼ cup ground hazelnuts

MEDIUM
1½ cups strawberries
⅔ cup butter, softened
¾ cup sugar
2 eggs, beaten
1 tablespoon milk
1⅛ cups self-rising
flour, sifted
⅓ cup ground hazelnuts

LARGE
1¾ cups strawberries
¾ cup butter, softened
⅝ cup sugar
3 eggs, beaten
1½ cups self-rising
flour, sifted
½ cup ground hazelnuts

MAKES 1 TEABREAD

1 Remove the kneading blade from the bread pan and line the pan with nonstick baking paper or greased waxed paper.

2 Hull the strawberries and chop them roughly. Set them aside. Cream the butter and sugar in a mixing bowl until pale and fluffy.

3 Gradually beat in the eggs and milk (if you are making the medium cake), beating well after each addition to combine quickly without curdling.

4 Mix the self-raising flour and the ground hazelnuts together and gradually fold into the creamed mixture, using a metal spoon.

5 Fold in the strawberries and spoon the mixture into the prepared bread pan. Set the machine to the bake only setting. Set the timer, if possible, for the recommended time. If, on your bread machine, the minimum time on the bake only setting is longer than the time suggested here, set the timer and check after the shortest recommended time. Bake the small or medium teabread for 45–50 minutes and the large teabread for 55–60 minutes.

6 Test by inserting a skewer in the center of the teabread. It should come out clean. If necessary, bake for a few minutes more.

7 Remove the bread pan from the machine. Leave the teabread to stand for 2–3 minutes, then turn out onto a wire rack to cool.

SUPPLIERS

UNITED STATES

MANUFACTURERS

APPLIANCE CO. OF AMERICA
P.O. Box 220709
Great Neck, NY 11021
Tel: (800) 872-1656

BREADMAN (subsidiary of Salton)
www.salton-maxim.com

OSTER
www.oster.com

PANASONIC
www.prodcat.panasonic.com/shop

REGAL
www.regalware.com/breadmakers.html

Toastmaster (subsidiary of Salton)
www.salton-maxim.com

WEST BEND HOUSEWARES
www.westbend.com/house.html

ZOJIRUSHI
www.zojirushi.com/bread.html

RETAILERS

DEAN & DELUCA
110 Greene Street
Suite 304
New York, NY 10012

Tel: (800) 221-7714

JCPENNEY
www.jcpenney.com

MACY'S
www.macys.com

WILLIAMS-SONOMA
P.O. Box 7456
San Francisco, CA 94120-7456
Tel: (800) 541-2233

ARROWHEAD MILLS
P.O. Box 866
Hereford, TX 79045
Tel: (806) 364-0730

BOB'S RED MILL
5209 S.E. International Way
Milwaukie, OR 97222
Tel: (503) 654-3215

CATHY'S COUNTRY STORE
2125 N. Richmond Street
Appleton, WI 54911
(920) 830-3311
www.cathysbulkfoods.com

KENYON CORNMEAL COMPANY
Osquepough, RI 02836
Tel: (401) 783-4054

KING ARTHUR FLOUR
P.o. Box 876
Norwich, VT 05055-0876
Tel: (800) 827-6836
www.kingarthur.com

WALNUT ACRES ORGANIC FARMS
Penns Creek, PA 17862
Tel: (800) 433-3998

THE CHEF'S CATALOGUE
3215 Commercial Avenue
Northbrook, IL 60062-1900
Tel: (800) 338-3232

BREAD BAKER'S GUILD OF AMERICA
P.O. Box 22254
Pittsburgh, PA 15222
Tel: (412) 322-8275

ENGLAND

PRIMA INTERNATIONAL
4 Elland Park Industrial Estate
Elland Way, Leeds LS11 0EY
Tel: 0113 251 1500
www.prima–international.com

PANASONIC
Panasonic House, Willoughby Road
Bracknell
Berks RG12 8FP
Tel: 01344 862 444

PIFCO
Failsworth
Manchester M35 0HS
Tel: 0161 947 3000
Brand: Russell Hobbs

HINARI
Harvard House
14–16 Thames Road
Barking
Essex IG11 0HX
Tel: 020 8787 3111

PULSE HOME PRODUCTS LTD
Vine Mill, Middleton Road
Royton
Oldham OL2 5LN
Helpline: 0800 525 089
Brand: Breville

AUSTRALIA

ADELAIDE

MYER
22 Rundle Mall, Adelaide
(08) 8205 9111
Brands: Panasonic, Remington,
Breville, Sunbeam, Easybake,
Ronson

HARVEY NORMAN
822 Marion Road, Marion,
South Australia
(08) 8375 7777
Brands: Breville, Ronson, Sunbeam,
Panasonic

BRISBANE

CHANDLERS
Shop 88, Myer Centre
Queen Street, Brisbane
(07) 3221 2011
Brands: Panasonic, Breville,
Sunbeam

BETTA ELECTRICAL
6 Victoria Street
Celvin Grove, Brisbane
(07) 3831 0950
Brands: Panasonic, Breville,
Sunbeam, Ronson

MELBOURNE

DAIMARU CNR
Elizabeth St and Swanson Walk
(03) 9660 6666
Brands: Panasonic, Breville,
Sunbeam

RETRAVISION
310 Clarendon Street
South Melbourne
(03) 9699 4577
Brands: Panasonic, Breville,
Sunbeam

PERTH

HARVEY NORMAN
1363 Albany Highway,
Cannington
(08) 9311 1100
Brands: Breville, Ronson, Sunbeam,
Panasonic

MYER
Murray Street, Perth
(08) 9221 3444
Brands: Breville, Remington,
Sunbeam, Panasonic

SYDNEY

DAVID JONES
Elizabeth Street, Sydney
(02) 9266 5544
Brands: Panasonic, Breville,
Sunbeam

GRACE BROS
436 George Street, Sydney
(02) 9238 9111
Brands: Panasonic, Sunbeam,
Ronson, Remington, Breville

BING LEE
Shop 1, HIA Building & Renovation
Supa Centre,
Homebush
(02) 9763 5077
Brands: Sunbeam

USEFUL HOTLINES

WESTON MILLING
   Hotline: 1800 649 494
BREVILLE
   Hotline no: 1800 807 911
PANASONIC
   Hotline no: 13 26 00
SUNBEAM
   Hotline no.: 1800 025 059
RONSON
   Hotline no: 1800 654 614

INDEX